PASTORAL COUNSELING FOR ORPHANS AND VULNERABLE CHILDREN

PASTORAL COUNSELING FOR ORPHANS AND VULNERABLE CHILDREN

A Narrative Approach

Tuntufye Anangisye Mwenisongole
and
Elia Shabani Mligo

RESOURCE *Publications* · Eugene, Oregon

PASTORAL COUNSELING FOR ORPHANS AND VULNERABLE CHILDREN
A Narrative Approach

Copyright © 2018 Tuntufye Anangisye Mwenisongole and Elia Shabani Mligo. All rights reserved. Except for brief quotations in critical publications or reviews, no part of this book may be reproduced in any manner without prior written permission from the publisher. Write: Permissions, Wipf and Stock Publishers, 199 W. 8th Ave., Suite 3, Eugene, OR 97401.

Resource Publications
An Imprint of Wipf and Stock Publishers
199 W. 8th Ave., Suite 3
Eugene, OR 97401

www.wipfandstock.com

PAPERBACK ISBN: 978-1-5326-4864-9
HARDCOVER ISBN: 978-1-5326-4865-6
EBOOK ISBN: 978-1-5326-4866-3

Manufactured in the U.S.A.

Contents

Acknowledgements | vii
Abbreviations and Acronyms | ix

1. **Introduction** | 1
Rationale of the Book
Background, Problem and Thesis
Purpose, Objectives and Study Questions
Scope and Limitations of the Book
Definitions of Key Terms
Book Outline and Synopsis

2. **Exploring The Context Of Study In Tanzania** | 42
Introduction
Overview of Geographical Area
Magnitudes of HIV and AIDS
Impact of HIV and AIDS
HIV/AIDS and Human Sexuality
Challenges of HIV and AIDS
Orphans and Children Living with HIV and AIDS
Organizations and the Fight against HIV and AIDS
Pastoral Counseling Ministry to Children
Conclusion

3. **Surveying Narrative Approaches And Practical Theology** | 60
Introduction
Theories, Definitions and Challenges
Pastoral Care to Orphans and Vulnerable Children
Definition of Terms that encompass Narratives
Why is Narrative Approach Important for This Book?

The Use of Narrative Approach in Counseling
Narrative Approach in Pastoral Counseling to OVC
Narrative Pastoral Counseling to OVC: The Way to Resilience
Skills and Methods of Narrative Approach in Pastoral Counseling to OVC
Conclusion

4. CONDUCTING EMPIRICAL RESEARCH | 130
Introduction
Research Design
Methods of Research
Population, Samples and Sampling Procedures
Instruments for Data Collection
Data Analysis and Presentation
Ethics in Research
Conclusion

5. MAKING SENSE OF OBTAINED RESEARCH DATA | 142
Introduction
Interview Schedule Results
Focus Group Activities Results
Reflections and General Assessments
Conclusion

6. TOWARDS AN INTEGRATIVE MODEL FOR PASTORAL COUNSELING TO OVC | 230
Introduction
Narratives
A Narrative Model for Healing and Resilience to OVC
Narrative Approach to Pastoral Counseling
Integrating Practical Theology and Narrative Approaches
Conclusion

7. CONCLUSION | 250
Summary of the Book
Challenges encountered during Study Process
Recommendations

References | 255

Acknowledgements

We would like to confess at the outset that the task of writing a massive work like this one can hardly be done by only one person. All well-written documents are, in most cases, outcomes of initiatives from a number of people. It is the same thing with this book. The first initiatives started with Tuntufye Anangisye Mwenisongole in his studies at the University of South Africa in South Africa. At this stage, we thank all those who made his initiatives successful. The following are worth mentioning: First, his research supervisor the late Dr. C.J. Hugo for his diligent supervision throughout the study process. His advice and comments were enriching to Mwenisongole's academic career and progress. Thanks are provided to him for the patience he had toward the completion of Mwenisongole's study. Second, to Dr. Edwina Ward of the University of KwaZulu Natal, South Africa, who established Mwenisongole's background for his study and who actually began the process of this work with him. Her guidance and supervision thus far brought him to success in his studies. Third, to the late Dr. Glenn Asquith, Professor of Practical Theology at the Moravian Theological Seminary in the USA for his patience, love, and guidance to Mwenisongole which helped Mwenisongole to see the path of his life and career to be followed. Professor Asquith's knowledge and wisdom was extremely important to Mwenisongole's academic progress. And fourth, to various other contributors: Dr. Lechion Peter Kimilike, UNISA and UKZN librarians and his sponsors (the Mission 21 in Switzerland, the Moravian Church in Tanzania and the Teofilo Kisanji University), each according to the role played to facilitate his studies.

The second initiative was accomplished by Elia Shabani Mligo, especially in doing all the necessary revisions and nourishments of the material into a publishable book. The revision involved the addition of up-to-date literatures and the follow-up interviews at the research area in order to have up-to-date information about what was going on at Amani Orphanage

Center during the revision process. At this revision and data follow-up stage, we are indebted to various stakeholders: first, to children in general, but specifically the children of *Amani* Center in Nsalaga, Mbeya–Tanzania, and to all who were concerned with such children (orphans and vulnerable children), thank you all for being the valuable resources toward the completion of our study. Second, to fellow lecturers both at Teofilo Kisanji University and Tumaini University Makumira Mbeya Teaching Center both located in Mbeya Tanzania for the various discussions we had in order to sharpen the argument of this book. Third, we are grateful to our family members (Mwenisongole's wife Grace and his children Steven and Anipa, and Mligo's wife Ester and Children Upendo, Grace and Faraja) for their perseverance, prayers and encouragements. Fourth, we appreciate the editing and typesetting work done by the editors and typesetters at Wipf and Stock Publishers, Eugene OR., for making the book appear in the form it has now. Their work is excellent!

The final initiative was beyond our human comprehension. God provided us health and ability to think and use other people's ideas in order to accomplish the argument of this book. God did not leave us, even a single minute. To this providence, we owe glory and honor to God Almighty in whom we live, move, and have our being. Amen!

Abbreviations and Acronyms

AACC	All Africa Conference of Churches
AIDS	Acquired Immune Deficiency Syndrome
ANGONET	Arusha NGO Network
CAA	Children and Adolescents Affected by AIDS
CABA	Children Affected by AIDS
CBO	Community Based Organization
CCT	Christian Council of Tanzania
CD	Children in Distress
CDH	Children from Disjointed Households
CEDC	Children in Extremely Difficult Circumstances
cf.	compare with
CLWHA	Children Living With HIV and AIDS
CNSP	Children in Need of Special Protection
ed/s.	editor/s
e.g.	for example
EHAIA	Ecumenical HIV/AIDS Initiative in Africa
FBO	Faith Based Organization
ff	and following pages
GTZ	Gesellschaft fur Technische Zusammenarbeit
HIV	Human Immunodeficiency Virus

KIWOHEDE	Kiota Women Health Development Organization
i.e.	that is
KJV	King James Version
MCT	Moravian Church in Tanzania
MCTSWP	Moravian Church in Tanzania, South West Province
NGO	Non-Governmental Organization
OVC	Orphans and Vulnerable Children
PEPFAR	President's Emergency Plan for AIDS Relief
PLWHA	People Living With HIV and AIDS
TACAIDS	Tanzania Commission for AIDS
UKZN	University of KwaZulu Natal
UNAIDS	The United Nations Joint Programme on HIV/AIDS
UNICEF	The United Nations Children's Fund
UNISA	University of South Africa
USAID	United States Agency for International Development
VCT	Voluntary Counseling and Testing
WCC	World Council of Churches
WHO	World Health Organization

CHAPTER 1

Introduction

> *"To enter into the world of children requires the ability to speak the language of 'play'. It requires freedom from adult preoccupations and reservations and a willingness to really humble oneself and become like a child. Social convention and cultural norms often make this difficult for adults. Adults are made to believe that they have outgrown childhood and that it is shameful to return to its habits and behaviour. This notions needs to be challenged, however. Jesus certainly did not see childhood as a shameful, worthless stage in the life of a human."*
>
> COETSEE & GROBBELAAR, "A CHURCH WHERE CHILDREN ARE WELCOME," 811.

Rationale of the Book

Brief Personal Backgrounds and Experiences

IN THIS SECTION WE describe our experiences as ministers of the Church in matters relating to counseling activities. In brief, Mwenisongole's journey in practical theology and counseling activites began in 1997 when completing his Bachelor of Divinity degree. At the said year he did his research on Christian education for children from the biblical perspective. It was an exegetical text taken from the book of Deuteronomy 6: 4–10, which basically is Moses' instruction on Israelites to teach their children about the great acts of God in history. Such instruction was being done orally through telling stories about God's great deeds.[1] Hence, the work with this text was his first exposure to dealing with biblical narratives.

---

1. Mwenisongole, "Religious Education of Children."

For his second degree in theology, Mwenisongole specialized in pastoral counseling, wherein his research was on using images and symbols with delinquent and troubled children using a Jungian analytical approach.[2] However, among the counseling approaches which intrigued and made him curious leading him to doing this research in pastoral counseling was the narrative approach. He saw that this approach was the way forward for him in doing further research on pastoral counseling to Orphans and Vulnerable Children (OVC). In relation to the study of children affected by the HIV and AIDS, he decided to do further research on theological and biblical response on the issues of the HIV and AIDS in Tanzania.[3] This helped him to have a wider view on how much the pandemic affected people in Tanzania and how to respond to it.

In addition to the above researches, in his pastoral counseling courses, he was interested in two subjects. The first was on understanding biblical passages and stories from psychological perspectives. The second was the Jungian analytical approach in pastoral counseling. He found narrative[4] approach in/to pastoral counseling to be close to those two approaches he had learned. In line with his motives, Capps also asserts: "any of the authors who are writing on narrative employ the perspective of psychoanalytic object relations theory, which emphasizes the ways in which we internalize and project parental and other culturally transmitted models and images."[5] Capps's quotation points to the idea relevant to what Mwenisongole intended to focus on in his counseling process as a paster, and in his theological reflections about what he was doing. Capps above assertion will further be discussed in details in the following chapters.

In addition to being a pastor and a volunteer at the Faith Based Organization (FBO) known as *Amani* Orphanage Center in Mbeya, Tanzania, he also engaged in teaching practical theology, and pastoral counseling in particular, in a church-oriented university in Mbeya, Tanzania. He was interested in teaching and counseling using stories, metaphors, proverbs, songs and other narrative aspects which seemed to be natural to people in Mbeya, Tanzania. That was also his passion and motivation for doing further research on narrative approaches because it was part of his experience

---

2. Mwenisongole, "The Use of Symbols."

3. Mwenisongole, "A Biblical and Theological Respose."

4. Through his experience of teaching pastoral counseling courses, reading different books, and attending to some seminars on narrative and counseling, he found that using narratives was a way forward for him to do further research in practical theology especially with traumatized children in the Tanzanian context. Why use narratives? This question will be answered in this book.

5. Capps, "Living Stories." 1.

throughout his life. He also personally liked to hear and tell stories, proverbs and metaphors to others.

One part of his story as he grew up was about his interest in playing and hearing stories about water in rivers, lakes and seas. He liked playing with water, looking and admiring at it. Water became one of his important symbols in life and in his pastoral ministry. Water was such a beautiful symbol in the life of many people and especially in the African context. To him, water symbolized life, beauty, and the presence of the Holy Spirit. From his childhood rivers were his best places to go and relax and have an opportunity to meditate on life and pray to God. They were places where he could go and regain his life. The waters revitalized his life and provided him strength for life. As a child, and even to this day, when he went to rivers or to places where waters were, he liked playing with water. Sometimes, he liked taking smooth stones around the rivers or ponds and throwing them into the water. When he threw a stone in the water usually what happened were waves in the form of rings or circles which went growing and expanding from the center to the edge of the pond or to the bank of the river. To him that was like a story of any person who had to experience much turbulence (waves) in life. Those turbulences were part of people's growth whether they were good or bad. What people did, acted or perceived and responded to all these turbulences in their lives was how they grew into becoming sick or healthy. Hence, these experiences, studies and research showed Mwenisongole's interest in working with children and young people who were more vulnerable in society due to poverty and the HIV and AIDS in particular. Mwenisongole is convinced that by the use of narrative approach, it is possible to build such a better health environment to traumatized children.

Mligo's experience is somehow different from Mwenisongole's, especially in terms of interests. Mligo graduated his undergraduate studies at a church related university focusing much on practical theological issues. His main focus was administration and caring of people. His postgraduate studies were done outside his country focusing on the use of biblical narratives as tools for emancipation from stigmatizing situation.[6] Narratives from the gospel of John were mainly studied.

Soon after completing his undergradute studies, Mligo engaged in administrative issues and caring for people. Contrary to Mwenisongole who was interested in water, symbols, and images, Mligo was interested in people, especially the downtrodden, those who were considered to be at the margins of society. This interest developed after several questions in his mind in relation to the ministry of Jesus. Mligo's contemplation about the

---

6. Mligo, *Jesus and the Stigmatized*.

ministry of Jesus convinced him that Jesus Christ, the Son of God, was not only a downtrodden himself in relation to the view of his contemporaries, but also the person who sided with the downtrodden with the aim of liberating them from their traumatizing situations.[7] Mligo used biblical narratives in his counseling and caring for people, especially those at the margins. This made him to see that biblical narratives are not only stories, but also powerful weapons for emancipation.

In his postgraduate studies, biblical narratives became the center for Mligo's reflections. His doctoral dissertation was on how the stigmatized and discriminated People Living with the HIV and AIDS read some narratives from the gospel of John as their tool for emancipation. The study enlightened Mligo that biblical narratives were powerful tools for people in the margins to find refuge. This is the conviction which Mligo has to this time, even as he approaches biblical narratives as tools for counseling orphans and vulnerable children in this book.

As they were conducting research and writing this book, Mwenisongole and Mligo were not children any more. They were adults. One can imagine the difficulty to write about something that does not belong to their age. However, their ability to write is justified by the fact that they are both Africans, writing about African children in their own context, and have in one time in their lives been children within the same context. And they were aware that effective communication with children was the sole means of entering into their world in order to acquire information from them. Coetsee and Grobbelaar have clearly stated this aspect, and we quote them at length here:

> Connecting to children requires an understanding of their preferred modes of communication. While children use speech to communicate as soon as they can master it, Gary Landreth, renowned play therapist, made an important observation when he stated: "Play is the child's language and toys are his words." Children of all ages use different forms of play to interact with each other and the world. They express their emotions and thoughts in concrete ways and toys become the visible manifestations of these concepts. Children find it easy to assign meaning to lifeless objects and can use time and space in a creative way to communicate. To enter into the world of children requires the ability to speak the language of 'play'. It requires freedom from adult preoccupations and reservations and a willingness to really humble oneself and become like a child. Social convention

---

7. Ibid., cf. Mligo, *Jesus and the Divorce Commandment*; Mligo, *The Kingdom of God*; Mligo, "Jesus Christ, the Compassionate Companion."

and cultural norms often make this difficult for adults. Adults are made to believe that they have outgrown childhood and that it is shameful to return to its habits and behaviour. This notions needs to be challenged, however. . . . [However,] Play is not the only mode of communicating and connecting with children. Stories, music, humour, touch, protection, encouragement—in short, activities reaching out to the hearts of children, showing respect and fulfilling their needs–all are expressions of love that strengthens relationships and enhances growth.[8]

Though contexts change with time, Mwenisongole and Mligo could still remember of what had happened in their own context of childhood and tried to reflect on what happened as they conducted research. Therefore, basing on the above experiences as members of the context and as researchers to children and their predicaments, and through shunning the beliefs about entering the world of children stated by Coetsee and Grobbelaar above, they managed to bring together biblical and children's narratives in order to propose the most suitable model of counseling for a life of hope to orphans and vulnerable children.

Biblical Narratives as Sources of Counseling

Narratives (stories) run in various places of the Bible. They can be found from the book of Genesis to the book of Revelation. The Bible is filled with different kinds of narratives which can be understood in different ways. As we read in the gospels, Jesus Christ himself was a good story teller. These stories came from different backgrounds and contexts. Some of these stories were told by God, some by individuals, and some by communities. Biblical stories have been very fascinating and helpful for our own lives and to the lives of others too. These stories teach and provide us the way to live a life which is worthwhile and the life of wholeness. Biblical stories show us different life experiences of men and women of God who were created in God's image. Hence, through reading biblical stories as they are, it is possible to grow in faith through identifying with the lives of characters used in the stories.

Biblical stories are in narrative form and require analysis in order to be understood and used. Our experience shows that in Mbeya Tanzania, the area of our study, the Bible is understood very literally. The Bible is a story book dealing with people's experiences and their relationship with God. It is a book which tells true historical stories. It is not much about the exegetical

8. Coetsee & Grobbelaar, "A Church Where Children are Welcome," 811.

understanding of the Bible, but as literal translations. Therefore, in this book all biblical texts will focus on the literal understanding of passages rather than the exegetical analysis of the texts. This is what we have experienced on the way people view the scripture as a collection of stories, which are real and true. It is about using a common sense when reading the Bible and not with systematic exegetical analysis of understanding the Bible.[9] Taking the texts as they are will be our approach to scriptural texts with children. In this case, we did not go into detailed systematic exegetical analyses of the texts which we used in this book. However, despite our literal approach to the text we suggest to use, this book does not reject or ignore the systematic exegetical methods of Scriptures; rather, we clearly understand their efficacy and limitations.

Narrative analysis is one of the ways to understand the Bible.[10] The Bible has been found through oral tradition because in those times, i.e., in biblical times, most people did not know how to read or write. This way of communication was very important to Jewish people. Training and instruction was through verbal communication. In order for someone to understand his or her life and where he or she came from, the history and background of an individual or a community, oral communication through stories was used most of the time. These types of biblical narratives were important to keep society in one place, in unity, and in solidarity. Narratives (stories) were told and retold from one generation to another. Narratives helped to keep the traditions and identities of people about who they were and where they came from and where they were going. Biblical narratives of the Jewish people are very similar to those of the African people.[11] In the African societies you find that from long time ago when the ancestors did not know how to read or write, they used to communicate orally. Stories were used for training and instructing people, for example in the initiation rites known as *Jando* and *Unyago*.[12] All these aspects gave them the identity of who they were in the community or society they belonged to.

Biblical narratives are stories we find in the Bible. These kinds of stories are many in the Bible; however, as an example, let us look at some of them. The first biblical narrative which we want to point out here, and which was very important for Jewish people, is the story of the great act of

9. See also Finucane, *In Search of Pastoral Care*, 233–240.

10. Note that the theory of narrative will be discussed in detail in the following chapters. It suffices to say here that narrative is one of the ways to communicate and understand the person through his or her life story.

11. Healey and Sybertz, *Towards African Narrative Theology*.

12. Mwenisongole, "A Biblical and Theological Response," 12; see also Mbiti, *African Religions*, 118–125; Mligo, *Elements of African Traditional Religion*.

God in the history of the Jewish salvation from the bondage in Egypt. This story is found in the book of Deuteronomy 6: 20–25. The passage so goes:

> When your son asks you in time to come, "What is the meaning of the testimonies and the statutes and the ordinances which the LORD our God has commanded you?" then you shall say to your son, "We were Pharaoh's slaves in Egypt; and the LORD brought us out of Egypt with a mighty hand; and the LORD showed signs and wonders, great and grievous, against Egypt and against Pharaoh and all his household, before our eyes; and he brought us out from there, that he might bring us in and give us the land which he swore to give to our fathers. The the LORD commanded us to do all these statutes, to fear the LORD our God, for our good always, that he might preserve us alive, as at this day. And it will be righteousness for us, if we are careful to do this entire commandment before the LORD our God, as he has commanded us.

This is one of the good biblical narratives (stories) we hear about the Jewish deliverance from the hand of Pharaoh in Egypt. This story was transmitted from one generation to another and was memorized by parents to teach their children of what happened in their lives, of where they came from, and where they were going to.[13]

Another good example which has drawn us to like the narrative approach is the story of Jacob in the book of Genesis. First of all, Jacob is described as being born while his "hand had taken hold of Esau's heel," and his name meant supplants, deceiver, or the one who takes by the heel (Genesis 25:24–26).[14] We also read that Jacob bought the birthright from Esau, his brother, by eating the red pottage which Jacob prepared (Genesis 25:29–34). Later, the story explains that Jacob cheated his brother Esau to acquire his father's blessings instead of Esau who was the firstborn child and who was liked by Isaac their father (Genesis 27:1–45). All these tricks of Jacob made him run away from his brother Esau who began hating him.

Esau, full of hate, began looking for the opportunity to kill Jacob. Jacob decided to run away from Esau, on the way he slept on the stone and dreamt a dream about a ladder which touched the heaven and the earth and on it he saw the angels of God descending and ascending on it. And God talked to him about his descendants and his prosperous future life (Genesis 28:10–17). Then, Jacob decided to live in Haran for some time where he received many challenges for his life and especially on his marriage; he married and

---

13. Henry, *Matthew Henry Concise Bible Commentary*.
14. Elwell & Comfort, "Jacob."

obtained children from two women and two maids. Finally, after serving Laban his father in law for many years, Jacob returned home. On his way home, he faced many challenges from Laban. Jacob kept thinking about his brother Esau, remembering what he did to him before. In his heart, Jacob was most likely looking for reconciliation with his brother Esau. The most striking experience for Jacob was about his dream. Jacob was challenged in his dream where he found God and knew who he was. The text says:

> And Jacob was left alone; and a man wrestled with him until the breaking of the day . When the man saw that he did not prevail against Jacob, he touched the hollow of his thigh; and Jocob's thigh was put out of joint as he wrestled with him. Then he said, "Let me go, for the day is breaking." But Jacob said, "I will not let you go, unless you bless me." And he said to him, "What is you name?" And he said, "Jacob." Then he said, "Your name shall no more be called Jacob, but Israel, for you have striven with God and with men, and have prevailed." Then Jacob asked him, "Tell me, I pray, your name." But he said, "Why is it that you ask my name?" And there he blessed him. So Jacob called the name of the place Peniel, saying, "For I have seen God face to face and yet my life is preserved. (Genesis 32:24–30)

The story of Jacob ends up with the reconciliation with his brother Esau and God blessed Jacob despite all the weaknesses and challenges he had throughout his own life and his twelve children. And God continued to guide Jacob throughout his life until died in his good old age.

The New Testament, and particularly the Gospels, is full of narratives told by Jesus Christ. Jesus used metaphors such as stories, parables, proverbs, and other sayings to teach his disciples and people who listened to him in most occasions. It is noted that without parables or examples, Jesus did not teach anything. Narratives have been regarded by others as the 'fifth gospel' in which God reveals himself through experiences of people.[15] This is not to take the place of the Gospel of Jesus down; rather, it is to make the Gospel more at home in the real life of people; and this is what is called the 'inculturation' of the Gospel—making the gospel at home in the cultural lives of people.[16] One of the good examples of how Jesus used narratives to make his message at home in the lives of his hearers are found in the synoptic gospels and John. The synoptic gospels teach about the parables of the kingdom of God and how the kingdom should be understood, while the gospel of John teaches us about eternal life and how to inherit it.

15. See Healey & Sybertz, 32–33.
16. Walligo, "Making a Church"; Crollius, "Inculturation."

These stories and experiences of ours point to our background in doing further research on orphans and vulnerable children (OVC) using a different approach more applicable in the Tanzanian context. The narrative approach, metaphors, stories, proverbs, and other sayings, have drawn us in doing further research for several reasons: First, it appears to be an appropriate approach for children in particular, and to all people as well. Second, it is for its wider perspective and application on different fields of psychology, theology, sociology, and philosophy especially in this postmodern time.[17] Third, the narrative approach invites pastors to engage in relationship that will build a meaningful story of hope in people's lives. Narrative approach makes people become more responsible for their actions and decisions. Metaphors in narratives help people to think beyond what is being spoken or portrayed. Therefore, since orphans and vulnerable children pass through difficulties and hard times in their lives, they require hope and assurance that come out of narratives from the Christian perspective.

Impact of the HIV and AIDS

After discussing the efficacy of biblical narratives in the counseling process, this part introduces the main impacts of the HIV and AIDS which require counseling attentions. It is reported that the southern part of Africa is the region that has mostly been affected by HIV worldwide. The percentage is nearly three quarters (72%) of AIDS related deaths in 2008. It was estimated by the UNAIDS in collaboration with WHO and other organizations that 1.9 million people were newly infected by the HIV in this part of the region (Sub-Saharan) in 2008, bringing to 22.4 million the number of people living with HIV. Children in the Sub-Saharan Africa who have lost one or both parents due to AIDS were more than 14 million in 2008.[18] These estimates indicate that the Sub-Saharan region of Africa is more highly hit by the pandemic than other parts of the world.

In Tanzania, a country among those in the Sub-Saharan region, the HIV prevalence was estimated to be 10% in 2000. And people living with

---

17. Postmodernism is a 21st Century phenomenon whose philosophy lies on looking and understanding the world in a more holistic ways rather than in individualistic and rationalistic ways which dominated the world of modernism (Woodward, "Theological Reflection," 133–140; cf. Finucane, *In Search of Pastoral Care*; Streets, "Love: A Philosophy of Pastoral Care," 11–12; Petta, "In Search of a Contextual Pastoral Theology," 199–207). The dawn of the postmodern phenomenon in pastoral care is attributed to Edward P. Wimberly's publication of his serminal book *Pastoral Care in the Black Church* in 1979; cf. Wimberly, *No Shame in Wesley's Gospel*.

18. UNAIDS, "Epidemiological Fact."

HIV were estimated to be 1.5 million in 1997. The number of orphans in Tanzania alone was estimated to rise to 2 million by 2005. According to UNAIDS the prevalence of the disease was 6.2% for 2007.[19] It is pointed out that Mbeya has the highest number of orphans, high HIV prevalence, few NGO's working in the region, and high level of regional and district response and commitment to other activities.[20] This means that the situation in this region is not good. It is also stated that the region hardly shows a good response towards the effects of the HIV and AIDS.

The UNICEF, UNAIDS and other partners launched a world-wide campaign focusing on the enormous impact of the HIV and AIDS on children. They state that it was a humiliation that fewer than 5 per cent of HIV-positive children receive treatment, and that millions of children who have lost parents due to the disease go without support. The UNICEF continues to point out:

> children affected by the disease are the 'missing face' of AIDS—missing not only from global and national policy discussions on HIV/AIDS, but also lacking access to even the most basic care and prevention services. Millions of children are missing parents, siblings, schooling, health care, basic protection and many of the other fundamentals of childhood....[21]

The HIV and AIDS pandemic does not discriminate between newborn babies and elderly people. Today children are becoming more vulnerable due to this tragic situation. Globally, in 2003, more than 15 million children under the age of 18 had lost one or both parents to AIDS. As a result of this tragic disease, children have undergone grief and abandonment; they have carried out family responsibilities beyond their own capability, and some have resorted to the streets for survival. Support for these children is lacking and for that reason they become very vulnerable.[22]

The challenge and impact of the HIV and AIDS is a global phenomenon despite being more prevalent in African countries. It is a multifaceted problem. The challenges go beyond technology and science, beyond philosophy and politics, and beyond social sciences. The problem of the HIV and AIDS becomes more complex; the impacts go beyond social, traditional, and cultural norms, beyond science and philosophy. There have been different discussions on the relationships between the HIV and AIDS on economy (poverty), healthy (other opportunistic diseases), ethics, human

---

19. TACAIDS, The United Republic of Tanzania: Prime Minisster's Office.
20. Ibid.
21. UNICEF, "Africa's Orphaned and Vulnerable Generations."
22. USAID, "From the American People."

sexuality, gender, politics, faiths, and science. Furthermore, the WCC reports that the impact of the HIV and AIDS is beyond statistics. The HIV and AIDS has caused people to be poor, they have even been affected both psychologically and spiritually. It is pointed out that,

> Many who suffer do so in rejection and isolation. In a striking way HIV/AIDS has become a "spotlight" revealing many iniquitous conditions in our personal and community lives, revealing our inhumanity to one another, our broken relationships and unjust structures. It reveals the tragic consequences of personal actions which directly harm others, or of negligence which opens people to additional risk.[23]

We really agree with the WCC's statement above as we contemplate about the existing situation in regard to the impact of the HIV and AIDS. The HIV and AIDS have caused the decline in responsibility of one to his or her neighbor, one to his or her children and one to his or her community. This irresponsibility has further caused harm to people and children have been more vulnerable in this case.

The former Executive Director of UNAIDS and Microbiologist, Peter Piot once noted that every minute:

- A child dies of an AIDS-related illness
- A child becomes infected by the HIV
- Four young people aged 15–24 become infected by the HIV.

In addition to the Director's note, an estimated 15 million children have lost at least one parent because of AIDS. Yet less than 10 percent of children orphaned and made vulnerable by AIDS receive public support or services. In sub-Saharan Africa, where the impact is greatest, coping systems are stretched to the limit. The then Secretary General Kofi Annan said, "Nearly 25 years into the pandemic, help is reaching less than 10 percent of the children affected by HIV/AIDS, leaving too many children to grow up alone, grow up too fast or not grow up at all. . ."; he stressed that, "AIDS is wreaking havoc on childhood."[24]

Putting more emphasis on the impacts of the pandemic, Veneman also pointed out that in some of the most suffering countries, particularly in sub-Saharan Africa, the AIDS pandemic is "unravelling years of progress for children."[25] She asserts that concrete steps to address the impact of AIDS

23. WCC, *Facing AIDS*, 97.
24. UNICEF, "Unite for Children."
25. Ibid.

on children are essential for meeting the Millennium Development Goals. Veneman says again, "A whole generation has never known a world free of the HIV and AIDS, yet the magnitude of the problem dwarfs the scale of the response so far."[26] Therefore, it is the goal of the whole world to take appropriate steps for children in particular fulfilling the mission we have been called to. These steps include establishing effective ways of providing proper counseling in order to help them mitigate their own hurting situations.

What are the global campaigns to counteract the hurting situations of children and community as a whole? The document from UNICEF, points out the aims of global campaign are as follows:

> *Prevention of mother-to-child transmission*: The vast majority of the half-million children under the age of 15 who die from AIDS-related illnesses every year contract HIV through mother-to-child transmission. The campaign aims by 2010 to provide 80 percent of women in need with access to services to prevent transmission of HIV to their babies. Currently less than 10 per cent of women have access to these services.
>
> *Pediatric treatment*: Less than 5 per cent of HIV-positive children requiring AIDS treatment are receiving it, and only 1 per cent of children born to HIV-infected mothers have access to cotrimoxazole, a low-cost antibiotic that can nearly halve child deaths from AIDS by fighting off deadly infections. The campaign aims by 2010 to provide antiretroviral treatment and/or cotrimoxazole to 80 percent of children in need.
>
> *Prevention*: Adolescents and young people age 15–24 account for roughly half of all new HIV infections, but the vast majority of young people have no access to the information, skills and services had to protect themselves from HIV. The campaign aims by 2010 to reduce the percentage of young people living with HIV by 25 per cent, in line with agreed international goals.
>
> *Protection and support of children affected by AIDS*: By 2010, it is estimated that there will be 18 million children who have lost at least one parent to AIDS in sub-Saharan Africa alone. Well before parents die, children–especially girls–have to take on adult tasks such as caring for the sick, looking after younger siblings, generating income to pay for health costs, or producing food. Often they must drop out of school. The campaign aims by 2010 to reach 80 per cent of children most requiring public support and services. . .

26. Ibid.

The former UNAIDS Executive Director Peter Piot says,

> "AIDS continues to tear apart families and communities, leaving behind 15 million orphans and robbing countries of their future... If countries are to develop, we must put children first. Children must therefore be a major priority when it comes to the way we allocate and use resources. The above stated goals have to be taken seriously by the Church and society as a whole. They should be utilized properly, and be responded actively by all sectors in our communities. In particular the children should be protected and helped to cope with the needs and problems they face in the midst of the HIV and AIDS."

The impact of the HIV and AIDS in Tanzania, and Mbeya in particular, should not be ignored. The above alarming statistics and all the challenges of the HIV and AIDS also triggered our minds to examine and find ways we should respond to this issue as pastoral counselors and the Church as a whole. The Church and society as a whole have to act on the challenges of the HIV and AIDS squarely. What is required there is for the Church and society to be more open to the true knowledge which reflects Christ's love and compassion to the ministry which Christ called us. The Church has been called to be a vigilant Church in any circumstances it finds herself. Hence, the pandemic calls the Church to be alert with all what it brings in society, instead of being ignorant or uninformed about the impacts of HIV and AIDS. Strategic and effective ways are required to help children who have become more vulnerable because of the pandemic. By exploring different ways or approaches in the midst of the HIV and AIDS, we are of the opinion that the narrative approach can make a significant contribution in pastoral counseling to OVC in Tanzania.

Importance of this Book

The previous section explored the impacts of the pandemic to Sub-Saharan Africa, Tanzania, and Mbeya region in particular. This section answers the question "Why is this book important?" This book explores and looks at the contribution of narrative approach in the pastoral counseling context in response to the HIV and AIDS pandemic, especially to orphans and vulnerable children (OVC) in Tanzania. The narrative approach in the pastoral counseling context invites pastoral counselors to look at the challenges of the HIV and AIDS pandemic and other issues related to this pandemic (i.e., human sexuality, poverty, and gender issues) as a serious crisis which calls the Church to exploration, response, stewardship and faith-seeking understanding. Theologically, narrative approach through metaphors, stories, proverbs, plays and arts is the way of resilience for OVC. Through narrative approach, the OVC can build coping mechanisms, faith, hope, and live a life of wholeness, which is the salvation through Christ. The book explores the lives of children and their experiences as they try to live a life of worthiness, self-esteem, and self-control.

Moreover, this book is important to the Church and its mission in general. The mission of the Church is to serve the whole organism. The Church is an organism of Christ called to be a servant of God. There is no adequate service of the Church if part of it is sick; it is suffering with AIDS. Children form part of the organism; they are part of the Church. The Church will benefit from this book by using the findings to enhance a better understanding of the way narratives can be a resource for the provision of counseling services to orphans and vulnerable children. In this case, the book uncovers the potentials of biblical narratives towards resilience and self- emancipation.

Why Children?

The reality of the problem leads researchers to explore, examine and evaluate the narrative approach in pastoral counseling to OVC. Children have for much of the time been rejected and neglected. They are one of the groups that are vulnerable and at risk.[27] It has been indicated that, "the pastoral care and counseling of children has only *recently* received specialized attention."[28] This is what also drew us towards exploring how we can offer counseling to OVC in Tanzania. Benjamini Kiriswa calls for urgent pastoral ministry when he writes: "There is a need to establish pastoral policies and structures of implementation for effective ministry and service to the sick with special reference to persons living with HIV/AIDS. These include instituting guidelines for the protection and rights of the poor, marginalized and socially disadvantaged or vulnerable groups, especially *orphaned children*, widows and widowers."[29]

Kiriswa's words above show not only the importance of pastoral services to people, but also to specific groups—orphaned children, widows, and widowers. These groups require special attention because they are groups considered to be at the margins of society, vulnerable and require

---

27. Sisemore, "Christian Couseling," 117; cf. Atkinson, et al. (eds.), *New Dictionary of Christian Ethics*, 225.

28. Hunter (ed.). *Dictionary of Pastoral Care*, 143 (emphasis is ours).

29. Kiriswa, "Pastoral Care and Counseling," 97 (emphasis is ours).

special attention. Kiriswa's quotation reminds us that in our pastoral ministry, children should not be neglected or forgotten. They are part of the larger context of the Church of Jesus Christ. Children are as important as the older ones. Jesus Christ paid attention to children when he told his disciples to let children come to him for such the kingdom of God is theirs (Mark 10:14). Therefore, children have all rights just as are the grown up people in our churches and societies.

Pastoral Counseling to Children

Doing pastoral counseling to OVC, most of them being affected by and even living with the HIV and AIDS, is a difficult and sensitive challenge. Authors of this book have found very few literatures (or none at all) on pastoral counseling to children, especially those who have been infected and affected by the HIV and AIDS in the Tanzanian context in particular. Perhaps a good place to start with is exploring how other people have tried to respond on the issue of children and the HIV and AIDS in general.

This approach brings us to what we learnt from the Circle of Concerned African Women Theologians, particularly on how they have responded to the issue of the HIV and AIDS in Africa.[30] The challenge and suggestions which the women theologians offer can help in our research for various reasons. The first reason is that the problem of the HIV and AIDS is a worldwide problem. Second, it is because children (mainly little girls) have been included as part of the problems that, women as a whole are facing. Third, the technique, skills or art of pastoral ministry with women living with the HIV and AIDS can stimulate an approach with children. Hence, the infected and affected people with the HIV and AIDS experience some common problems and needs.

As we work with OVC we have to be very sensitive and attentive. Louw validates the necessity of being sensitive in ministering to people with AIDS. He speaks about the "unconditional love, understanding, acceptance, listening to person's feelings and emotions, showing compassion and being sensitive to the person as a human being."[31] Louw again insists on sensitive listening, as does Kirkpatrick. He quotes from K. Wendler who calls for the openness to listen carefully in order that people receive good and hopeful news in the deepest of their hearts. Hence, listening is such an important skill for the pastoral counselor which helps the person (the counselee) to

---

30. Phiri, Haddad & Masenya (eds.), *African Women*.
31. Louw, "Ministering and Counseling," 45; cf. Abashula, Jibat & Oyele, "The Situation of Orphans".

recognize that 'I am acceptable', because of the time, effort, energy and love that the counselor has provided up for someone important[32]

According to Fredrickson as quoted in Streets, "Love is the momentary upwelling of three tightly interwoven events: first, sharing of one or more positive emotions between you and another; second, a synchrony between your and another person's biochemistry and behaviors; and third, a reflected motive to invest in each other's well-being that brings mutual care."[33] The concept of love is defined succinctly and differentiated from the concept of charity works by a theologian Paul Tillich, as quoted in Streets, thus:

> Here, when I use the term love . . . I certainly do not mean the love which is emotion; nor do I think of philia—of friendship which only really develops between the social worker and his patient, nor do I think of the love which is Eros, which creates an emotional desire towards the patient that in many cases is more destructive than creative; rather, it is the love whose name in Greek is agape and in Latin caritas—the love which descends to misery and ugliness and guilt in order to elevate. This love is critical as well as accepting, and it is able to transform what it loves. It is called caritas in Latin, but it should not be confused with what the English form of the same word indicates today– namely, Charity, a word which belongs to the many words which have a disintegrated, distorted meaning. Charity is often identical with social work, but the word 'charity' has the connotation of giving for good causes in order to escape the demand of love. Charity as escape from love is the caricature and distortion of social work.[34]

In order to implement the above described definition of love, for Ward, there are five challenges that are important in working with people who are dying. These challenges are caring, comfort, company, uncovering coping mechanisms and giving a sense of control.[35] All these aspects show the love and concern to OVC. Love, as described by Tillich and Fredrickson above, is not just a theory; it is love, which means acceptance, listening, and understanding. It is unconditional love, which extends the grace of God in comfort, empathy, hope and healing in the midst of problems. Love opens the door to such change and opportunity. The Church has been called for the holistic ministry in the midst of crises. Therefore, love brings about and

32. Ibid., 46; Abashula, Jibat & Oyele,"The Situation of Orphans."
33. Streets, "Love: A Philosophy of Pastoral Care," 3.
34. Streets, "Love: A Philosophy of Pastoral Care," 3.
35. Ward, "The Contribution of Clinical Pastoral Counseling," 252.

opens doors for the coping and healing phenomenon for OVC. The study of pastoral counseling has been very well addressed through various theorists and years of research. It is through scholarly studies and research that we will explore some of the works relevant to the subject topic in the following chapters.

Background, Problem, and Thesis

The previous section established the rationale for conducting this study to OVC using biblical narratives as an approach. In this section we survey the background challenges, state the underlying problem and the main thesis defended by this book. The following parts of this section deal briefly with some challenges in pastoral counseling in general, narrative approach and the HIV and AIDS. However, the more details of these subjects or topics will be dealt with in Chapter Three where the review of literatures is conducted. Therefore, let us provide briefly the background of this research.

Challenge of Pastoral Counseling in General

Pastoral counseling has been challenged of its emphasis on employing secular approaches of psychology and social sciences more than theological approaches. Whether these challenges are unfair or good, challenges and good criticisms are enriching for practical theology as a whole. We have to look for better approaches that will benefit pastoral counseling now and in the future as Capps points it out.[36] It is obvious, as Capps observes that pastoral counseling has to expand its horizon of its approaches and methods. However, some scholars such as Charles Gerkin, Daniel J. Louw, Howard Clinebell, Emanuel Lartey, and Donald Capps have tried to suggest some of the methods that can be applied with pastoral counselors in the ministry of the Church. Capps, for example, says that, "it is true that many pastoral counseling specialists have been using a variety of methods, including some not addressed in either edition of Clinebell's textbook."[37] Clinebell also sees the challenges facing pastoral counselors. In his revised version of *Basic Types of Pastoral Care*, Clinebell recognizes the limitedness of methods in pastoral counseling by saying: "It gradually became clear to me that the relatively passive, long-term model of psychotherapy that I had learned was not particularly effective with many persons who came for

---

36. Capps, *Reframing*, 1–2.
37. Ibid., 2.

pastoral counseling. Gradually, my conviction grew stronger—that pastoral counseling must broaden its conceptual base and revise its working model in order to flourish more fully."[38]

Clinebell's invitation here is to be always creative and inspired for our ministry to make pastoral counseling more holistic in its methods. We concur with Clinebell who admits that the Church should be more creative and innovative in its approach to people who are being afflicted by many problems and challenges of life. The Church should look for ways that will help pastoral ministry to be more holistic than it was before. The ministry of care, healing, and growth must be relevant to the people concerned in their own context and needs. The current Church should look for models and methods of pastoral counseling that would be more integrative, broad, and holistic in its approach.[39]

Challenges facing pastoral counselors in the ministry of the Church have resulted into the increase of wider perspectives in the field of practical theology. Several approaches and methods which have been employed from disciplines of psychology, sociology and others have been enriching to practical theology despite the challenges it faces. Louw is of the opinion that practical theology should look for a model that will base on the central message of the gospel which is salvation, which is also understood in the context of our human relationships. The important thing here is how to communicate the good news of Christ to people's lives according to their contexts. Therefore, this communication requires a good skill and knowledge of translating the gospel in what Louw calls 'hermeneutical mode.'[40] Louw continues to argue that the basic task of practical theology is to integrate theological ethics and the social sciences so that the life of the person and its existence can be effective and applicable in meaningful ways. He says: "pastoral theology, as well as practical theology, needs theological ethics."[41] Hence, these integrative models or methods are ways to go if we want our pastoral ministry of care and counseling to be more holistic to people we serve.

Challenge Facing the Narrative Approach

After stating the challenge of pastoral counseling in general, this part focuses specifically on the narrative approach. The word 'narrative' has been

38. Clinebell, Basic *Types of Pastoral Care*, 9.
39. Ibid., 16.
40. Louw, *A Pastoral Hermeneutics of Care*, 1.
41. Ibid., 11.

used by different disciplines in the academic arena. It has been used mostly by social sciences and the humanities. Narrative has been used by sociologists, psychologists, philosophers and theologians.[42] In this book we will use narrative approach as a way for pastoral counseling to OVC. Narrative approach involves life stories, stories, metaphors, proverbs, riddles, songs, plays, arts and other sayings that we hear and tell about our lives and experiences. Particularly, we use narrative approach for the sake of the focus of this book, which is practical theology, in pastoral counseling. However, we concur with the definition of narrative by Hinchman and Hinchman quoted in Elliot's book which says: "Narratives (stories) in the human sciences should be defined provisionally as discourses with a clear sequential order that connect events in a meaningful way for a definite audience and thus offer insights about the world and/or people's experiences of it."[43] According to Elliot the definition enlightens us to three important aspects: the chronological nature of events within the narrative, the meaningfulness of the narrated story, and the odience oriented nature of any narrated story.[44] Moreover, this definition means that narratives are stories or conversations which people tell or listen inspired by their own lives, others, and by all the events and experiences of life. Hence, through stories people try to interpret, explain, and comment in order to find meaning for their lives.

On the narrative approach, Louw describes Capps's understanding by pointing out that "the task of pastoral care [involves] helping people to locate 'their personal stories within the framework of the Christian story.'"[45] Narrative approach helps people, including children, to find purpose and meaning for their lives. Moreover, Gerkin describes the ministry of pastoral counseling by interpreting the life of the person through the narrative approach. Narrative approach means a way of knowing the person's story, an account, or a description of the person's life. Pastoral counselors should understand the person as God's creation who has been created in a form of a story that has to be interpreted through understanding, the relationship between the story and this person, and being open to God's revelation portrayed in the story. This hermeneutical approach tries to interpret the person's life experience to provide it a purpose and meaning.[46] Therefore, it is clear that narrative approach can also be used within the field of practical theology as it has been pointed out above. Despite the wider perspective

42. Herman, Jahn & Ryan, *Routledge Encyclopedia*.
43. Elliot, *Using Narrative*, 3.
44. Ibid., 4.
45. Louw, *A Pastoral Hermeneutics of Care*, 15.
46. Gerkin, *Widening the Horizons*, 100–101.

and usage of narrative approach in various fields of study, the approach can well be used in practical theology and particularly in pastoral counseling of OVC in the context of Mbeya and Tanzania as a whole

Problem Statement

There have been little or no effective ways in working with orphans and vulnerable children have been documented in Mbeya and Tanzania as a whole.[47] Researchers are exploring and investigating pastoral ways through narrative approach that can be better or effective in responding to the prevalence of OVC in the research area (Mbeya, Tanzania). The Church and pastoral counselors have to find other alternatives or broadening ways which can be effective in the ministry of working with these children. The number of orphans is increasing everyday and there have been no enough and appropriate ways to help them realize their potentials within society. Most children end up in streets, and even those who live with their relatives hardly have enough support. This research explores one alternative to help such children who have been affected by the HIV and AIDS—the use of narratives to revive their human potentiality and dignity within the communities they are.

It is our assumption that narrative approach can be a better way of pastoral counseling to OVC affected by the HIV and AIDS. This approach helps these children in enhancing the process of resilience (i.e., coping and healing phenomenon). The approach is especially applicable in the African context and the Tanzanian context in particular. This is the approach which is more of a cultural practice than a skill or technique to them. Narrative approach which involves the use of storytelling, metaphors, proverbs, riddles, symbols, rituals, plays and songs is the ways of expressing daily experiences of life in times of peace or difficulties in an African context.

The Tanzanian cultural environment is different from that of other countries, particularly of the West, where most of the African people are affected. When Tanzanian people deal with their problems and difficulties, they always reflect on their own environment and culture so that they deal appropriately with those challenges. Practical theology must also bear in mind this attitude of the contextualization of its practice. It must fit the context of people where they are at particular time and place; and this is what we really call 'practical theology', a theology of action based on people's

---

47. Interview with Pastor W at Jacaranda, Mbeya on 13/01/2007 (He was the chairperson of the Moravian Church in Tanzania, the South West Province)

real experiences.[48] However, the world is becoming more of a village where people have become closer and the knowledge has become a worldwide network (i.e., globalization). Networking and sharing of knowledge is very important in postmodern times. People learn and experience from each other, expanding their horizon of knowledge and experience. Despite this interconnectedness of the world order, still, people live according to their contexts and backgrounds, according to where they belong. People still have to find their own ways and means to solve problems and challenges of life. Hence, this research is part of that struggle, of looking for appropriate and adequate ways which are better and effective in dealing with difficulties in the Tanzanian context, especially in regard to the effects of the HIV and AIDS pandemic to OVC.

Thesis Statement

A thesis is inevitable in a qualitative study like this one. According to Mligo, a "thesis is the main idea which your [study] endeavors to support. . . . It represents your position (conviction or opinion) about an issue . . ."[49] The thesis is a statement which the researcher argues for or against when presenting his or her argument. The thesis statement of this study is that narrative approach with its use of stories and metaphors in pastoral counseling is an effective way of responding to different issues surrounding OVC affected by the HIV and AIDS in Tanzania. Narrative approach helps children in their process of coping and healing where they finally find peace and harmony for their lives (wholeness). This resilient phenomenon is very important for these children because it helps them come to terms with the challenges of the HIV and AIDS. It is our hope that in the long run the above-stated thesis statement will be explored and confirmed by the result of the research in the field, where different theories, methods, and themes or ideas will be used for exploration and analysis.

Purpose, Objectives and Study Questions

Purpose of the Book

This book explores problems facing OVC identified above. In dealing with the discussed problems, the main purpose of this book is to explore and

48. Heitink, *Practical Theology*.

49. Mligo, *Writing effective Course Assignments*, 27; Mligo, *Introduction to Research Methods*, 32–36.

examine in detail the adequate and effective ways of ministering to OVC. The Church and its ministry (pastoral counseling) must look at ways that will be helpful for children's resilience in the midst of the HIV and AIDS. Narrative approach through stories and metaphors allows children to express their issues in ways that are very natural for them. It is the method that leads children in the coping-healing process. Hence, narrative approach aims at helping children to know themselves and others much better for the well-being of their lives.

The book is not much about therapeutic approach or methods, but it is about detailed explorations and thick descriptions of children's experiences of pain and suffering as the result of the HIV and AIDS pandemic. The thick descriptions of children's experiences are explored in detail using a narrative approach resulting into ways which are better and effective in responding to issues of OVC in Mbeya, Tanzania. Therefore, this narrative approach is basically a method from the grassroots, from common people in our societies. The approach also applies theology from below. Children are the primary resources and important just like the grown up people. They have all the rights to enjoy and experience the fullness of life. Despite all the challenges and difficulties which children face in the midst of the HIV and AIDS, they have to be respected, helped, and served like other human beings with dignity as we call in Swahili *utu*. In respecting the dignity (*utu*) of OVC, narrative approach respects all people despite the differences they might have.[50]

Objectives of the Book

The objectives of this book point to the thesis statement that has been put forward. First, the book intends to identify possible ways that can be most helpful to reach OVC in Tanzania and other places apart from Tanzania. Pastoral (theology) counseling employs interdisciplinary methods such as psychology and sociology. Examples of these methods are family systems theory, psychoanalysis, client-centered approach and more others. However, narrative as an interdisciplinary approach in counseling is the method which, to our opinion, brings about the better well-being of the person as the result of telling and listening to stories in a pastoral context.

Second, the book intends to investigate and examine the challenges of the HIV and AIDS in Tanzania. There are several challenges which have evolved since the spread of the HIV and AIDS, these challenges are like new perspectives on ethical, political, religious, economical, health, social,

50. Cf. Evans, *Lazarus at Table*, 11–25.

and cultural issues like poverty, human sexuality, gender, death and grief. These issues will also be analyzed and studied in brief as we proceed with this book.

Third, this book investigates and provides an adequate model for pastoral counseling and for the practical theology as a whole in working with children in an African context. It is our assumption that narrative approach can be incorporated in practical theology as a pastoral approach. Furthermore, we will examine and provide adequate approaches for pastoral counseling using the narrative methods for the well-being of OVC in Tanzania. Pastoral counseling is being challenged every day for a good theological, psychological, and ethical foundation. Pastoral counseling is explores different ways to enrich itself so that it can reach out to people of different backgrounds. In this way pastoral counseling will be in a position of responding appropriately to the needs of people in different ways which are more inclusive and divertive, relying on the richness of Christian traditions and social science methods. When it comes to OVC in particular, pastoral counseling tries to be very sensitive to their language and needs. With the help of appropriate methods, pastoral counseling is able to meet the needs of these children.

The goal of pastoral counseling is to help people to grow into fullness of life. Pastoral counseling aims to heal, sustain, comfort, guide, reconcile, and nurture. As OVC pass through different passages of loss and grief, they long for what pastoral counselors can offer. Children are people like any other people who have to grow into their fullness of life even in the midst of the HIV and AIDS pandemic. These children should be listened to stories they tell. They should know themselves as people who are able to do things on their own, and who have to be respected. Children can find their own way of coping and healing if they are provided with guidance and opportunity to share their stories in a sacred space of safe environment. Therefore, it is anticipated that these objectives and results of the book will enable us to find possible solutions and make suggestions for pastoral counseling to the Church as a whole. The highlighted objectives relate to one another and can hardly be separated. They must be integrated as being of one goal—to make the ministry of the Church more effective.

Research Questions

A research question, according to Mligo, is the question which the researcher will mainly focus in executing his or her study. It is a question which the researcher intends to provide answers.[51] In this study, several questions have to be asked about our selected research topic. However, research questions for this book are based on the above objectives, and are as follows:

- Why is the narrative approach using stories and metaphors appropriate in pastoral counseling to OVC in the context of the HIV and AIDS in Mbeya, Tanzania?
- In what ways will the use of narrative approach to OVC in a pastoral counseling context improve the quality of life of OVC?
- How will this research project impact the wider pastoral ministry and society as a whole?

Therefore, the main concern of this book is to endeavor to provide appropriate answers to the above question as a way of fulfilling the purpose of the book.

Scope and Limitation of the Book

The word scope points to the *confinement* of the study while limitation points to the *obstacles* which hindered the proper execution of the study. Our study was confined to Mbeya city area in Tanzania. Among several organizations which dealt with orphaned children, we selected only one organization to do field research in the city. This center is known as "*Amani* Orphanage Center." It is a Faith Based organization (FBO) is located at Uyole Ward in Mbeya urban district. However, other organizations will be mentioned or used for further elaboration or other intended reasons cited in the progress of the book. Hence, through the above orphanage center and others cited and mentioned sources the purpose of obtaining the required research information was fulfilled. The orphanage Center was selected because of its location. It was located within the city where orphans and vulnerable children mostly flocked requiring care.

In our study, we worked with children from the age of 5 to 19 years old. However, in this book we only deal with children who are 12 to 17 years old and of both sexes (i.e., boys and girls). These are referred to as children according to several constitutions. The total number of children which we worked with was more than eighty. For this research purposes, we limited the book to only twenty four children with their case studies recorded in details. Hence, it was our conviction that the ages selected and the number of children whose cases were recorded provided appropriate and adequate research information to answer the stated research questions.

51. Mligo, *Introduction to Research Methods*, 39.

Though we used the narrative approach in studying the sampled children, we were aware that studies on narrative theories are broad and wide subjects. Narrative is a postmodern approach and many scholars have been writing about it in different fields, especially in social science subjects. The theory and philosophy of postmodernity is the 21st Century phenomenon. It came as a result and a challenge to modernity, which emphasized on rationalism (reason), objective truth or knowledge, individualism, facts, and the quest for absolute truth. Postmodernity, in the other hand, does not emphasize on the above assertions of modernity. It goes beyond reasoning. It explores the plurality and diversity of the world and truth. According to Couture, "'Postmodernity' is a cultural state. It identifies changes in global culture associated with the decline of metanarratives, the respect for human difference, the analysis of power, the fragmentation of communal life, the loss of confidence in scientific reason, the rise of technology and virtual reality, the reemergence of an integrated global economy, and the development of post-colonial identity."[52] Therefore, it was not our intention to go into historical details of psychological and sociological research, methods, and techniques in this book. We employed the narrative methods generally, in a way which enabled us to integrate them in the pastoral counseling to OVC. Our main emphasis was applying narrative approach in practical theology. We also used several scholars from the field of practical theology whose subjects related to the concern of this study.

Moreover, the study on the HIV and AIDS also focuses only on the objectives of the book stated above. Therefore, the study on the HIV and AIDS does not go into historical and scientific details of the problems and challenges of the HIV and AIDS. The book only points to those basic and important issues about the HIV and AIDS, which are relevant to the undertaken study. All biblical texts used in this book are from the Revised Standard Version (RSV) unless stated differently.

Definitions of Key Terms

Some of the technical and important terms have to be explained here for the clarification of how they are used in this book. However, the detailed definitions and theories of crucial terms will be discussed in chapter three

---

52. Couture, "The Effect of the Postmodern on Pastoral/Practical Theology," 85; cf. Speedy, *Narrative Inquiry*. For more discussions on modernity and postmodernity, see Finucane, *In Search of Pastoral Care*, 113–150; Jun, "The Paradigm Shift"; cf., Speedy, *Narrative Inquiry*, 11–14.

that deals with literature reviews. Moreover, other terms will be discussed in the respective chapters within this book.

Pastoral Care

The first term is pastoral care. Pastoral care is a ministry which is offered by Christian believers. It is the ministry which uses resources from Christian traditions background and social science theories. Pastoral care as one aspect of pastoral theology is generally described as the 'cure of souls', which is used "to describe the consoling effect which God's empowering and transforming presence has in the world."[53] Pastoral care includes support, advocacy, comfort, guiding, healing, sustaining, and reconciling and nurturing the lives of those who are in need.[54] Lebacqz and Driskill define pastoral care as, "the broad term used by mainline Protestants to encompass any caring action performed by pastors and other recognized religious leaders who minister by virtue of their ordination or office on behalf of a community of faith."[55]

Moreover, Engedal defines pastoral care as "the more comprehensive concept covering any act of compassion administered by members of a Christian community, that aim at preventing or relieving the suffering of a troubled person."[56] The difference between the two (pastoral care and pastoral counseling) is that one is within the other—pastoral counseling is within pastoral care. Pastoral counseling is a more specialized form of pastoral care characterized by strong relational bonds between the care provider and the care-seeker characterized by confidentiality.[57] Ramsay, as quoted in Petta, further defines pastoral counseling to be "a specialized form of pastoral care and accountable to religious communities through skilled representatives of such communities who practice this ministry within and alongside the communities. It is a ministry of relational humanness that intends to integrate critically and skillfully therapeutic resources with theological understanding in order to facilitate healing and justice for individuals, relationships [and] communities."[58] Moreover, Benner cements this difference by saying: "Much as pastoral ministry is broader than pastoral care; so too, pastoral

---

53. Louw, *A Pastoral Hermeneutics of Care*, 4.

54. Ramsay, *Pastoral Care and Couseling*, 3–4.

55. Lebacqz & Driskill, *Ethics and Spiritual Care*, 61; cf. Truter & Lotze, "Spirituality and Health," 275–276.

56. Engedal "The Couselor's Competence," 113.

57. Ibid.

58. Petta, "In Search of a Contextual Pastoral Theology," 178.

care is broader than pastoral counselling. To attempt to reduce all pastoral care to counselling is to fail to recognize both the breadth of pastoral care as well as the distinctive nature of counselling."[59] Therefore, caring for the sick, the needy, those who sufferer various anguishes and OVC is the task of the Church through its ministers.

The most important question in a caring relationship is this: "What is good care? Vosman and Baart list the important aspects for the good care:

1. "It must have a proper identity; it must be actually care.
2. It must be relevant, fine-tuned to specific needs.
3. It must be true, that is, effective.
4. It must be legitimate in more respects than the legal.
5. It must be do-able, technically and humanly speaking.
6. Good care is beneficence, a caring good in itself an *sui generis*."[60]

Following the above-listed aspects, good care involves recognizing the care seeker and his or her identity and being present when the care-seeker needs the caring intervention.

Pastoral Counseling

The second term is pastoral counseling. The American Association of Pastoral Counselors, as quoted in Streets, write: "It was recognized long ago, however, that in many cases specialized professional therapy was necessary for effective treatment and healing . . . Pastoral counseling has evolved from religious counseling to pastoral psychotherapy which integrates theology and other faith tradition knowledge, spirituality, the esources of faith communities, the behavioral sciences, and in recent years, systemic theory."[61] Pastoral counseling, as a specialized profession, goes together with pastoral care described in the previous section. It is a ministry within the larger context of pastoral care done by the person who is accountable to a certain type of religious organization or community. It is a professional ministry done by the person who is well informed by Christian traditions and skills in social sciences processes and methods.[62] Lebacqz and Driskill quoting from J. Patton define Pastoral

---

59. Benner, *Strategic Pastoral Counseling*, 19.
60. Vosman & Baart, "Relationaship Based Care," 201; cf. Ibid., 202–225.
61. Streets, "Love: A Philosophy of Pastoral Care," 3.
62. Ramsay, *Pastoral Care and Couselling*, 4; McClure, *Moving beyond Individualism*," 21–22.

counseling as "a specialized type of pastoral care offered in response to individuals, couples, or families who are experiencing and able to articulate the pain in their lives and willing to seek pastoral help in order to deal with it."[63] Following this definition, Louw further asserts that, "pastoral counseling indicates the procedures, attitudes, and responses which are introduced during the course of the pastoral conversation so that a helping relationship, with its objectives of healing and growth can be established."[64]

Moreover, Engedal quoting from Lartey defines pastoral counseling as follows: "Pastoral counseling . . . is a way of relating and responding to another person or persons so that the person is helped to explore his or her thoughts, feelings and behavior, to reach clearer self-understanding; and then to find and use strengths and resources so that he or she copes more effectively with life by making appropriate decisions or by taking relevant actions. Pastoral counseling is essentially then a purposeful relationship in which persons help others to help themselves."[65] In this definition, Engedal emphasizes that several aspects are important. These aspects include the following: "*empathy*—the ability to enter into the other's experience and being aware of the other's feelings; *respect*—valuing and recognizing the worth, dignity and self-responsibility of the other; *non-possessive warmth*—a welcoming attitude of hospitality and acceptance; *genuineness*—to be as true, authentic and forthright towards the other as possible."[66] The above aspects work within the concrete network of relationship of hospitality and trust between the counselor and the counselee which make the counselee free to explore his or her deepest feelings

Pastoral counseling is not mutually exclusive from pastoral care but part of it. It is very difficult to make a clear distinction between them. However, Clinebell says that both "pastoral care and counseling involve the utilization by persons in ministry of one-to-one or small group relationships to enable healing empowerment and growth to take place within individuals and their relationships."[67] Pastoral counseling, in addition to other psychological methods and skills, helps pastoral counselors to be more equipped with counseling people. Pastoral counseling is done in the context of the ministry of the Church, where the gospel is proclaimed in words and deeds, in worship, prayer, and sacraments. Hence, these instruments of faith help

---

63. Lebacqz & Driskill, *Ethics and Spiritual Care*, 63.
64. Louw, *A Pastoral Hermeneutics of Care*, 4.
65. Engedal, "The Counselor's Competence," 112.
66. Ibid., 113; cf. Evans, *Lazarus at Table*, 11–25.
67. Clinebell, *Basic Types of Pastoral Care*, 25–26.

people to live a life of well-being through different approaches used by pastoral counselors.

Practical Theology

The third term is Practical Theology. Practical theology is a branch in theology which includes Christian practices such as Christian education, homiletics, worship, liturgy, pastoral care, administration, and Church polity. As a discipline, practical theology "emerged in the German Protestant tradition as part of the academic theological curriculum in the late eighteenth century. Although pastoral care was seen as one important area of concern in practical theology, its concerns extended beyond this to specialist interest in worship, preaching, Christian education, and church government."[68] It is the theology of experience and action which applies the "contemporary situations and realms of individual and social action."[69] Practical theology is "concerned with the whole of the church's life in the world, not the functions of clergy alone as was the case with most traditional pastoral theology."[70] Practical theology is applied in a wider sense depending on the context of where it is being used. In some sense practical theology and pastoral theology are used simultaneously, but in the actual sense pastoral theology is part of a big umbrella of practical theology. Therefore, the two terms are complementary to each other despite the differences they might have. Pattison and Woodward, quoted in Petta, confirm this similarity when they state that "there is a lot of common ground between pastoral theology and practical theology. Ultimately, both are concerned with how theological activity can inform and be informed by practical action in the interests of making an appropriate, effective Christian response in the world."[71]

Pastoral Theology

The fourth term is Pastoral Theology. There are several theologies with different focuses: systematic theology, biblical theology, contextual theology, pastoral theology, etc. Each of these theologies has its knowledge bases. As noted above, pastoral theology is a theological discipline which is in most

---

68. Petta, "In Search of a Contextual Pastoral Theology," 177; cf. Streets, "The Pastoral Care of Preaching," 835–836.

69. Hunter (ed.). *Dictionary of Pastoral Care*, 934.

70. Ibid., 867.

71. Petta, "In Search of a Contextual Pastoral Theology," 177.

cases similar to practical theology. What makes the two terms distinct is the wait of the term '*pastor*' and how it is reflected in the one doing theology. The word "*pastor*" is a Latin word which means "shepherd" suggesting the caring work of the shepherd to his or her sheep. Basing on the definition of the term "pastor" pastoral theology is not a mere application of theological principles to issues of worship, Christian education, preaching, counseling, etc. as conceived by practical theology. Rather, pastoral theology bases its knowledge on the ministry of care done by *ordained pastors* where the contextual and biblical theologies are applied and integrated with social science approaches in promoting healing and transformation (wholeness).[72] Pastoral theology uses "biblical and theological resources to inform a faithful use of secular psychological wisdom. The behavioral sciences are integrated into the practice of care in ways that preserve the integrity of a particular theological or biblical perspective."[73]

Seward Hiltner is considered to be the father of modern pastoral theology who was influenced by the clinical pastoral educationist Anton T. Boisen and systematic theologian Paul Tilich.[74] Quoting Hunter, Petta notes: "Hiltner remains a major conceptual resource...because he was the first systematic theorist of clinically based pastoral theology, and because his theory attempted to be a comprehensive methodological framework for all of the theology including practical theology, and of course, pastoral theology which was its principle concern."[75] Hiltner, the founder of pastoral theology, defines it in light of shepherding thus: Pastoral theology is "that branch or field of theological knowledge and inquiry that brings theshepherding perspective to bear upon all the operations and functions of theChurch and the minister, and then draws conclusions of a theological order fromreflection on these observations."[76] However, the shepherding perspective of Hiltner has suffered considerable criticisms. According to Petta, Hiltner's "pastoral theology is often critiqued as being individualistic, clerical based, and blind to the contextual and cultural factors that shape particular pastoral situations. Moreover, he 'relied heavily on the practical wisdom and theoretical

---

72. Ramsay (ed.), *Pastoral Care and Counseling*, 5–6.

73. Ibid., 6.

74. Petta, "In Search of a Contextual Pastoral Theology," 65–69.

75. Ibid., 169.

76. Hiltner, *Preface to Pastoral Theology*, 20. Before Hiltner, pastoral theology was considered to be part of systematic theology. Theologians doing systematic were considered to be doing what was called 'real theology' while those doing pastoral theology were considered to be applying systematic theology to the real lives of people (see Petta, "In Search of a Contextual Pastoral Theology," 165.

foundations of psychology."⁷⁷ In the same background, Barbara defines: "Pastoral theology is the branch of theology that is concerned with the basic principles, theories, and practices of the caring and counseling offices of ministry."⁷⁸ In this case, "pastoral theology seeks to bring meaning religious and moral meanings to bear on the needs, problems, and activies of everyday human experience to interpret their significance, understanding their etiologies, and guide appropriate and healing interventions."⁷⁹

However, other scholars have challenged the "shepherding" metaphor which Hiltner used in developing his clinical psychologically based pastoral theology. Kenneth R. Mitchel, as quoted in Petta, for example, writes:

> The metaphor was a relic of rural, agricultural times, unfit for use in modern urban society. Besides, sheep are notoriously unintelligent, stubborn animals; the comparison of intelligent human beings to stupid sheep is insulting and inaccurate. The metaphor involves the assumption that there is the person who knows what is good for the sheep far better than do the sheep themselves. They may be true with sheep, but it is a dangerous, ill-founded assumption to make about relationships between pastors and parishioners.⁸⁰

Therefore, the above challenge indicates that the methaphor used in modern society is not context sensitive and dangerous, especially due to its holding of the individualistic and paternalistic natures of the classical paradigm of pastoral care which "limits pastoral functions to healing, sustaining, guiding and reconciling."⁸¹

Several other definitions of pastoral theology were provided after Hiltner's pioneer work. Ramsay, for example, further defines pastoral theology thus:

> Pastoral theology is that branch of theology that constructs theories and practices of personal and corporate care, and contributes to the constructive theological task and to the common good by identifying, evaluating, and modifying the technical practices, core meaning systems, and normative value structures operating within and between all of the efforts of care brought to bear upon individuals and groups within our common life. To accomplish its task, pastoral, pastoral theology develops for

77. Petta, "In Search of a Contextual Pastoral Theology," 171.
78. McClure, *Moving beyond Individualism*," 19.
79. Ibid., 20.
80. Petta, "In Search of a Contextual Pastoral Theology," 172.
81. Ibid., 181.

public debate and policy interpretations of our common life, norms by which this life will be lived, and practical strategies for healing, sustaining, guiding, and liberating individuals, cultures, and the natural order.[82]

It is in the matter stated by Ramsay above that pastoral theology is refered to as being the "caring of souls."[83] It is a theology that confronts human daily predicaments to advocate healing and wholeness and contributes to human growth in faith. This theology is mainly enshrined in the caring experiences of the pastor to his or her sheep. In this book, however, both terms pastoral theology and practical theology will be used; it should be understood that these terms are different but related to each other. Ramsay's above definition indicates that what distinguishes between pastoral and other theologies is its applicability to people's lived lives. Pastoral theology involves in the lives of Christians; it is the practical formulation of other theologies incorporating it in the real lives of Christians.

The *Dictionary of Pastoral Care and Counseling*, the New Edition, further defines pastoral theology as "the branch of theology which formulates the practical principles, theories and procedures for ordained ministry in all of its functions (though in the nineteenth century often excluding homiletics)"; it is also defined as "The practical theological discipline concerned with the theory and practice of pastoral care and counseling. In addition to a study of methods of helping and healing, this includes studies of moral and religious life and development, personality theory, interpersonal and family relationships, and specific problems like illness, grief, and guilt."[84] The dictionary continues to defines pastoral theology as,

> A form of theological reflection in which pastoral experience serves as a context for the critical development of classic theological understanding. Pastoral theology in this sense generally focuses on topics like illness, death, sexuality, family, and personhood, though in principle and theology topic may be considered from a pastoral perspective—faith, hope, love, salvation, and God, for example. Here pastoral theology is not a theology of or about pastoral care but a type of contextual theology, a way of doing theology pastorally. Pastoral theology in this sense is complementary, not competitive. . . .[85]

---

82. Ramsay (ed.), *Pastoral Care and Counseling*, 15.
83. Benner, *Strategic Pastoral Counseling*, 13–28.
84. Hunter (ed.), *Dictionary of Pastoral Care* (2007).
85. Ibid.

Basing on the above definition, there is no pastoral theology without pastoral experiences. The experience of shepharding the sheep is what makes the theology "*pastoral*." Stating on the reasons for pastoral counseling, which belongs to this theology being pastoral, Snodgrass states: "The adjective *pastoral* refers to the metaphor of the shepherd present in Jewish and Christian scriptures; shepherds are key figures throughout these texts. David, a young shepherd, was chosen by God to become king. God was depicted as shepherd in Psalm 23, highlighting God's caring and protective natures. 'The Good Shepherd," guided, protected, and gave his life for his 'sheep." An Abel, Abraham and Rachel spent time in the pastures caring for and guiding their flocks. The adjective *pastoral* not only refers to this rich religious heritage, but also indicates how, through 'careful listening, through sensitive responses, and with compassionate understanding, the pastoral counselor sherpherds persons into a new grazing land, leads people to cooler waters."[86]Therefore, the experiences of ordained ministers as they handle various issues facing Christians they minister forms the bases of the theologizing process to lead to the formation of pastoral theology.

Ministry

The fifth term is ministry. The concept of ministry is confusing in our current time. This is because there are numerous ministries, each claiming to be a genuine ministry. In the Christian sense, ministry involves two people: the one who offers it and the one to whom it is offered. Ministry is a service offered by Christian believers in the Church and community, which includes feeding, healing, preaching, comforting, guiding, caring, counseling, reconciling, and shepherding. Moreover, ministry also includes of Eucharist, Baptism, prayer and worship. Hence, these are refereed as the ministry of care. It is the ministry of all people of God.[87]

Narrative

The sixth term is narrative. Narrative (life story) is a story which communicates something (life experience) about the teller or the listener. It is an interactive conversation. In regard to narrative in social research, Elliot quoting from Hinchman and Hinchman defines narrative as follows:

---

86. Snodgrass, "Pastoral Counseling," 2–3.

87. Hunter (ed.), *Dictionary of Pastoral Care*, 737; Segler, "The Concept of Ministry," 141–142; Benner, *Strategic Pastoral Counseling*, 18.

"Narrative (stories) in the human sciences should be defined provisionally as discourses with a clear sequential order that connect events in a meaningful way for a definite audience and thus offer insights about the world and/or experiences of it."[88] Following Elliot's definition, in this book the term narrative will be widely explored and used to fit into the African (Tanzanian) context of our study. Narrative will not only deal with life stories, but also go further on using metaphors, stories (fiction and non-fiction), proverbs, allegories, riddles, symbols, images, plays, songs, poems, and dramas which come as a way of expressing things or experiences of people's lives.

We also agree with Speedy who says that narrative is a way of using the language which makes sense of things. It is not only about narrative used as literary or academic term, but also as a 'story' which is used in a daily basis.[89] In this book, the reader might sometimes find that the terms narrative and story as overlapping one to another despite the distinction or differences which we respect will be discussed in the third chapter. Children are much more interested in such methods in integration with pastoral counseling when used appropriately with their own condition of coping and understanding. Therefore, narrative approach in/to pastoral counseling is, to our opinion, an appropriate method for OVC.

Metaphor

The seventh term is metaphor. The word 'metaphor' is derived from the Greek word *metapherein* which means to transfer or to carry something across. It is a figurative language where the word or phrase is being used to refer to something else. It is a "word or group of words used to give particular emphasis to an idea or sentiment.[90] The *Concise Oxford Dictionary* also defines metaphor as "a figure of speech in which a word or phrase is applied to something to which it is not literally applicable." Metaphors can be found in our daily use of language such as in narratives (stories), and other sayings. In the Christian context as well as in the African context metaphors are being used. For example, the gospels tell us the story of Jesus as the 'lamb of God' (John 1:29, c.f. Revelation 5:6), a 'good shepherd' (John 10:1, c.f. Psalms 23:1), or the 'lion of Judah' (Revelation 5:5). Moreover, Jesus called himself as the 'bread of life' which came from heaven (John 48, 51). In Tanzania we also have this figurative language; for example, one might say: *Mchumia juani ulia kivulini*, which means that the one who gathers in

---

88. Elliot, *Using Narrative*, 3.
89. Speedy, *Narrative Inquiry*, 45–46.
90. *Microsoft Encarta Encyclopedia*.

the sun will eat in the shade. This is a proverb which teaches people to be patient to work hard in life despite the hardships showing that people expect to reap from their work at the end.

Story

The eighth term is story. The *Concise Oxford Dictionary* defines story as "an account of imaginary or real people and events told for entertainment" It is an "account of past events, experiences, etc."[91]. A story can either be fiction or non-fiction. A story can be used in everyday conversation about life and the way we experience that life. We are surrounded with stories everywhere. There are different kinds of stories; as it has been pointed out, there are "folk stories, virtual stories, latent stories and untold stories, and 'narrative' as in the telling of stories. 'Story' 'is something that is delivered by narrative but seems to pre-exist it', whereas 'narrative always seems to come after, to be a representation.'"[92] In the distinction between a 'story' and a 'narrative,' it is pointed out:

> A fundamental element that makes a distinction between story and narrative possible is one of intentionality, in the sense that a story communicated intentionally and is governed by certain formal rules of structure and content. . . .Narrative, on the other hand, can be viewed as being embedded within the conversation or interaction between people and is not formalised in the sense that a story is and not necessarily experienced as a story by the listener.[93]

The above distinction still indicates that there is an overlap between the terms 'story' and 'narrative' despite the differences they have. And in these two terms most of the times metaphors are being used and applied in daily conversation. Narratives can come in the form of stories (life story), stories (fiction and non-fiction), metaphors, riddles, songs, poems, proverbs, images and symbols. In this case, the term narrative as will be used in this book means many things. It is used interchangeably representing the mentioned terminologies, story, metaphors, riddles, songs, proverbs, images symbols etc., depending on the context of its use.

---

91. *Concise Oxford Dictionary.*
92. Speedy, *Narrative Inquiry*, 46.
93. Cattanach (ed.), *The Story so far*, 49.

Church

The ninth term is church. The Church with a capital letter "C" refers to the Christian community, a universal community of believers who believes in the life and death of Jesus Christ. It is a community of believers who follow and lives on the teachings of Jesus Christ. It is the community of fellowship which has agreed to live a life of sharing, caring for the wellbeing of individuals (i.e., members).[94] The church with a small "c" is just a denomination or sect within the universal community of believers. Both of the two uses of the term church will be seen in this book

In this book, the service of the Church goes beyond its boundaries when it comes to the services in the community. Most of the FBOs in Tanzania, and Mbeya in particular, are not restricted to the service of their own people of the same faith; but they go beyond their denominations and faiths. When it comes to the community service, it involves all people of all faiths: Christians, Moslems, and others. Moreover, in this book, a distinction is made between the Church as a universal community of believers in Jesus, and the church or churches as denominations or sects within the universal Church. The universal Church will have a capital C while denominations will have a small letter c.

Orphans and Vulnerable Children

The tenth term is Orphans and Vulnerable Children. The definition of 'orphan' is complex and varies between countries, cultures, and ethnic groups within Africa. In most cases its definition comprises of two main variables: age (below 18 years) and parental loss (both or one parent dead).[95] However, in most African countries, orphans are children under the age of 18 who have lost one or both parents. Most of the children's parents die from AIDS related diseases, but others die from other causes. These children also have been vulnerable to or infected and affected by the HIV and AIDS. Being vulnerable to the HIV and AIDS, they are known by various names: "children affected by AIDS" (CABA), "children and adolescents affected by AIDS" (CAA), "children in distress" (CD), "children in extremely difficult circumstances" (CEDC), "children in need of special protection" (CNSP) and "children from disjointed households" (CDH).[96] In whatever name is

---

94. Hunter (ed.), *Dictionary of Pastoral Care*, 202.

95. Smart, Policies for Orphans, 3; cf. Boss, "The Trauma and Complicated Grief"; Price, "Walking through the Dackness"; Jones, "A Theology of Hope."

96. Smart, *Policies for Orphans*, 4.

ascribed to orphans, the main issue encompassing all of them is their vulnerability to acute life circumstances, which in most cases does not face children only but even adults.

The concept of vulnerability has to do with being at high risk to a particular situation. One can be at high risk of dying due to hunger, being infected by a particular disease, being surrounded by robbers, etc. In the context of this book, vulnerable children are those who become at high risk because of different circumstances in life within communities they live. They become vulnerable because of their parents' deaths, diseases, and poverty. These are the children who are in great risk of being abused, displaced, infected and affected by the sexually transmitted infections (diseases).[97] Abashula, Jibat and Ayele clearly state that "Orphans and vulnerable children have been suffering from a lot of problems associated with these vulnerability factors. Some of the problems they face include hunger, lack of access to health and education, physical and psychological abuse, lack of love and affection and negative communities' attitude towards them. . . ."[98] However, Chogo distinguishes bwtween orphanhood and vulnerability when she states: "Not all orphans are vulnerable and also not all vulnerable children are orphans."[99] This means that someone who is vulnerable can be dependent and looks for support, or independent from anybody. What makes both of the two groups equal is the susceptibility to facing a particular harshi situation. Both face harsh situations, though in different extents.

Resilience

The eleventh term is resilience. The term "resilience" refers to the capacity for successful adaptation despite challenging or threatening circumstances.[100] It is the ability to cope well with difficult situations in life. In the case of children, resilience is the ability for them to cope with their parents' illnesses and deaths, with loss and grief. Children find coping skills when they are supported by adults to know and tell stories about their families. In this case, narratives can play great roles as tools for children's resilience, an investigation done by this study.

---

97. Hunter (ed.), *Dictionary of Pastoral Care*, 273; cf. Lekule, "Investigating School Experience," 44–48; Ng'ondi, "Characteristics of Most Vulnerable Children," 1.

98. Abashula, Jibat & Ayele, "The Situation of Orphans," 247; Ng'ondi, "Characteristics of Most Vulnerable Children," 1–2; Kacholi, "Assessment of Factors," 8–9.

99. Chogo, "Improved Income," 2.

100. Foster, Levine and Williamson (eds.), *A Generation at Risk*, 107.

Coping

The twelfth term is coping. The concept of coping is applied where there is a counter situation. Coping is the act of someone to adapt to circumstances that can be challenging or difficult to him or her. It is the way of being firm, strong, and flexible to unexpected or shocking situation. It is a defense mechanism which every person has been created with. The person tries to adapt and maintain or preserve what he or she thinks and believes it is his or her right.[101] Here, in this book, coping will be used in relation OVC and the way they try to deal with issues related to their needs and problems.

Healing

The thirteenth term is healing. In the article called "Love: A Philosophy of Pastoral Care and Counseling," Streets writes thus in regard to illnesses and the human endeavor for the restoration of health:

> We have, since our beginning as a human species, sought to defne illness and health and assign to it a meaning. We seek advice and help for what troubles us from a variety of healers and sources depending upon our physical and emotional needs and cultural context. Healers are called by many different names ranging from physician and psychotherapist to priests and diviners. Healing practices vary to include our calling upon divine intervention in addition to engaging in other non-traditional and traditional therapeutic practices in our effort to feel better. These practices . . . "function as important epistemic and generative resources for how Africana populations [people everywhere . . .] deploy religious meaning, invoke counter strategies of resistance, and seek to create remedies of restorative health and wholeness as protective shields from individual and collective affliction, disease, threat, and annihilation."[102]

As just pointed out by Streets above, healing is a very wide term, frequently used but hardly well defined. This term originates from the Greek word *"therapeuo"* which literally means "to heal". It is the word which signifies more than a physical wellbeing of the person. It comprises of peace and harmony in the person's life. It also denotes calmness, and wholeness. Pastoral care involves healing and caring *"cura animarum,"* cure of souls. According to Benner, the concept of cura animarum is a Latin and embraces both

---

101. Hunter (ed.), *Dictionary of Pastoral Care*, 267–269.
102. Streets, "Love: A Philosophy of Pastoral Care," 1.

'caring' and 'curing' or 'healing.'[103] Healing also involves spiritual and psychological growth.[104] Wendler provides the following definition: "Healing is an experiencial, energy-requiring process in which space is created through a caring relationship in a process of expanding consciousness and results in a sense of wholeness, integration, balance and transformantion and which can never be fully known."[105] In this definition, several aspects can be identified: the experience of the one whom the healing encounter, the need for energy in order to experience healing, a caring relationship with a specific space for it, an expansion of consciousness about the existing situation, and the feeling of integration and wholeness as final encounters. Following this definition, healing is an encounter which someone faces as he or she moves from low consciousness about a particular situation which hinders him or her from being whole and integrated towards a certain consciousness which leads that person to wholeness and integration. The whole of this encounter is a process in ones experience which requires energy. It required energy and relationship in order for Jesus to heal the world and its universal sickness. And this is this energy requiring healing which Jesus commissioned to his disciples and to the whole Church.[106]

Wholeness

The fourteenth term is wholeness. Wholeness is the process of becoming whole. It is the process of maturity into both spiritual and physical. It is the word which is associated with what the Bible calls 'salvation', which means harmony and peace with oneself, with other people, with creation, and with God. It is the relationship of a human web in creation. Carl Gustav Jung calls it as the process of individuation, where the person comes to terms with his or her inner being.[107] Similarly, Louw asserts that "The use of the term *soul* in Scripture refers to human wholeness and not to a different substance...."[108] The term has its origin from Hebrew *nephesh* and Greek *psyche* which refer "to the whole person, including the body, but with particular focus on the

---

103. Benner, *Strategic Pastoral Counseling*, 14.

104. Lebacqz and Driskill, *Ethics and Spiritual Care*, 62.

105. Wendler, "Understanding Healing," 836.

106. Cf. Bate, "A Theological Model of Healing," 69–70; cf. Salt, "Healing in the Context of Palliative Care," 10.

107. Hunter (ed.), *Dictionary of Pastoral Care*, 36–37; cf. Louw, "A Theological Model," 2.

108. Louw, "A Theological Model," 2.

inner world of thinking, feeling and willing."[109] Human wholeness entails a life of hope, an inner hope. As Louw further notes, "Without hope, the human soul is killed; hope is the music of a heuristic soul. Furthermore, if the Christian caregiving cannot open up a vista of hope what then is the character of comfort and compassion and what kind of 'future music' we are going to play in making the soul whole?"[110]

Book Outline and Synopsis

This book comprises of seven chapters. The first chapter is an introduction, which provides the rationale and the background of the study. The problem and the thesis statement are also discussed in this chapter. The research question and objectives of the study, scope and limitation of the book, and the definition of key terms are explained here in the introductory chapter. The second chapter surveys the context of the study in general. The background of the area studied, and the general overview of several issues related to the book are discussed in this chapter. From the context of Tanzania in the region of Mbeya, the issues related to the HIV and AIDS and Sexuality, orphans and vulnerable children in Mbeya, and the pastoral ministry to children in Mbeya is discussed in this chapter.

Chapter Three surveys the relevance of literatures in the study of different theories and approaches as have been used and applied by different scholars in this context of the study.

Chapter Four discusses the methods used in the research (i.e., empirical research). The methodological part deals with how the study was conducted. The population of the study, data collection and instruments used, data analysis and presentation, validity and reliability of the methods are discussed in detail in this chapter.

Chapter Five discusses the results and analysis of the research findings. In this chapter we discuss in detail all what happened in the field research. From what was seen and observed, the chapter discusses the interactions and interviews, the recorded and written documents, the focus group and case studies. The analysis of the data will also be discussed in details and interpreted to fit the objectives which have been laid in this introduction. The focus of discussion of data collected is mainly based on exploring, interpreting and understanding OVC and how they can be helped. Hence, the discussion of obtained data helped us to see whether the method has been effective and worked to the intended goals or objectives that were set.

109. Benner, *Strategic Pastoral Counseling*, 14
110. Louw, *Wholeness in Hope Care*, 14.

Chapter six presents and discusses our own creative model that can be helpful and applied in pastoral counseling to OVC. The model comes as a result of the study in the field research to find any other effective and workable alternative approach in the field of pastoral theology. The goal of this model is to come up with a model which is more integrative in its approach. This is the model which will be applied in practical theology and particularly with pastoral counseling. The model is known as "integrative narrative cycle" for pastoral counseling to OVC. Further, this chapter will also deal with the outcome of the result found from the research findings and analysis. It is seen that the model developed has a good connection between the pastoral theology and the narrative approach in pastoral counseling in particular. The integration of narrative approach in practical theology is applicable in working with OVC in an African context. Eventually, chapter seven is the conclusion of the book, where the summary of research is provided; moreover, the challenges, recommendations, and suggestions for further research are discussed in a conclusive way.

CHAPTER 2

Exploring the Context of Study in Tanzania

"The children of the world are innocent, vulnerable, and dependent. They are also curious, active, and full of hope. Their time should be one of joy and peace, of playing, learning, and growing. Their future should be shaped in harmony and co-operation. Their lives should mature, as they broaden their perspectives and gain new experiences."

—World Declaration on the Survival, Protection, and Development of Children
Quoted in Smart, *Policies for Orphans*, 1.

Introduction

THE RESURGENCE OF THE HIV and AIDS has been the reality in countries within Sub-Saharan Africa in such a way that it has various connotations and denotations in both popular and academic discourses. To some, it is a "silent killer" that takes the lives of most people; and to others it is a "weapon of mass destruction," a "disease without cure," and a "killer disease" that does not pay attention to age, nationality and ethnic group to which one belongs. However, in whatever representation the HIV and AIDS have been done in popular and academic discourses, no nation, race, or ethnic group should be submerged into a false hope of not being affected or infected by the pandemic. This is because, in the real sense, the pandemic is devastating to the whole human race making all people vulnerable to death, caring for the dying, or caring for orphans.[1]

1. Bongmba, *Facing a Pandemic*, 9–39.

This chapter surveys the background of the study. It provides the reader an understanding of the context of the study where the research was undertaken. The context of the study is Mbeya region in Tanzania. The question is: Why Mbeya region? Mbeya region is one of the regions which are most affected by the HIV and AIDS in Tanzania, and that is where we decided to undertake our research work. The study surveys some issues surrounding the area of study. The issues or questions which have to be addressed in this chapter are the following: How much have the HIV and AIDS affected the region of Mbeya and Tanzania in general? What challenges have been brought to the Church and the Tanzanian society as a whole since the HIV and AIDS pandemic came into existence? The possible challenges are such as the increase of orphans and other vulnerable children, poverty in communities, ignorance, and stigma in the Church and in societies. Finally, this chapter looks at what should be the response of the Church, and how pastoral counseling ministry should be exercised as part of the pastoral ministry in society, especially to orphans and vulnerable children in Mbeya. Therefore, this chapter establishes the background and context of the study following the questions posed above.

Overview of Geographical Area

Tanzania, officially known as "The United Republic of Tanzania," is a country in the coast of the eastern part of the African continent. Countries which border Tanzania are Kenya and Uganda in the north, Burundi, Rwanda and the Democratic Republic of Congo in the west, and in the south are Zambia, Mozambique and Malawi. The Indian Ocean is in the eastern side of Tanzania. The country's name 'Tanzania' was named after Tanganyika obtained independence from the British colony in 1961. Tanzania was a result of the union between Tanganyika (the mainland) and Zanzibar (the islands in the Indian Ocean) which happened after the independence in 1964

Politically, the country was dominated by the right wing of socialist system of one ruling party since independence. Since 1985, the politics of Tanzania changed towards the democratic systems of multi-parties. By the time this study was conducted, Tanzania had 26 regions having more than 120 tribes with different ethnic groups and languages; however, only two languages were official: Swahili and English. Swahili language was widely and almost being spoken by everyone; but English was a foreign language learned in schools and used in official matters.[2] Therefore, Swahili was the

---

2. Mligo & Mwashilindi, *English as a Language of Teaching and Learning*.

dominant language in normal life communications and in most schools, especially primary schools.

By the time when this research was done, Tanzania had a population of more than 38,000,000 and the growth rate per year was about 2.61 percent. It was one of the poorest countries in the world with a US$ 320 GNI per capita.[3] Its economy was mainly dependent on agriculture, whose technology was yet very poor; the hand hoe was still being used by most people. This poor technological advancement was also one of the factors which made this part of Africa more vulnerable to the HIV and AIDS and their effects.

Tanzania mainland had three main religions (Christianity, Islam, and African Traditional Religion): nearly 40 percent of the population was Christians, 30 percent were Moslems, and 30 percent were traditional religious adherents. Surprisingly, in the islands of Zanzibar the population was largely Moslem who occupied about 99 percent. This was mainly because Zanzibar was dominated by the Arabs in the 18th and 19th centuries and even before that, while the mainland Tanganyika was under the protectorate of Germany and then the British by that time.[4] Most of the people were educated in primary and secondary levels but not in college or university levels. This factor of low educational levels and other factors discussed above still contribute to problems in Africa and particularly to Tanzania. Tanzania, as well as other countries in Africa, is affected socially, politically, economically and religiously by the various factors which resulted from the colonial legacy. This means that, relief, foreign aids, corruption, abuse of power, drought, overpopulation, violence, poverty, the HIV and AIDS, civil and ethnic conflicts are some of the factors which contribute to the many problems in Africa.[5]

It is our conviction that through African resources and initiatives such as using heritages of African wisdom of using the narrative approach, such as using proverbs and other techniques, Africans can overcome their many problems. As it will be seen in the following chapters, narrative approach provides creativity in the person, which eventually leads to knowledge and change. Narrative approach teaches how the importance of a human being (dignity) is. The Swahili people would say, '*utu*,' to mean 'the human-ness.' It is all about the holistic growth of the person who has to grow into the fullness of life in the midst of other beings. Therefore, the real growth of countries and people starts from below and not from above (i.e., it hardly

---

3. UNICEF, UNAIDS AND PEPFER, "Africa's Orphaned and Vulnerable Generations."

4. *Microsoft Encarta Encyclopedia*.

5. Cf. Kimilike, "An African Perspective on Poverty," 67–70.

starts from people who are elite and are in authority, but from people who are poor and marginalized in society).[6]

Magnitude of the HIV and AIDS

After an overview of the geographical area, this section surveys the resurgence of the HIV and AIDS in Tanzania and its consequences. In sub-Saharan Africa, it was estimated that by the end of 2001 the number reached over 11 million children who lost one or both parents due to AIDS. By 2010 that number was expected to increase to 20 million. It was said, "about 5.7 per cent of all children in sub-Saharan Africa will be orphaned by AIDS by 2010."[7] This means that many orphans range at the age between six to seventeen years old.[8]

The HIV and AIDS in Tanzania were reported since the early 1980s in Kagera region, the northern part of Tanzania which is neighboring Uganda, Rwanda and Burundi. Since then the pandemic spread throughout the country making it one of the most affected countries in the southern part of the Sahara. It is estimated that there is more than 1,300,000 reported cases of the HIV and AIDS. The prevalence rate of the HIV and AIDS infection is about 8.8% of the population among those aged 15-49 years. Children orphaned by AIDS are estimated to be 980,000 (2003 estimation). By 2010, Mbeya region was leading with the highest number of AIDS cases while Rukwa region had the lowest.[9]

Tanzania has a population of more than 38 million and almost half of the populations are children under the age of 14 years which is 43 percent of the general population. The life expectancy at birth is only 46 years (2000—2005 estimation). The reduction in life expectancy due to AIDS is 12 years. People living with the HIV and AIDS (15+ years) in Tanzania in 2005 were estimated to be 1.3 million. Children living with the HIV and AIDS in 2005 under 14 years was estimated to be 110,000. The AIDS death by 2005 was estimated to be 140,000 (UNICEF, 2006). These population–death estimations indicate that AIDS takes the lives of people to a greater extent leaving a great number of children without care. Moreover, the rates of AIDS infections indicate that children are one of the most vulnerable groups.

---

6. Cf. Ibid., 120–121; cf. Evans, *Lazarus at Table*, 11–25.

7. USAID et al. in Foster, Levine, and Williamson (eds.), *A Generation of Risk*, 5; cf. Kacholi, "Assessment of Factors," 8.

8. Foster, Levine, and Williamson (eds.), *A Generation at Risk*, 5.

9. WCC, *Facing AIDS*; cf. Kacholi, "Assessment of Factors," 8.

The above estimations had greatly changed by the year 2014. By the year 2014, the estimated population in Tanzania was more than 40 milion people (according to the census of 2012) and a half of this was children of the age below 18 years. The SOS Children's Villages International reports that "The 2012 Population and Housing Census results showed that, Tanzania had a population of 44,928,923. Children under 15 years made up 44.1% (19,813,655) of the total population. To date the number of MVCs in the country is about 3,000,000. These children are living without parental care or at risk of losing it. These include double orphans (230,256), maternal orphans (462,688), paternal orphans (1,283,067), children cared by elderly (327,514) and those cared by siblings (200,091). In 2012, 11,565 children were living in residential homes. 453children were in conflict with the law and kept under prison, 578 were in detention, 80 in retention, and 80 in approved schools. . . ."[10]

For Tanzania, UNICEF estimated the number of orphans by AIDS under the age of 17 years to reach 980,000 by 2003. The orphans under the same age, but due to all causes are estimated to be 2,500,000, while the population (in 2004) of the children under 18 years old was estimated to be 18,833,000. It is almost half of the population of the whole country of Tanzania, which was about 38 million by then. Most of the data for this study were collected in 2008, which means that from the year 2004 to 2018 the above figures have probably increased greatly.

In Tanzania, it was estimated that people living with the HIV and AIDS to be 1.4 to 1.6 million (2003 estimation). And people who died due to AIDS were estimated to be between 140,000 and 180,000. Children who lived with the HIV and AIDS were estimated to be 110,000 to 210,000 under the age of 14 years. The orphans due to AIDS under the age of 17 years were approximated to be between 1.1 million to 1.2 million. In one of the speeches of the then Tanzanian President Jakaya Mrisho Kikwete, he showed that the total number of all orphans in Tanzania was estimated to be 2 million.[11] This shows that the number of orphans has not remained stagnant; it has increased by this year when this book is written.

Mbeya is the most affected regions in Tanzania. Mbeya city which has 36 wards had about 30,000 children who were most vulnerable. The population of Mbeya urban district was 266,422.[12] This number of most vulnerable children was about 10% of all children in the city of Mbeya. These children included orphans, street children, disabled children, and children

10. SOS Children's Villages International, *Assessment Report*, 10.
11. Mwendapole, "Kikwete: Tusiwanyanyapae wenye UKIMWI."
12. Tanzania National census, 2002.

who came from poor families.[13] Moreover, Mbeya is one of Tanzania's 26 original administrative regions, excluding the newly added regions of Katavi, Njombe, and Songwe.[14] The regional capital is Mbeya. Before the division of the region into two (Mbeya and Songwe), it was bordered to the northwest by Tabora region, to the northeast by Singida region, to the east by Iringa region, to the south by Zambia and Malawi and to the west by Rukwa region. Mbeya region is currently occupied by several different ethnic groups including the Nyakyusa, Ndali, Lambya, Nyiha, Nyamwanga, Safwa, Malila, Wanji, Bungu, Sangu, Wanda, and Sichela. Most of these tribes are found as mixture of people living at Mbeya City despite those found in rural areas of the region. Mbeya urban is one of the districts of the Mbeya region of Tanzania and comprises of the area of Mbeya town. It is bordered to the north by the Mbeya rural district, to the east by the Rungwe district, to the south by the Ileje district and to the west by the Mbozi district which now belongs to the new Songwe Region. Mbeya region is rich in agricultural food and cash crops such as banana, coffee, maize, beans, tea, cocoa, tomato, groundnuts, and pyrethrum.[15]

Mbeya City is one of the largest cities in Tanzania after Dar es salaam, Mwanza, and Arusha. It is the City where the Great North road passes through (i.e., Cairo to Cape Town). This road is also one of the main roads in Tanzania which begins from Dar es Salaam to Tunduma (the city in Mbeya region which borders Zambia). It is a busy road especially with truck cargoes which go through the city to Malawi, Zambia, and the Democratic Republic of Congo. Hence, this has been one of the reasons why Mbeya has been one of the most affected regions in Tanzania for the HIV and AIDS and other sexually transmitted diseases because of these routes and businesses of truck drivers.

The UNICEF reports that by 2005 the number of orphans was 2.4 million; this was about 12 percent of all the children in Tanzania. However, the AIDS orphans were about 1.1 million which was 44 percent of these children. By 2006 the number of orphans in Tanzania was approximated to reach 2,500,000.[16] Many people become infected by the HIV but without seeing the symptoms for years. It is good to recognize that the HIV and AIDS is not the disease or infection of 'bad people' or 'sinners', it is the in-

13. See TACAIDS, The United Republic of Tanzania, Prime Minister's Office.

14. The information in this subsection was adapted from the document entitled *Mbeya Region Socio-Economic Profile*, in joint publication by the Planning commission Dar es Salaam and Regional Commissioner's Office Mbeya, April 1997.

15. Cf. Mligo & Mwashilindi, *English as a Language of Teaching and Learning*, 70–71.

16. *Tanzania Daima*. "Hakuna Takwimu za Wajane," 6

fection or disease that anybody can be infected or affected by it. Negative attitudes and prejudices towards some people, we label them as 'sinners,' should be eliminated in our minds. This indicates that the HIV and AIDS have affected men and women, heterosexuals and homosexuals, children and adults, black and white, poor and rich, lay people and pastors, believers and unbelievers, and all sorts of people we may know on earth.

Let us again purposely point out how the HIV and AIDS have affected this part of the world statistically. We have already shown statistically how the HIV and AIDS affected the sub Saharan countries in the above paragraphs. These statistics will probably make the Church and society as a whole to be more alert and sensitive to listening and seeing how big the problem is, and then finding ways that will be proper, effective, and applicable in response to all the challenges that the HIV and AIDS bring to this world.

Impact of the HIV and AIDS

The previous section indicated the magnitude of the HIV and AIDS in Tanzania, and in Mbeya Region in particular. This section discusses the impact of the HIV and AIDS in Tanzania. The HIV and AIDS in Tanzania has affected all sectors concerned with the development of the country. The disease has affected the people who have potential for the growth and development of the country; the HIV and AIDS have affected both women and men, young and old. Death has left many children orphans, and has left grief and suffering among people. The HIV and AIDS have caused many other psychosocial problems including poverty and the increase in mortality rate. This pandemic has become a great enemy and threat to society as a whole. There is no cure to AIDS until now. It is a reality with shocking truth that everybody remains affected even though not infected. Therefore, the impact of the HIV and AIDS is vivid in the way it silently kills the responsible people in society and leaves orphans and vulnerable children.

HIV/AIDS and Human Sexuality

This part surveys the relationship between the HIV and AIDS and human sexuality. The study of human sexuality cannot be ignored if we want to understand clearly the issue of the HIV and AIDS especially in Tanzania. Human sexuality is all about who we are as human beings and how we relate to each other. Human sexuality is a very complex subject, often treated in a simplistic way by faith communities and society as a whole. Sexuality is a God-given gift, it is the way God has created us as persons with feelings, intellects, emotions, and acts related to sex in our bodies. People are sexual beings who have been created as female or male; it is the way we are as persons. In this case, the WCC is right when it states that sexuality "is an integral part of human identity."[17]

Sexuality is not only a physical phenomenon; but it is also something directly related human spirituality. Sexuality and spirituality go hand in hand; they should not be separated. If the person wants to know about his or her spiritual life with God he or she must also know her or his own sexual life. The Bible clearly shows that the body is the temple of the Holy Spirit (1 Corinthians 6:19–20; cf. 2 Corinthians 6: 16). The body, which includes sexual organs, has to be a place where God can be worshiped and honored. By understanding the complexity of sexuality in human's life and its potential, one has to be aware of how human relationships work. Misunderstandings and ignorance of our sexual relationships bring about negligence and abuse of health relationships among people. Myths, taboos, and some cultural practices surrounding human sexuality are some of the factors contributing to the spread of the HIV and AIDS in Tanzania. The misuse of our sexual relationships can result in the increase in vulnerability to the HIV infection. Therefore, personal responsibility has to be recognized to prevent the misuse of our sexual relationships.

Directly related to sexuality is the issue of gender which is not the same as sex. Gender is what society defines about people of who is a male or female. Gender inequality is another factor contributing to the spread of HIV infection among people of Mbeya, Tanzania. Education and empowering of people particularly girls/women among Tanzanian people should be advocated strongly if the Church and society as a whole want to break the vicious spread of HIV infection. Negative cultural beliefs and some wrong value systems which tend to suppress women and condone loose sexual life among people should be challenged and criticized. Data show that girls tend to be more vulnerable to HIV infection at earlier ages than boys.[18] In this case, the way girls and boys are treated by society in Tanzania should be considered and challenged, especially the discrimination against girls.

In Tanzania, 90% of the transmission of the HIV infection is through heterosexual relations.[19] In Mbeya, and Tanzania in general, people mostly do not prefer to talk about sex, AIDS, and issues relating to sexual health education. As we observed and listened to various people, we saw that many people believed that if people were allowed to talk openly about issues of

17. WCC, *Facing AIDS*, 30.
18. Foster, Levine & Williamson (eds.), *A Generation of Risk*, 149–150.
19. TACAIDS, The United Republic of Tanzania, The Prime Minister's Office.

sexuality it would result into promiscuous behaviors. Following this notion, which is in most cases erroneous, it is the responsibility of the Church to minimize or break the silence among people and be open to speak out about sexual health relationships. The Church should empower people for sound moral decisions on sex education.

Challenges of the HIV and AIDS

Having discussed the impact of the HIV and AIDS in Tanzania, we turn to Mbeya Region where our research work was done. The first case of HIV in the Mbeya region was diagnosed in 1986. In the past five years or more Mbeya was the second worst hit region in the country after Dar es Salaam. From 2004, Mbeya became the worst hit region in the country by 15.9 percent, while Dar es Salaam was 10.9 percent.[20] Dr. Siyame of the Prime Minister President's Office for Disaster and HIV/AIDS desk said that not all people who were infected by HIV were known; but for the whole country the prevalence rate of HIV infection was approximated to be between 15 to 20 percent.[21] Moreover, in 2002 Mbeya urban district had a population of 266,422. In 2006 the Mbeya urban was approximated to have the population of more than 300,000. The HIV prevalence in the urban area was 14%. The number of orphans was estimated to be about 32,400. Mbeya urban had 36 wards; only six wards had been surveyed, which were reported to have 5,888 orphans and vulnerable children of under 18 years of age (according to one of the leaders of the Step Forward Project Initiative,[22] and one of the Medical Officers of health in Mbeya City[23]). These statistics indicate that the HIV and AIDS are a great challenge to the well-being of both adults and children in Mbeya Region.

Since 1999, AIDS has been the main cause of deaths among adults between 15 and 59 years of age in the country leaving behind children without people to take care of them. It is reported that "The social, economic and human impact of AIDS already has severe consequences for the entire region and the country as a whole. It affects economic productivity and disrupts families and communities, leaving thousands of orphans. It is also reflected in development indicators such as school enrolment, infant

---

20. TACAIDS, The United Republic of Tanzania, The Prime Minister's Office.

21. *Tanzania Daima*, "Hakuna Takwimu za Wajane," 6.

22. This Project leader worked under the office of Mbeya City council. She was interviewed at Mbeya on 10 January 2006.

23. This Medical Officer was interviewed at Mbeya on 11 January 2006.

and child mortality and life expectancy at birth."[24] This means that AIDS has affected all aspects of human life, especially children have been damaged psychologically and socially and cannot develop and grow well in their lives. In other words, the effects of AIDS are too many in societies. AIDS has affected many sectors of life in the region, and the economy of people individually and of the region grows in the pace in which it should be growing. The pandemic causes many negative consequences to communities in Mbeya region to be detailed later in this chapter.

Orphans and Children Living with the HIV and AIDS

This section focuses on the target group: vulnerable children in Mbeya urban. The children living with the HIV and AIDS in Mbeya urban are not distinctly tested and recorded as HIV positive or having AIDS. The number which is usually offered is only an estimation of what researchers approximate according to those few who are tested and records are being taken by some of the health care centers.[25] This is also true to children at *Amani* Orphanage Center where the research was conducted. Generally speaking, the number of children who have been infected or even affected by the HIV and AIDS at Mbeya urban and especially the Uyole area is extremely high. However, any data available are just approximations of those few people who have gone for counseling and testing.

Orphans in Mbeya

As the result of the increased adult deaths in Mbeya region, the number of orphans also increases rapidly. Orphans are the results of one or both parent's death. Death is caused by different circumstances of life including accidents and sickness such as that caused by AIDS. The number of orphans in Mbeya urban also increases tremendously. These orphans bring challenges to the ministry of the Church and the community as a whole. Accommodating and meeting the needs of all orphans in Mbeya is very challenging. The exact figures of these orphans in Mbeya urban are not known; however, the magnitude of how many these children are in Mbeya is the reality which calls every individual to notice. The squatters and streets of Mbeya town are full of these children and some of them do not even have a place to sleep or

---

24. GTZ.
25. TACAIDS, The United Republic of Tanzania, The Prime Minister's Office.

eat, except begging and sleeping in sewage tunnels or at bus stands.[26] The increase of orphans in Mbeya, our study area, most likely due to the HIV and AIDS, points to the need to help these children overcome their situation.

HIV/AIDS and Poverty in Mbeya

As it has been discussed above, one of the impacts of AIDS is the stagnation of economic growth which finally causes poverty to society. The increase in poverty in Tanzania has been caused by many young people who die as a result of AIDS.[27] These young people have potential for the growth of economy in the country. As a result of poverty in Mbeya, Tanzania, children have become more vulnerable to other problems such as becoming more risky to diseases and sicknesses, and to abuses and risky behaviors. Poverty in society also has influenced the rapid spread of the HIV. Poverty increases the risk of becoming more vulnerable to HIV infection due to malnutrition and little or no access to health social services. Poverty causes death to many people who are very dependent in society. When these strong people die in society, people who remain are orphans and old people who suffer from being overburdened with all sorts of difficult situations. It is further stressed:

> Where poverty and HIV coexist, children and households are at risk of great deprivation. The effects—often combined—of decreased income, increased expenses and higher dependency ratios can generate impoverishment in affected families. As the AIDS epidemic takes its toll on communities, there is some indications that orphaned children can end up in poorer households, perhaps because households able to care for an additional child are becoming saturated.[28]

According to the statement above, poverty is one of the factors which make children to be more vulnerable and at great risk of various problems such as HIV, abuse, and other ill factors. Therefore, the impact of AIDS and poverty has to be dealt with simultaneously and effectively to rescue the perishing generation due to the pandemic.

---

26. Interview with one of the Leaders of Step Forward Project Initiative and one of the Medical Officers at Mbeya City on 10 February 2007.

27. TACAIDS, The United Republic of Tanzania, The Prime Minister's Office.

28. UNICEF, "Africa's Orphaned and Vulnerable Generations."

Organizations and the Fight against the HIV and AIDS

Despite all the sufferings and impact of the HIV and AIDS in Tanzania, which includes deaths of potentially responsible people and poverty; the government and the whole society including the Church are not to remain silent about the issue. It is the responsibility of these institutions to educate and respond to the issues brought by the HIV and AIDS. These includes issues of human sexuality, gender, poverty, stigma, healthy, social and other cultural issues which influence the spread of the HIV and AIDS in the country. All these institutions should try their best to fight against the HIV and AIDS. They all have to stand together to fight with this pandemic. All the institutions have to find various ways that are thought to be helpful to fight against the HIV infections. For example, the issue of using condom as one of the ways to prevent the HIV infections has been dividing people of Tanzania. In this case, Institutions have to find their position so that people of Tanzania are not confused with mixed messages.[29]

Organizations Involved

There are several organizations working with the HIV and AIDS in Mbeya urban. These organizations belong to different institutions, such as government institutions, Church institutions, private, and community institutions. They are commonly known as governmental organizations, non-governmental organization (NGOs), faith-based organizations (FBOs), or community based organizations (CBOs). However, Most of these organizations rely on donations and charity from within the region, from outside the region, and even from outside the country. Still, the finances are very much limited to these organizations. It is very difficult for these organizations to meet the basic needs of the resurgent orphans.

Amani Orphanage Center[30]

As pointed out above, there are several FBOs in Mbeya urban. However, researchers conducted research only in one of these FBOs. This is known

29. TACAIDS, The United Republic of Tanzania, The Prime Minister's Office.

30. Interview with Pastor X at Uyole Mbeya on 05January 2007. She was the director of the *Amani* orphanage center. Some of the information on this section was taken from the report on the history of this Center given by the director. The word "*Amani*" used in naming the Center is a Swahili word which means "*peace.*" It indicates that the Center is a place of "peace" for orphans and vulnerable children. In this case, there are

as *Amani* Center which belongs to the Moravian Church in Tanzania, the South West Province (MCTSWP). *Amani* Orphanage Center is a Faith Based Organization (FBO) located at Nsalaga, Uyole Ward in Mbeya Urban District of Mbeya region. *Amani* Orphanage Center is located at the main road which comes from Dar es Salaam to Tunduma, Mbeya (a boarder between Tanzania and Zambia). Uyole, where *Amani* is located is about 12 km before entering the city of Mbeya from Makambako, another town within Njombe Region. Uyole is also a junction to the road which goes to Malawi via Tukuyu town. Uyole is a business area having many activities and with different kinds of ethnic groups from different parts of Tanzania.

As said above, *Amani* Orphanage Center belongs to the Moravian church in Tanzania, the South West Province (MCTSWP) under the Department of Women and Children. By the time this research was conducted, the Church had appointed Rev. Tulinagwe Kibona to be the director of the *Amani* Orphanage Center. *Amani* Orphanage Center had three teachers who were volunteering to help these children. However, as this book was written, the Center was headed by Rev.Bahati Mshani and her assistant Phoibe Kisambwe. Moreover, the Centre had three more teachers and four carers who took care of orphans. Hence, the aim of the center at the beginning was to help those children who were in difficult circumstances such as poverty, abuses, broken marriages, teenage pregnancy, and AIDS orphans.[31]

The center was established in difficult circumstances; it had no smooth beginning. The Moravian church as a whole under the women and children department did not have enough buildings and funds to run the center. Moreover, the department did not have any specific budget for the center. It depended greatly on voluntary contributions of funds, clothing, food and other necessary materials from different people and groups with good wills. This difficult beginning indicated the intention and attitude of the Church towards people in unfavourable situations.[32]

---

several other Amani Orphanage Centers in Tanzania located in various other parts of the country apart from the one located at Nsalaga in Mbeya City with the same connotation of a place of peace.

31. Cf. Nsangalufu, "The Contributions of Local NGOs," 1–2.

32. A similar organization was started at Mpiji village, Maili Mbili Ward in Kibaha District Pwani Region in Tanzania. The name of this organization was Huruma Trust Fund. The word 'huruma' is a Swahili word which means 'mercy' or 'compassion.' Its beginning was as difficult as the Amani Orphanage Center at Uyole Mbeya. Nsangalufu reports that the main aim of Huruma Trust Fund was to provide support to orphans and vulnerable children with the initiatives of the community. Other NGOs for supporting OVC include KIWOHEDE, ANGONET, etc. (For more details about these organizations, see Nsangalufu, "The Contributions of Local NGOs.")

To demonstrate this intention, the center received children from different life circumstances through the help and support of ten cell-leaders and ward executive officers because they were the ones who knew them and the acute lives facing them. These orphans were those whose mothers, fathers or both died from any cause. However, despite trusting the ten-cell leaders, the leadership of *Amani* Orphanage Center also followed up to see whether the children who came to the center were the kind of children who real required help from the Center. The number of children who join the Center has been increasing rapidly since then. At the opening of the center there were only twenty one children, by 2010 the center or the department as a whole took care of more than 200 children who come from different areas such as Mbozi district, Mbeya rural district, and in the streets of Mbeya city, with the majority coming from Uyole area. These 200 children were too many to take care of them with all their needs, especially if there were no any strategic plan or a planned budget on how to finance the center.[33] As we write this book, the Center has children from different parts of Mbeya urban and other parts of Tanzania.

There were about four people or instructors who directly involved with these children when the study was being conducted. Only one instructor was employed by the Church and who was the Director of the Center. This is Rev. Tulinagwe Kibona. The other three instructors worked as volunteers and were taken because of their experience in teaching Sunday schools in their congregations. These teachers tried to help these children in whatever circumstances there were in. These three teachers were only helped with transport fares from their places of residence to the Center. As we write this book, the Center is headed by Rev. Bahati Mshani and her assistant Rev. Phoibe with some servants who help children according to the areas they come from.[34]

These children were sometimes visited by those teachers at their homes. Most of the children were reared by their caregivers such as grandparents and aunts; but some of them had a single parent and some did not have anyone to take care of them. They depended on themselves. The children met at *Amani* Orphanage Center every Saturday from 11am to 3pm. They did several things and activities when they met together with their teachers. They played different games especially football and netball, which were more familiar games to those children. They also did the cleanliness of the surrounding environment. They cleaned the rooms, swept the grounds, watered the trees, and washed dishes. They cooked food for their lunchtime

---

33. Cf. Nsangalufu, "The Contributions of Local NGOs," 6–7.
34. Cf. Nsangalufu, "The Contributions of Local NGOs," 7.

every Saturday, learned the Bible, songs, and other skills such as painting and drawing. Moreover, they learned health and ethical issues related to their daily lives. Sometimes teachers made some follow ups of their home and school progresses and asked them some questions in order to understand their progresses at school and at homes.

The Women and children department had several objectives for *Amani* Orphanage Center. Some of them were as follows:

- Rearing children holistically (i.e., physically, psychologically, and spiritually).

- Educating children by providing them with opportunities for going to school, buying uniforms, exercise books, and paying for school fees.

- Counseling and teaching children various skills of life such as physical exercises, games, health, agriculture, environmental care, and spiritual life.

With these objectives, the future plan of the department was to put some more buildings to be able to accommodate those children and their needs. The department thought of becoming a hostel where some children would voluntarily be able to eat and sleep at the Center.

The second plan of the department was to establish a school from a nursery level to a secondary education level where those children would have a privilege to study by the support of the Church and society as a whole. The third plan was to create income generating projects for the Center. The vision which the department had in mind was the project of animal husbandry, such as cattle, pigs and chicken, and a small garden around the center for vegetables and fruits could be very helpful. All these plans of the Center focused on providing as adequate services to children as possible.

Despite all the progresses and moves which the department had done, it obviously had several obstacles and challenges to face as it continued to reach its goals and objectives. Some of those obstacles were such as lack of enough funds to take care of all those needy children, and meeting their home and school needs (i.e., food, clothing, school fees, medical expenses etc). The department also required some more teachers and counselors trained in issues related to orphans and vulnerable children. The teachers they had were not trained and were not educated in a level where one could think they were of more help to such children. Therefore, funds were also required to educate and train teachers and counselors who could take care of them. Funds were rrequired for educative materials such as books, pictures, boards and other educative materials. The department required having some projects which would help the Center to meet some of the needs it might had. It was hoped that those projects would generate some incomes to help the center be more self-reliant.

With all the progresses and challenges which the Church faced, it is yet hoped that the vision of the church continues now and in the future; and that it comes to its fruition. It is further hoped that the Church will finally be able to help the needy children, especially the OVC as much as it can to meet all their physical and spiritual needs and problems they face.

Pastoral Counseling Ministry to Children[35]

The Church has been called to be a healing community within society. The Christian ministry of Jesus Christ is the model for the Church today. It means that the Church should follow the good example of Jesus Christ on his ministry while on earth. Jesus showed love to people who were downtrodden, the lepers, and sinners; moreover, he showed love to women and children (Luke 4:18–19). The AIDS pandemic calls the Church to think about its ministry towards people of God on earth who have been affected by this pandemic and respond to their situation accordingly. The ministry of the Church is the ministry of love and compassion towards all people no matter what their gender, background, race, sexuality, and faith are.

The majority of inhabitants of Mbeya urban are Christians. Mbeya is also a region with a great number of faith communities (denominations) in the country. However, the most recognized churches are Roman Catholic and Protestant mainline followed by Pentecostal churches. In one way or another, they are all involved in pastoral ministry of care and counseling in communities, congregations, streets, schools, hospitals, prisons, and other organizations. Most ministries being done by the Moravian church and other Protestant churches in Mbeya Tanzania have been doing visitations to sick people in hospitals, visiting prisoners, visiting orphans in the orphanage centers, and visiting the homes of people.[36] This assertion is also supported by the leadership of the Church.[37] Other ministries include some pastoral care of prayers to different kinds of people in society who have been afflicted by the power of evil and darkness, the power of Satan. The minis-

---

35. This subsection is the result of our own experiences and observations as pastors in the area; moreover, we rely on the interviews with leaders of the Moravian church conducted on 24th May 2007 at Mbeya.

36. Interview with Pastor Y on 23 May 2007 at Mbeya. He was one of the pastors in Mbeya city under the MCTSWP.

37. Interview with Pastor Z on 23 May 2007 at Mbeya. He was one of the top leaders of the MCTSWP.

try of anointing, comforting the bereaved people, counseling people who are expecting to be married, expecting a child, and other issues of work, finance, and life in general have also been practiced.

Moreover, it is pointed out that, for voluntary organizations, churches have a large percentage of curative health care system in Mbeya region.[38] Almost every district and many wards have opened health centers for voluntary counseling and testing (VCT). These centers have helped people to be more cautious about their health. These organizations or institutions include faith-based ones, such as churches. Speaking and researching for member churches of the Christian Council of Churches in Mbeya, Tanzania (CCT), the pastoral ministry for children is mostly practiced in different ways. Churches are called to serve people for their moral, spiritual, and physical needs; not only within their own communities, but also in the larger society about issues raised by the HIV and AIDS pandemic. Therefore, the Church has to expand its horizon of ministry to orphaned children in the region more than it is now. Pastoral care and counseling should be broadened to reach such children at risk. To be more responsible to make sure that these children are not forgotten and denied. Different strategies have to be sought for effective ministry in the Church and society as a whole. New revelations and more skills are required for the Church and society as a whole to cope with the challenges of globalization and other forces that are in the world and which are so destructive. New revelations and skills are required in order to cope with the works of evil, the work that are contrary to the good work of God who means good for humanity and other God's creation.

Theologically speaking, the responsibility of the Church towards orphans and widows has been there for centuries. The Bible clearly speaks of Christians to be upfront to take care of orphans and widows (Deuteronomy 10:17–18; 14:28–29; Psalms 82:3–4; Proverbs 23:10–11; James 1:27). The gospels continue to emphasize on how we should treat children when it says, When Jesus saw what was happening, he was angry with his disciples. The text says, "But when Jesus saw it he was indignant, and said to them, 'Let the children come to me, doNot hinder them; for to such belongs the kingdom of God. Truly, I say to you, whoever does not receive the kingdom of God like a child shall not enter it." (Mark 10:14–15) This biblical text indicates that the ministry of care for the wellbeing of children acquires its essence from Christ himself who urges his Church to do the same.

---

38. GTZ.

Conclusion

This chapter has deductively analyzed the context of the study starting from the general Tanzanian context to regional Mbeya urban, and eventually to *Amani* Orphanage Center. It tried to lay the basis for the whole book together with Chapter One. The historical background of the research title and the context of research are such important parts of this book because they open the eyes of the reader towards knowing where, why, how, and what has to be known before going further with other detailed information. The next chapter will go into details of what other scholars have tried to do in relation to this particular study. It reviews literatures on the subject of our concern in order to help readers discern how other scholars have used their approaches, theories, models and methods in different fields of study in order to deal with the question of counseling to people in vulnerable situations.

CHAPTER 3

Surveying Narrative Approaches and Practical Theology

"People are always tellers of tales
They live surrounded by their stories and
The stories of others; they see everything
That happens to them through those stories
And they try to live their lives as
If they were recounting them."

—Webster & Martova, Using Narrative Inquiry, 1.

Introduction

In the preface to their book *Using Narrative Inquiry*, Webster and Martova state: "By its very nature, the use of stories in research means that the researcher has a desire to probe the human centered nature of learning and the associated issues of complexity in a way that is holistic and transcends traditional discipline divides."[1] The above statement indicates that narrative research is centered upon human stories of experience trying to make sense of the retold and lived stories. As they state in the preamble above, human beings are story tellers and are surrounded by stories about themselves and about others. These stories form a rich source of information and analysis to understand what could not be conveyed in other means, except in the form of retold narratives.

Following the above understanding, this chapter reviews literatures in order to survey the current state of knowledge in regard to various issues

---

1. Webster and Martova, *Using Narrative Inquiry*, ix.

of this study as portrayed by other researchers, especially in the theological discipline. According to Mouton, literature reviews are "studies that provide an overview of scholarship in a certain discipline through an analysis of trends and debates."[2] It is further noted that literature review "involves the identification and analysis of information resources and/or literature related to one's research project."[3] Following the above definitions of literature reviews, this chapter reviews different literatures, which are relevant to the study. It reviews studies which have been done in this field of study by other scholars. It explores and examines different concepts and perspectives for the sake of bucking up the thesis statement and objectives set up in the first chapter of this book We aim at being well-structured and systematic in presenting this literature review because "a literature review should be organized around a particular theme, and is written from the perspective or standpoint of the reviewer."[4]

In reviewing literatures, this chapter limits itself to concepts and perspectives which different scholars of psychology, sociology and theology have discussed in their researches. It only discusses these concepts and perspectives focusing on the set objectives. It means that the chapter answers the proposed questions for this study on what other scholars have been using in their studies. What models have they been following in developing their perspectives? Therefore, this chapter aims at surveying different perspectives on narrative approaches and related subjects from various fields, especially from subjects under human sciences such as sociology, psychology, and theology.

In accomplishing the review of literatures and scholarly discussions anticipated in this chapter, the following are some of the aspects that will be focused: the definitions and discussions of various perspectives and their challenges, the discussion of perspectives like Practical Theology, Contextual and narrative theologies, the discussion of concepts like Christian theology, Pastoral Care, pastoral counseling, and human sexuality, and surveying the relationship between HIV/AIDS and pastoral counseling. The chapter dwells greatly on discussing about the care and counseling of orphans and vulnerable children by the use of metaphors, plays, and arts within the narrative approach. The chapter ends with a suggested model of pastoral counseling to orphans and vulnerable children. It is our hope that the chapter covers the necessary aspects to ground the interpretation and discussion of the field research data in the following chapter.

2. Mouton, *How to Succeed*, 179.
3. Terre Blanche, Durrheim & Painter (eds.), *Research in Practice*, 19.
4. Ibid., 21.

It should be clearly noted at the outset that there are no direct parallel works so far in this area, especially as it concerns with the narrative approach integrated with pastoral counseling for OVC in the context of Mbeya in Tanzania. We have also found that there is relatively little written on pastoral counseling to OVC in the African context and even less written in the Tanzanian context in particular. However, there are some researches on pastoral counseling and the HIV and AIDS in which sometimes orphans and vulnerable children are mentioned. In this case, most of the discussions of pastoral counseling to OVC will base on literatures from outside Tanzania.

Moreover, there is no particular literatures that have been written in regard to narrative approach in pastoral counseling to OVC in the Tanzanian context. It is our aim to use different literatures on narrative from outside Tanzanian context and integrate them together to defend our thesis statement whose focus is examining and analyzing the possible use of narratives in pastoral counseling to OVC in Tanzania. Hence, we use the available literatures from the field of pastoral theology, particularly those on counseling, to make a case for the narrative approach as a more suitable model in working with OVC in Tanzania.

Theories, Definitions, and Challenges

We begin the chapter with theories, definitions and challenges. There have been prominent theorists in theology, psychology, sociology, philosophy, and other different fields which sometimes differ in theory, definition, approach, and use of technical terms in counseling. We examine these challenges and approaches in the following subtitles. All subjects or subtitles are relevant and very crucial towards contributing to the research topic we examine in order to fulfill the objectives laid before. Therefore, the following subtitles or themes have to be taken into careful consideration.

Practical Theology and/or Pastoral Theology

The first theme to deal with is about Theology. Theology as discipline has several branches. *Practical theology* is one of these branches. The term itself has been a complex subject for many years till now. It is not my intention to go into details of its historical development. There are several scholars who use the term 'practical theology' synonymously with the term 'pastoral theology'; however, some scholars differentiate between them.[5]

---

5. See Swinton & Mowat, *Practical Theology*; Ramsay (ed.), *Pastoral Care and*

What then is practical theology? What is the difference between practical theology and pastoral theology? We briefly look at the essence of practical theology and its place in this study. On the one hand, practical theology is a theology of faith in action through reading, understanding, and applying the Gospel of Jesus Christ in the experiences of daily lives. However, this definition should not mislead people to understand the term "practical" in the opposition to the term "theoretical". Practical theology deals with matters of life that are applicable, practiced, acted, and performed. In congruence with the statement above, it is noted that "practical theology deals with God's activity through the ministry of human beings."[6] Hence, according to Heitink, practical theology is a theological theory of action (i.e., theory and praxis).[7]

On the other hand, practical theology has been defined, translated, and used or applied in a wider sense than ever before. When it comes to the term *pastoral theology*, some have preferred to use the term as contextual theology or public theology which comes with its style of common or public interest (i.e., resisting, empowering, and liberating).[8] This is mainly because pastoral theology deals with people's lives and their daily challenges and experiences in the community. Pastoral theology is thus defined as follows:

> Pastoral theology as other theologies such as systematic theology, biblical theology, and others, is one of the branches in the field of theology. Pastoral theology deals with theories and practices in the life of individual people and the Church as a whole for the betterment of theology and its tasks. Pastoral theology is not static but it is dynamic whereby it can be renamed, changed, analyzed, criticized, modified, and recreated. Pastoral theology looks for what is best and beneficial for individuals as well as for groups. Pastoral theology looks for the life of the people in the way that are more practical and real, the life that can be lived for the common good of the society and the whole universe. The goal of pastoral theology is to heal, sustain, guide, comfort, and liberate for the purpose of living the life that is whole in the universe.[9]

In regard to the above definition, the concept of *practical theology* means that the theology is practical as well as theory in its content and intent. It is

---

Counseling.

6. Heitink, *Practical Theology*, 7.
7. Ibid., 151–154.
8. Ramsay (ed.), *Pastoral Care and Counseling*, 62, 157.
9. Ibid., 15.

the theology which is done in practices in its theory. The theory of practical theology relies more on its practices. The practices of practical theology include pastoral care and counseling, visitation for the sick and disabled people, prisoners and individuals or groups who are in need and suffer from different challenges of life.

Practical theology and pastoral theology relate to each other. Practical theology takes a bigger and wider view than pastoral theology. We can say that pastoral theology is within the practical theology realms. Pastoral theology is more specific and limited in its application than practical theology. Practical theology does not limit itself on pastoral issues in Church's context alone; it is wider than that. It involves other activities that can be done even by lay people in different contexts and backgrounds. In this case, the two terms are sometimes very difficult to differentiate; they can be used alternatively.[10]

Practical theology as contextual theology is the theology from below; it is theology from people in the grassroots. It is theology which has to be applied in the context where we are doing theology and pastoral counseling, in the African context in particular, the context of marginalized people and people who fall under the great risk of poverty, homelessness, sicknesses, and other hurting social factors. We concur with Bosch in Morkel who summarizes the epistemology that informs contextual theology. Bosch conceives contextual theology as:

> A suspicion that western science, philosophy and theology were designed to serve the interest of the west;
>
> A refusal to endorse the world as static, as something that only has to be explained, but rather as something that has to be changed;
>
> A commitment as the first act of theology and then specifically commitment to the poor and marginalized;
>
> The notion that theology can only be done *with* those who suffer;
>
> An emphasis on doing theology since doing is more important than knowing or speaking (hermeneutics of the deed), and

---

10. For more definitions of these two terms of "practical theology" and "pastoral theology," please see the definitions of terms in the first Chapter of this book.

The notion that hermeneutic circulation starts with praxis or experience, and shifts to reflection on theory with an intersubjective relationship between the two.[11]

We concur with Bosch's highlights of contextual theology above because what he states has been the concern of contextual theologians all over the years since it evolved in the 1970s.[12] From the above description of practical theology, the task of practical theology is to interpret and respond on issues happening to people's lives. Osmer provides four core tasks of practical theological interpretation:

- *"The descriptive-empirical task.* Gathering information that helps us discern patterns and dynamics in particular episodes, situations, or contexts.
- *The interpretive task.* Drawing on theories of the arts and sciences to better understand and explain why these patterns and dynamics are occurring.
- *The normative task.* Using theological concepts to interpret particular episodes, situations, or contexts, constructing ethical norms to guide our responses, and learning from "good practice."[13]
- *The pragmatic task.* Determining strategies of action that will influence situations in ways that are desirable and entering into a reflective conversation with the "talk back" emerging when they are enacted."

The understanding and interpretation of practical theology and its tasks highlighted by Osmer above explain how much it is integrated in its approach. It shows that the process of interpretation is integrative, broader, interconnected, contextual, open and dynamic. Hence, practical theology is pluralistic and integrated to other fields such as arts and social sciences. As Osmel states, "It is not self-enclosed."[14]

The Gospel of Jesus Christ must be understood and applied to our daily living, critically, practically, and contextually. It means that we will understand the gospel and the Christian tradition much better if we apply it to our African traditions and customs, which relates to our daily experiences. It is the way we live as human beings in relation to what we always have

---

11. Morkel, "When Narratives create Community," 26–27; cf. Bevans, "Models of Contextual Theology"; Okafor, "The Challenge of Contextual Theology."

12. See for ExampleWheeler, "The Legacy of Shoki Coe"; Nocholls, *Contextualization*; Bevans, "Models of Contextual Theology."

13. Osmer, *Practical Theology*, 4.

14. Osmer, *Practical Theology*, 240.

and all what God reveals to us through different ways, where we sometimes cannot even imagine. This is what is known as 'faith seeking understanding' where people ought to be questioning, challenging, and seeking new things they cannot understand at the time, especially when it comes to the stories people read from the gospels and other biblical stories.

In this book, our approach to practical theology will be more of narrative hermeneutical approach as explained by theologians such as Charles Gerkin,[15] and Daniel Louw.[16] People live in a story; however, in relationship to the story of God. These stories are interpreted and reflected to find an alternative story (externalizing story) that brings meaning through the process of pastoral hermeneutics. Hermeneutics itself is the way of understanding and interpreting a human being. Hence, this hermeneutics must transcend the normal realm of understanding to understanding human beings in particular contexts and cultural surroundings.

African Christian Theology

All the above stated definitions and explanations on theology, and practical theology in particular, are primarily based on a Western kind of understanding. As African theologians, we are indebted to the use and application of this knowledge to fit to our own African context. What we object from Western theology as Setiloane says is "the accretion of western civilization and culture which have come to be considered as inseparably part and parcel of Christianity."[17] Therefore, as it has been elaborated by the AACC Assembly: "by African theology we mean a theology which is based on the biblical faith and speaks to the African's soul . . . It is expressed in the categories of thought which arise out of the philosophy and world view of Africans."[18]

Our faith, as Africans, should be molded in our own ways of living through the gospel of Jesus Christ. African theology should be rooted in the life and experience of African ways of living (i.e., norms, culture, customs, and traditions). African theology bases its theory on the concept of *utu* in Swahili or *ubuntu* in Zulu. It is the concept which lacks a good translation in English, but just defined as 'humanity'. However, in Swahili or Zulu language, *utu* is more than just humanity; it is dignity. The African worldview of a human person lies not on individuation but on relatedness. Basing on

---

15. Gerkin. *The living Human Document*; and Gerkin, *Widening the Horizons*.
16. Louw, *A Pastoral Hermeneutics of Care* (2003).
17. Setiloane, *African Theology*, 49.
18. Setiloane, *African Theology*, 49.

this relatedness, the human person lives in the community of hospitality and relationships; and this is the African view of a 'person'.[19]

The African perspective on theology bases its understanding on how people live with God, with each other, and with all the creation in the world (cosmos). Most African theologians and Christians emphasize in the theology of health, healing,[20] and liberation.[21] From an African perspective, life is both sacred and secular; that is why in African context one can hardly find contradictions or separations between the two.[22] In African perspective, relationship with the whole cosmos is more important than anything else. Harmony with the forces in the cosmos is the crucial thing. Living a holistic life is the goal of humanity in the community where every human being is seen to belong to society where all people belong and value each other. From this kind of relationship and life, healing happens in society.

This study is all about practical theology in the African context (i.e., contextual approach). Narrative approach is integrated within practical theology so as to bring this study to the aims and objectives intended. Within narrative approaches we find valuable essence, which if translated and applied properly can enrich the ministry of pastoral care and counseling with its focus or base on practical theology. Therefore, as we observe and interpret our daily Christian living and experiences, we try to live the life that God has intended for every one of us, the life of hope and wholeness.

African Contextual Narrative Theology

This subtopic goes much deeper into exploring narrative theology in the African context. African narrative theology is the term which goes deep into the Africans ways of understanding the Bible in their own background and context. It is what many African theologians have called as the 'contextualization or inculturation' of African theology.[23] The continent of Africa and its people has passed the journey of life with many difficulties and problems.

---

19. Magesa, *Anatomy of Inculturation*, 177–180; Evans, *Lazarus at Table*, 11–25.

20. Hunter (ed.), *Dictionary of Pastoral Care* (1990): 12–13; cf. Magesa, *Anatomy of Inculturation*, 94.

21. Mugambi, *From Liberation to Reconstruction*; cf. Mugambi, *Christian Theology*, 61–67.

22. Kunene, "Research in African Literature"; cf. Mbiti, *African Religions*; Mligo, *Elements of African Traditional Religion*.

23. Magesa, *Anatomy of Inculturation*; Cortez, "Creation and Context"; Mugambi, *Christian Theology*; Nicholls, *Contextualization*; Wheeler, "The Legacy of Shoki Coe"; Walligo, Making a Church"; Crollius, "Inculturation"; Bevans, "Models of Contextual Theology."

It is the continent which has experienced and gone through the slave trade, colonialism, neo-colonialism, imperialism, civil, and ethnic wars. It is the continent which has been exploited from its resources. Economically, Africa is probably the poorest continent, and the most stricken with the HIV and AIDS pandemic and with other diseases such as malaria of all other continents in the world. It is the continent which most of the leaders are corrupt having no direction for their countries and people. It is the continent which has to liberate itself from the economic, political, social, and religious problems. It means therefore that liberation can be obtained through self-consciousness about their situation and taking deliberate actions against the dehumanizing forces of this world.

The Church in Africa has the responsibility to make sure that its people are free from most of those problems facing the African continent. It has to address issues related to all aspects of life. It is in this oppression and the brokenness of Africans where theologians have to find means of acquiring true freedom in political, social, economic, and religious life.

Africans, and especially Christians, have to liberate themselves from the bondages they have experienced in history and still experience in other forms. The first place to start with is to understand themselves who they are and recognize the real problems they face. Liberation theology is trying to help African Christians (the Church) and others who experience the same kind of bondage to come to true freedom in all aspects of life. Liberation is one of the ways of making the gospel at home in Africa, especially when it attends to the subjugating situations of people. It is the method of inculturation or the theology of inculturation. Mugambi, quoting from Joseph Healey and Donald Sybertz who also cite from Justin Ukpong, observes that "The theologian's task consists in re-thinking and re-expressing the original Christian message in an African cultural milieu. It is the task of confronting the Christian faith and African culture. In this process there is interpretation of both. . . . There is integration of faith and culture and from it is born a new theological expression that is African and Christian."[24]

While we find a difference in the theology of liberation and that of inculturation, we agree with Mugambi's above statement. It is very difficult to separate between religious (sacred) and secular in the life and minds of African people. They are all connected to each other; there must be an interaction between the two. However, this is not syncretism; it is a relationship that is very important in African theology of inculturation. It is the way the African mind works as a cyclical mode of life, which is the holistic life. For the Africans, secular life is also a sacred life. As Healey and Sybertz have

---

24. Mugambi, *Christian Theology*, 73.

pointed out: "African religion and culture contain seeds of God's Word."[25] This statement means that African traditions and gospels can relate to each other. It is further pointed out that God's grace cannot be limited only to human's understandings. Whether it is religion or culture, God's grace can be seen and manifested. However, what is required is the new understanding of the gospel of Jesus Christ, which comes with new light and understanding God's grace apart from our preconceived ideas and theories; this is God's work alone.[26] Inculturation and contextualization are ways of understanding the Bible in our African context and through the resources (i.e., symbols, images, traditions) that are within our own means. African Christian theologians use several terms to imply the ways to true freedom.[27] Hence, the terms used are such as the following: liberation theology, reconstruction theology, black theology, and narrative theology. All these theologies try to make Christian theology at home in Africa.

What does it entail narrative theology? We now describe narrative theology in general in order to guide us towards seeing its importance in the practical theology, and particularly in the process of pastoral counseling to OVC. African narrative theology involves cultural practices and experiences mostly passed orally in the form of stories, proverbs, myths, songs, plays, riddles and cultural symbols. African narrative theology is one of the ways of inculturation in which the gospel is translated and understood in its cultural context. Healey and Sybertz pointed out thus:

> One type of inculturation theology is an African narrative theology of inculturation. The starting point is African culture, but specifically African oral literature and the wide range of narrative and oral forms: proverbs, sayings, riddles, stories, myths, plays and songs explained in their historical and cultural contexts. Anne Nasimiyu-Wasike states: "The oral literature of the African people is their unwritten Bible. This religious wisdom is found in African idioms, wise sayings, legends, myths, stories, proverbs and oral history."[28]

25. Healey & Sybertz, *Towards an African Narrative Theology*, 50.

26. Healey and Sybertz, *Towards an African Narrative Theology*, 51; cf. Mligo, *Teolojia ya Kimazingira*; Donkor, "Criteria for Developing"; Garner, "Contextual and Public Theology"; Matheny, *Contextual Theology*; Cortez, "Creation and Context"; Okafor, "The Challenge of Contextual Theology."

27. Mligo, *Teolojia ya Kimazingira*; Donkor, "Criteria for Developing"; Bevans, *Models of Contextual Theology*; Shreiter, *The New Catholocity*; Walligo, "Making a Church"; Crollius, "Inculteration."

28. Healey & Sybertz, *Towards an African Narrative Theology*, 28; cf. Walligo, "Making a Church"; Crollius, "Inculturation."

As Healey and Sybertz have just pointed out above, proverbs, riddles, metaphors, and sayings are very common in everyday speech in Tanzania and in Africa as a whole. There is a great potential in using African proverbs in our teaching, preaching, and counseling.

Narrative theology, according to Healey and Sybertz's book, is one of the ways to understand people's lives, according to their own contexts. African narrative theology, with all its components, helps people to grow up in physical and spiritual maturity. Narrative approach speaks to the everyday lives of people. Narrative approach is all about relationships among people, as some Swahili proverbs say, *Asiyekula na wenzake ni mchawi* (The person who does not share food with his or her friends is a witch), and *Kidole kimoja hakivunji chawa* (one finger does not kill a louse). Both proverbs speak about relationships and unity among community members. Narrative approach is one of the ways to make African theology more at home; it is what people call the theology of inculturation. Therefore, narrative approach feels at home in the African soil. The theology of inculturation becomes very effective in helping people to move from different kinds of problems and challenges of life. Hence, narrative approach helps people to become more mature and live a life that is more meaningful, the life that leads to wholeness.

In this book, as pointed out in the previous discussions, we examine the problem of the HIV and AIDS in the Tanzanian context and its impact in society, especially to OVC by the use of narrative approach. Through narrative approach, we hope that OVC will be helped to cope with their problems. Narrative methods have some good Christian potential resources helpful for children's resilience. Narrative approach is what we can call African theology from below, from African local people (known within practical theology as contextual approach). It is a theology from the grassroots we have discussed in some paragraphs above. Therefore, what we do in this book is to theologize or do theology based on African narratives. This is a praxis theology, a practical theology which people have really experienced in their daily lives and continue telling their narratives (stories) from one generation to another.

Since our field research concerns children, it is also important to understand the theology of children or rather more specific, the children's spirituality.[29] Grobbelaar clearly states that "Child Theology (CT)...begins in the midst of pain and joy. It is a matter of seeing and hearing, of the heart and not just the mind, from God's point of view. Thus, CT, like other forms of theology,

---

29. Cf. Hoopes, "The Power of Story."

can never be impartial."[30] She further adds, "One characteristic of CT is that it is drawn into the grip of God's indignation and wrath towards those who cause children to sin (Matthew 18: 6–9) or hinder them from coming to God (Mark 10: 14). It is also gripped by God's happiness about lost children being found (Mattew 18: 12–14) and broken children being healed and welcomed by God's people into God's kingdom (Matthew 18: 5)."[31]

In the next subtopic we discuss how children understand God and their surroundings basing on the characteristic of children's theology stated by Grobbelaar above. In general, it suffices to say that every child in his or her inner being carries a story which he or she connects to the Higher Being, God, in one way or another. Therefore, it is assumed that every child has stories of spirituality in him or her no matter his or her background.

Children's Spirituality and Counseling

The language of children and the way they relate to the world is different from the world of adults. In order to understand children well, it is important to explore their developmental stages. Children we explore in this subtopic are between the ages of 12 and 17. Children at this particular age are known as adolescents. Adolescence is the time between puberty and adulthood. These are children who still depend on their parents. Erik H. Erikson describes that at that age a child tries to understand who he or she is. The child struggles to find his or her own identity.[32] It is the age whereby if the child is not guided well he or she ends up in role confusion; which means that the child cannot understand who he or she is. The basic question of the adolescents is, "Who am I?" Hence, understanding the developmental issues and changes in the child will help pastoral counselors meet the needs of these adolescents.

Physically, adolescents become active in their sexual urges. Boys and girls respond and feel differently to this sexual urge. Girls and boys start to feel attracted to each other. The challenging issue here for adolescents is to understand sexuality in relation to love. Intellectual, social development and moral issues also come into play at this stage. It is the stage whereby adolescents develop the personal value system or belief system; they develop rules that can identify with them. Most children at this stage look for belongingness, someone they can socialize, trust, and believe in. Their mind at this stage is mostly abstract in the way they try to relate to the

30. Grobbelaar, *Child Theology*, 9.
31. Ibid.
32. Erikson, *Identity: Youth and Crisis*.

world and to God. Because of the egocentrism and idealism in them, it is hard to accept the responsibilities of what they think they can master and have control over. Adolescents face negative pressures that force them to make bad decision. This is the place where adults have to come in and help adolescents for companionship, support, and compassion so that they can develop and grow into meaningful and healthy maturity. Otherwise, adolescents start feeling anxious, afraid, ashamed, guilty and embarrassed. Adults have to understand adolescents so that they can understand how to take care of them. In this case, adults must look for ways that allow adolescents to participate in decision making and choose wisely and responsibly for all the consequences that can be the result of their choice.[33]

Adolescents' language is abstract and ideal. In order to understand them, adults have to understand their language. Some of the means of understanding children is through metaphors, dairy keeping, writing letters, songs, drawings, poems and stories. All these ways are important to understand themselves in relation to others and God. The way they understand themselves is the way they understand the world and God. Children's identity helps them to know who they are in relation to the universe. However, this identity must be developed through good relationship with people around them. It is in this stage that children have to develop self-esteem and self-identity in order to have a good image of God and grow in faith that is more practical and stable.

Pastoral care and counseling to children have been neglected or even marginalized. Despite all challenges which children go through such as anxiety, fear, shame, guilty, grief and traumas of life, people have hardly paid enough attention to them. Lester understood this situation and some have started paying attention with them. He points out several issues that show how children have been neglected. The first is the misunderstanding of children's language as we have pointed out above. For example, the way they express grief, or communicate the crises they have experienced in life is very different from the way adults do. Most adults think that children do not understand or hardly feel the pain of crises in life as adults do. Second, it is about the cultural issues, especially in patriarchal societies where most of the time the one that takes care of the child is the mother and not the father. Children are thought to be unproductive and cannot contribute anything. The third is about the fear that goes around people, that they are afraid of making mistakes or misunderstanding—which in turn can result into more traumas in the child's life. The lack of recourses and proper training about

---

33. Hunter (ed.), *Dictionary of Pastoral Care*, 9; cf. Van Dyk, *HIV/AIDS Care*, 163–166; Hoopes, "The Power of Story."

children's counseling also contributes to this negligence.[34] Children also go through crises and hardships of life just as adults do. They require care and counseling just as adults do.[35] The work of pastoral care and counseling therefore must be treated seriously to children and with dignity as equally independent human beings.[36]

Narrative approach in pastoral care and counseling is one of the ways that can help adults work with adolescents in non-threatening ways. It is an approach that is neither authoritarian nor *laissez-faire*, but a democratic style that suits the developmental stage of adolescents. This stance helps children (adolescents) to master, and control many challenges they face at that stage and be able to develop a good identity of trust that is meaningful and purposeful.

After understanding children's spirituality and how to communicate with them using narrative approach, it is good to survey the general understanding of pastoral counseling: its approach, theories, and philosophy behind it. This understanding will help us to see how and what others have done and used, in order to determine alternative or integrated methods more applicable in the context of the study, the method which we try to examine and explore.

Understanding Pastoral Counseling in General

In general, counseling is defined as a skill and principle used in creating a relationship that aims at developing self-knowledge, emotional acceptance, growth, and personal resources. The goal is to make sure that life is much better, that problems are solved, crises coped, and that life becomes at ease, in the state of becoming whole, even in the midst of conflicts, problems, sickness, and challenges of life. Following the above definition of counseling, pastoral counseling is different from other types of counseling. The *Dictionary of Pastoral Care and Counseling* defines pastoral counseling as "a specialized type of pastoral care offered in response to individuals, couples, or families who are experiencing and able to articulate the pain in their lives and willing to seek pastoral help in order to deal with it."[37] It is obvious from this definition that there are several people involved in pastoral counseling context. Both the pastoral counselor and the client are involved

---

34. Lester, *Pastoral Care*, 23–35; Lester (ed.), *When Children Suffer*, 11–12; cf. Shim, "Pastoral Care," 9–10; Hoopes, "The Power of Story."
35. Lester, *Pastoral Care*, 36.
36. Cf. Evans, *Lazarus at Table*, 11–25.
37. Hunter (ed.), *Dictionary of Pastoral Care*, 849.

in the counseling process; however, in the Christian kind of counseling we believe that the Holy Spirit is also involved.

Pastoral counseling can be done in different kinds of contexts. It can be done in the parish or congregational context, in homes, prisons, hospitals, armies, orphanage centers, schools, and in private or public offices. What is most important in the pastoral counseling context is the relationships. It is being accountable and responsible to create good relationships according to the Christian ministry of the Lord Jesus Christ. It is the ministry of reconciliation for an individual or people who require this specialized ministry of pastoral counseling. This ministry of pastoral counseling is a pastoral ministry which means that the pastoral counselor must be the person who is responsible to make sure that he or she creates an atmosphere which is conducive to both parties (i.e., good relationship). The pastoral counselor is like a shepherd who knows how to take care of his or her flock, especially those who are lost or are in great need.

However, pastoral counseling is different from other types of counseling because of its mission of pastoral relationship. This relationship is seen in the role, accountability, understanding, and expression of the pastoral counselor.[38] The pastoral counselor focuses his or her relationship on the meanings of life in connection to the faith found in Jesus Christ. It means that the pastoral counselor is surrounded not only by the Christian faith and tradition, by his or her role, function, identity as a pastor, but also by all that surrounds him or her in the community in which he or she is responsible to.[39]

The term pastoral counseling has been used differently in different times and contexts. Other terms that have been used are such as biblical counseling, Christian counseling, and pastoral psychotherapy. "By psychotherapy," Wise as quoted in Streets writes, "we mean a process, engaged in by two or more persons in which one is accepted as a healer or helper, who aims at assisting the other to change feelings, attitudes, and behavior, or, in other words, become in some ways a different person. Psychotherapy deals with intrapsychic processes, with interpersonal relationships, and with the person's response to his total environment, including his cultural milieu."[40] It is from these differences that the emphasis or approach has been also different. For example, some insist using or applying the secular approach in counseling (i.e., psychology) and some insist using the Bible alone as an approach to counseling. Pastoral counseling imploys different approaches;

---

38. Ibid., 850.
39. Ibid.
40. Streets, "Love: A Philosophy of Pastoral Care," 2.

SURVEYING NARRATIVE APPROACHES AND PRACTICAL THEOLOGY

it is not our intention to go deeper into discussion of these approaches here in this research report. These approaches are such as client-centered approach, family (system) therapy, brief therapy, Cognitive, Gestalt, Jungian, Ericksonian, text-focused therapy, and psychoanalysis.[41]

In this study, pastoral counseling uses both psychological and theological resources to strengthen its understanding of pastoral relationship. This means that the pastoral counselor must know how to do the 'intake and referral' in a professional manner.[42] This is an important stage in creating conducive relationship with the client. To organize and plan is an important step in counseling. It is a step where pastoral professionals real know their clients' needs or problems, whether they really require help or not or require referral. However, the most important work of the pastoral counselor is making sure that pastoral relationship is built. This building of pastoral relationship means that the pastoral counselor has to be trusted and be honest in his or her caring as a human being.

In this study, pastoral counseling process is by the way we hear and tell our stories of life (i.e., narratives). We understand and interpret stories in ways we like or choose. The pastoral counselor enters into the play by trying to hear and tell or retell the story in different ways, to interpret the new story in the Christian light to bring the meaning that is acceptable and healthy.[43] Therefore, the pastoral counselor tries to assist the counselee to experience and interpret new possibilities of being the person whom God intends to be.

In the article "Toward Envisioning the Future of Pastoral Counseling and AAPC," Clinebell points out some very crucial points in the field of pastoral counseling. He urges that pastoral counselors should be aware of new revolutions in the world. Being aware of new revolutions involves seeing the world in different views globally and not only concentrating with the western culture and one sidedness of the brain methods (left brain) of healing and growth. Integration of methods globally and widening the horizons or visions of pastoral counseling is especially required now. Clinebell calls for spiritual and ethical revival in our society, to go back to the values and beliefs that have been neglected and looked down in this pluralistic society. He calls upon the Church to be more creative in its methods to use more contextually integrated and psychotherapeutic methods with our biblical resources. Hence, all these efforts aim at the search for wholeness

---

41. Hunter (ed.), *Dictionary of Pastoral Care*, 850.
42. Ibid., 852.
43. Ibid., 853.

through holistic pastoral counseling. The integrative methods will ultimately strengthen the practice of spiritual healing and pastoral counseling.[44]

One of the ways to be creative and widening the vision of pastoral counseling is applying what Clinebell calls the right brain methods of healing which involve storytelling (narratives), imaging, symbols, intuition, and metaphors.[45] Healing and growth involve this integration between the right and left-brain methods. We find that, in narrative approach, there is an essence of what we can call the Christian or theological themes or concepts. Applying narrative approach in the life of people through pastoral counseling conveys meaning, hope, and wholeness in this light of theological terms or Christian faith.

This application of narrative approach to bring meaning, hope and wholeness leads us to the ministry of care. Engedal defines pastoral care as "the more comprehensive concept covering any act of compassion administered by members of a Christian community, that aim at preventing or relieving the suffering of a troubled person."[46] Despite the specialized activity of pastoral counseling, pastoral care also "includes such things as visiting the sick, attending to the dying, comforting the bereaved, encouraging reconciliation of the estranged, supporting those who are struggling or facing difficulties of any kind, nurturing and protecting the faith of those within the congregation, preaching, teaching, intercessory prayer, and administering the sacraments."[47] The difference between pastoral counseling and pastoral caring is that one is within the other—pastoral counseling is within pastoral care. Pastoral counseling is a more specialized form of pastoral care characterized by strong relational bonds between the care provider and the care-seeker characterized by confidentiality.[48]

Human Sexuality and Pastoral Care

One of the subjects in pastoral caring and counseling within the African context, that should not be ignored, is the study or doctrine of human sexuality. It is very crucial to study and understand the doctrine of the Church concerning our human sexuality. The study of human sexuality is important because it involves the whole being of the person.[49] Understanding human

44. Clinebell, "Towards envisioning the Future."
45. Clinebell, *Counseling*, 193.
46. Engedal, "The Counselor's Competence," 113.
47. Benner, *Strategic Pastoral Couseling*, 20.
48. Engedal, "The Counselor's Competence," 113.
49. Carroll & Wolpe, *Sexuality and Gender*.

sexuality provides an opportunity for the person to relate and experience the world in more responsible ways. In this time, especially where Africa, and Tanzania in particular, struggles with the problem of the HIV and AIDS and its consequences of poverty, deaths, and orphans, the study of sexuality should not be ignored. Human sexuality is the study which relates to who we are as human beings. Therefore, this subsection studies how this is such an important subject and how it relates to the whole research work.

The devastating effects of the HIV and AIDS have brought many challenges and questions about our humanity which have been paid little attention before. More specifically, the HIV and AIDS have brought many questions about our sexuality. In Africa, especially the Sub-Saharan Africa, much of the HIV transmissions have been through sexual relationships (heterosexual relationship).[50] Therefore, as the Church and society as a whole, we have to understand our sexuality much better than before, otherwise this HIV and AIDS pandemic continues to devour us and torment the world. Then, what is sexuality to do with the HIV and AIDS, or is the HIV and AIDS largely a human sexual issue? Therefore, what is a human sexuality? What is the importance or advantage of understanding or learning about our sexuality?

The *Dictionary of Pastoral Care and Counseling* states that the concept of, "sexuality includes but is not limited to genital expressions and procreative capacities."[51] It further defines sexuality as "the human way of being in the world as female or male persons, including varied experiences and understandings of sex roles, sexual-affectional orientations, perceptions of one's own embodiedness and that of others, and capacities for sensuousness, emotional depth, and interpersonal intimacy."[52]

Hunter's definition above indicates that the study of human sexuality is one of the controversial subjects in the human history. It has separated people and their religious or denominational affiliation. It is one of the complex subjects in Christian theology, philosophy, psychology, sociology, and ethics. As Christians, we have to understand this study of human sexuality in the light of Christian faith and tradition as we interpret the scripture with faith and experiences of our daily life as we try to relate to each other, to God, and with the whole creation.

Human sexuality is an issue of the whole world; it is not an issue of Africans themselves or of an individual alone. The whole society is invited to look at the issue of sexuality as a must subject to every individual in this

---

50. Stine, *AIDS Update*, 290.
51. Hunter (ed.), *Dictionary of Pastoral Care*, 1154.
52. Ibid.

world to be open at it. Human sexuality must be understood from different and various views, from theological, sociological, psychological, philosophical, biological, and ethical points of view. Human sexuality is not limited to sex or to genitals only; it is more than that. Sexuality involves emotions and feelings.[53] It is our role to learn and understand the way we are as human beings. How does God create us, and how does God want us to know about ourselves? It is in the light of what God reveals to us through revelation found in the Christian tradition and our daily cultural and traditional experiences. Through these experiences of scriptures and our daily experiences, it is hoped that the Christian faith is being built and strengthened. This has to do with the whole body theology. According to Musopole, body theology is "our human capacity as a whole persons to enter into love-giving, life-giving union in and through the body in ways that are appropriate. It is basically the power to share self. Sharing involves giving and receiving and not giving and getting."[54] Ini this case, it suffices to say that sexuality is a good gift that God has provided human beings. It is not a sin, as those who believed on dualistic ideas knew it. All human beings are sexual beings; it is how we have been created. No matter what the person is, married or single, or any other differences people may have, all people are sexual beings.[55] The issue of sexuality should not be separated from spirituality. They should be integrated within human spirituality; and this is the way or the process which will help human beings to become whole. This is the way to our true identity of being people.[56] In the integration of spirituality and sexuality Arthur Freeman has these words: "At times Christians have disassociated their spiritual life from their bodily life, allowing their bodily life its expression without integration with their spirituality, a different sort of dualism. The Church's exploration of flesh and sexuality must also reflect upon the nature of the authority of our traditional anthropological and psychological views and the role of the Spirit as a guide to new understandings of human existence beyond the traditions."[57] According to Freeman's statement above, whom we agree with, our lives especially in the African philosophy, both the physical and the spiritual life are very important. They should be honored and respected. The doctrine of dualism which favors the spiritual life should be neglected. Physical life (body) and spiritual life (spirit) are both about the whole human being. In other words sexuality and spirituality are both what

53. Carroll & Wolpe, *Sexuality and Gender*, 2.
54. Musopole, *Spirituality, Sexuality and HIV/AIDS*, 21.
55. Hunter (ed.), *Dictionary of Pastoral Care*, 1155.
56. Nelson, *Embodiment*, 17.
57. Freeman, "Sexuality," 2.

we are as human beings and should not be separated. Misunderstanding one of them brings disharmony in one's life; and denying or suppressing down one of them leads to disintegration of life.

James Polling goes further by elaborating the issue of sexuality not as an issue of threat but as a sacramental issue. This means that it is the issue which is very big and crucial in pastoral ministry. He quotes Boisen who writes:

> Instead of reducing religion to the level of the sexual, a correct understanding requires that the sexual be raised to the level of the religious.... What true love wants is union with the idealized other-than-self, which is also what religion wants. Sex love thus seeks not just the finite love object but the infinite, and when it ceases to do so it is no longer love.... These positive values are to be found first of all in the home. This might involve a rediscovery of the sacramental character of marriage.... It would set up the ideal of a self-mastery and consecration of will on the part of the individuals concerned which would enable them to practice self-control and to reserve the act of intercourse to such times and such occasions as would have for them a truly sacramental value and serve as the outward and visible symbol of communion, not merely with each other but with God.[58]

Following the above quotation, we should say that the issue of sexuality is very religious. At the heart of religion, love is so central. In Christianity love is all about God and us as human beings are just reflecting God's love. Love is so central in Christianity. Therefore, love must be found in every corner of our lives. Love lies at the center of both sexuality and spirituality. This is what has been referred to as a sacramental issue in the life of humanity.

In the African perspective, sexuality has been part and parcel of the African culture even before colonialism and the missionaries' era. It is the African understanding that sexuality is not only good, but also very powerful which requires much control and discipline. That is why in Africa, especially in Tanzania, young men and women are provided special training to understand who they are and their role in society. It is the time they come into adulthood where they are expected to act as men and women. Respect and honor are expected to both sexes. Appropriate relationship is expected to both sexes. This training is known in Swahili as *Jando na Unyago* (initiation process).

When the missionaries came, and after colonialism, our culture and tradition was greatly destroyed including the values we had, such as initiation ceremonies for boys and girls (i.e., *Jando na Unyago*) were seen as

58. Couture & Hunter (eds.), *Pastoral Care*, 117.

barbaric and primitive.[59] Africans were introduced to new and strange traditions and cultures, with western cultures. The Bible, which came through the hand of missionaries, also focused on the western packages of their cultures and traditions. As Africans, following the missionary destruction of our cultural values, we have to reframe our theology especially on sexuality. The African perspective should move away from western traditions or civilizations on issues relating to sexuality. The silence on issues of sexuality within the Church in Africa is the result of the influence of the western culture and it is not a biblical message. The Bible is very specific when it talks about our sexuality because it says that all what God created for the human being was very good. The Church's responsibility is to come back to a new understanding of human sexuality. It is time for the Church to enjoy what God has created for us. The Church should understand, accept, and enjoy her sexuality which is one of the ways to make her healthier and whole especially in this challenging time of the HIV and AIDS.[60] Therefore, Africans fall under great contradictions and misunderstandings of what they would believe or know.

Myths and taboos related to sexuality are great in African culture because of the western influence. We do not want to say that the African culture was pure by itself. We also do not mean that everything brought by missionaries was wrong or bad. On the contrary, what we say is that all cultures have some weaknesses and strengths. We all have some myths and taboos in our cultural practices. We concur with Agrippa Khathide who warns us thus: "there is a tendency for African theological students to have to concentrate on past problems of the European church. They have not been made to study how to resolve pressing problems facing the African continent. Because of this heavy Eurocentric slant in our theology, African problems are treated as if they were unimportant."[61]

What Khathide says in the above quotation is that the ministry of the Church must be sensitive to the context of people living in. The gospel of Christ must be contextualized to fit the needs of people. Christian theology and African culture must stay in conversation to make it more applicable and effective. Culture and Christ must live in the same ground through good understanding of contextual theology. The goal of contextual theology is to look for the relevance and identity where the person feels at home but at the same time finds wholeness in life. Therefore, the culture that does not

---

59. Mbiti, *African Religions*; cf. Mligo, *Elements of African Traditional Religion*; Mwenisongole, "A Biblical and Theological Response."

60. Cf. Phiri in Ammicht-Quinn and Hacker (eds.), *AIDS*, 43–44.

61. Dube (ed.), *Africa Praying*, 3.

promote this end of valuing life, identity of Christ, and people is doomed to failure. The Christian ministry is accountable to value the daily lives of people and apply Christian theology for the purpose of restoration and wholeness in the lives of people.[62]

What we develop here is a new understanding that promotes our knowledge of sexuality and a theological base. Hopefully, this understanding integrates our Christian faith with our African culture and experience. This is known as African Christian theology. This kind of theology is being interpreted and understood in the perspectives and contexts of African people. This theology is interpreted in the light of the Holy Scripture and the Christian tradition. It is the theology that fits the African people in their particular context. The problem of the HIV and AIDS with all its effects and challenges should be treated in the perspectives of the African Church and society in general.

Nelson calls for the reunification of sexuality and spirituality, where the Church should understand itself as a sexual community that requires relationship. It is a relationship that regards sexuality as part of our being in God's image; to see sexuality as personal and public. Sexuality is also about sexual salvation where people must be saved from the sin of sexual alienation. Sexuality is all about love and relationship, which is the central point of our Christianity.[63] Nelson in his book titled: *A Continuing Sexual Revolution*, urges the Church to move away from a patriarchal understanding of sexual dualism and recognizing the gospel as the *Word* which became flesh (incarnational). He alerts the Church saying,

> Joining vigorously in the fight against AIDS and in compassionate ministries to all affected by this scourge is crucial. As the AIDS worsens, it has the capacity to bring on an antisex hysteria. Beyond anything we have ever known, AIDS has linked in our consciousness the two greatest fears in our society—sex and death. For the Church to allow the fear of death to govern its sexual ethics would be an unholy capitulation. We need to help our children to understand and feel good about their sexuality, even in a time when sex seems almost synonymous with fear and death.[64]

Nelson continues to say that sexuality is always much more than genital expression which he urges to reconstruct our sexual theology. He explains that in order to understand the creation of God, it is better to understand

62. Cf. Eide et al. (eds.), *Restoring Life*, 95–107.
63. Nelson, *Embodiment*, 187–190.
64. Nelson, *Embodiment*, 563.

our sexuality first. Human beings have been created with both components of spirituality and sexuality and all relate to each other in a very harmonious relationship and not in isolation.[65]

Nelson's urges to the Church above cement that the center of spirituality and sexuality is love. It is a force which guides and joins one coin with these two sides. Our culture today has to understand much better about issues of sexuality so as to manage and train children and the coming generations. This kind of control will help even to reduce the possible risks of the HIV and AIDS and the myths or taboos we have about human sexuality.

Furthermore, Musopole analyses several points which we think are helpful if we want to manage our sexuality in responsible ways. These are paraphrased in our own understanding and interpretation as follows:

i. Understanding the theology of human sexuality involves understanding the relationship that exists between the human body and the spirit, or sexuality and spirituality in the light of the theology of creation.

ii. Emphasis on sex education from the Church level to secular education should be done. All the myths and taboos related to sexuality and the whole human body should be taught properly in churches and schools. The youth should understand who they are in society and be ready to face different challenges in life such as marriage.

iii. The Church should plan and establish educational and recreational camps to teach the youth some important issues related to moral issues and sexuality in general. These camps should be like what we used to have in the African societies such as initiation process or *Jando na Unyago* as called in Swahili.

iv. The Church has to change its teaching from dualistic traditional doctrines on spirituality and sexuality. Sexuality and spirituality are two things but of the same coin. They relate to each other and should not be separated from each other.

v. Love should be understood as the central or source of our spirituality and sexuality. Love is what God is of much concern, and God is love. Love is the very nature of God. We as human beings are God's creation and through God and in God we become the partakers of God's love. The love we have is the reflection of God's love. The doctrine of love is so central among doctrines in theology, and particularly practical theology. Love should always be understandable in God's perspective. Love is so broad and is a process. Love is not a simple

---

65. Ibid.

theory and empty words or statements; it has to be learned and acted upon, and is an action. Love should be practiced and lived on.

vi. Human sexuality; and all its relationships is like a communion or partnership in the lives of people. Therefore, it should be understood in the light of the Holy Communion or sacrament. This kind of sexual relationship is a mutual relationship between people and God. It is self-offering relationship to one another from the example of Christ himself as he self-offered on the cross to build a bridge that was broken between God and people. The act of sexual intercourse is the act of self-offering of one to the other. It is the act of communion, transparency and openness of one to the other. When this kind of relationship is not open and transparent, then there is no true love except hatred, fear, and hypocrisy. True love involves freedom and justice.

vii. God created a male and a female for partnership, to share and help each other. As males and females we are created in partnership with God in God's creational activities. People are placed here on earth to continue what God started to create; people are placed on earth to recreate the universe. Male and female alike should respect each other so as to fulfill God's command. All of us can be initiators of sexual activity; and this should be respected and praised.

viii. Sexual expression is both public and private; and this should be respected. Sexual relationship and the way we do things differ from one culture to another. In the African context we emphasize on the issue of sexual activity to be a private and not a public expression. However, even in Africa people can differ in what they mean by public and private depending on their heritages and customs on issues of sexuality. How they judge these different issues on sexuality is a difficult question to answer! The important thing is how they teach their children and youth on such issues.

ix. Exercises are very important to both women and men. They are important for the physical body and even spiritual health. Lack of exercises can cause many problems for human spiritual and physical life. Exercises also help in the process of sexual activity between men and women. Exercises help to discipline the whole system of the human body. Exercises help to prolong the life of a person. Generally, exercises are good for the life of a human being.[66]

---

66. Musopole, *Spirituality, Sexuality and HIV/AIDS*, 26–29.

There are many challenges which are not dealt with in detail here such as homosexuality, masturbation, and pornography. It suffices to say that the issue or doctrine of human sexuality is very important in this study to understand as much as we can. In the above-highlighted points, Musopole explores comprehensively on human sexuality in his context (i.e., Malawian context) and seems to be not very much aware of what is going on in other parts of the world. He seems not to be cautious of other controversial issues because he fails to discuss in detail the challenges of homosexuality, masturbation, pornography and the use of condoms in the African context. The emphasis to his discussion, which we agree, is on the general view of sexuality in the African context despite the challenges faced by society.

On his part, Khathide urges the African churches to view human sexuality critically and positively as they try to fight against the HIV and AIDS. The light of scripture allows Africans to see openly about the challenges of their daily lives despite the negatives, myths, and taboos we might have in our traditional beliefs about their sexuality. God has provided them the fruit of self-control, love, openness, and sensitivity in order to live like what God intends them to, with their true humanity or *Utu*.[67] In that case, they have to be open with their sexuality because it is a good gift that God has provided us to enjoy and use it properly because some have misused it and have not shown any responsibility towards each other as human beings with *utu*. Gender inequality, rape, incest, and other sexual misconduct have been widely practiced in our societies.

Good theological training is required, where Africans will learn to appreciate what they have in their own hands, the resources in the African mind and their cultures that promote life full of love; the theological training that the Church and society as a whole will learn to talk freely and openly about sex. Khathide invites us (ministers) "to be human beings and act as vulnerable creatures before our students (people), for them to be able to identify with us and with people ravaged by sexual frustrations and HIV/AIDS."[68] Hence, these words indicate that human sexuality is a wide subject as we have seen above.

We have to understand sexuality in our African context and theology. We are human beings with *Utu*; we are not animals. We have been created in the image of God. We have even been created with the love within us. To love people, God, and ourselves is the life we have been called to. Love stays at the core or center of our African spirituality and sexuality. The African philosophy believes in our relationship; that is why we have the saying

---

67. Dube (ed.), *HIV and AIDS*, 6.
68. Ibid., 8.

which goes, "I am because we are, and since we are, therefore, I am." We, as human beings, are vulnerable; therefore, we have to care for each other, and together we stay stronger as reflected in the Swahili proverb which says: *Umoja ni nguvu na utengano ni udhaifu* (Unity is strength and disunity is weakness). Paul also says to Corinthians that it is in weakness that we become stronger (2 Corinthians 12:9–10). Paul's statement means that human beings are vulnerable beings. Without the help of God humans are weak and vulnerable. It is in God that we can be strong. Human beings are supposed to humble under God's guidance.

HIV/AIDS and Pastoral Care

After discussing the issues relating to sexuality in the above sub-section, this sub-section discusses issues relating to the HIV/AIDS and pastoral care. However, it does not go into details of scientific, historical, and development of the HIV and AIDS, or its origin; such issues are beyond the scope of this book. Instead, it goes deeper into some important issues which are more relevant to transmission and pastoral caring of those infected by HIV and affected by AIDS. In order to have a focus, the following questions guide us to see some of the important issues for discussion: What are the HIV and AIDS? What are the effects and challenges of the HIV and AIDS to the Church and society as a whole, and to children in particular? Who are more vulnerable or at great risk from this pandemic? What is the church's response to the effects and challenges of this pandemic? By exploring these questions, this section contributes to the aim of the chapter: to deal with concepts and ideas in relation to the narrative approach and practical theology.

The Human Immunodeficiency Virus (HIV) is a virus that deteriorates or infects blood cells that are important in fighting against any strange guests in the body. They infect the immune system of the body in such a way that it cannot fight against the disease causing germs that enter the body. The body remains weak and defenseless to disease causing germs. Acquired Immune Deficiency Syndrome (AIDS) is not a disease in scientific sense; rather, it is a 'condition' which results after the weakening of the human immune system. It is a syndrome, an 'acquired' syndrome. This means that the syndrome was not there before; it emerged after the infection of HIV.

Unfortunately, the HIV and AIDS have neither found vaccines nor cure, despite the struggles of researchers and scientists. The complexities of the HIV have made scientists' researches to be more difficult and even impossible to have a vaccine or cure. What have been developed so far are the anti-retroviral drugs to maintain and prolong the life of people infected by the HIV. However, the struggle of fighting against the HIV and AIDS must continue. Governments, politicians, scientists, and religious people must continue to fight against it and be responsible in dealing with the whole issue of the HIV and AIDS. This means that in all sectors of life the problem relating to the HIV and AIDS must be addressed openly and properly.

Transmission of the HIV

The HIV is transmitted in different ways such as the transfer of fluids from the body of the infected person to an uninfected one. Stine asserts that "worldwide the predominant mode of transmission of HIV is through exposure of mucosal surfaces of the vagina, vulva, penis, rectum, or mouth to infected sexual fluids (semen, cervical/vagina, rectal) and during birth."[69] This statement means that the virus can enter the body through internal linings of organs such as the vagina, rectum, urethra in the penis, or mouth, or through the openings in the skin cuts or sores. The body fluids are such as blood, semen, and vagina fluids. Moreover, the virus can be transmitted through the prenatal and breast feedings.[70] Therefore, it is good to understand the ways in which the HIV is being transmitted, so that we caution ourselves not to enter into risks of not only contaminating, but also not avoiding people with other ways which are not linked to the ways elaborated above. Casual contacts with infected people are not dangerous at all because HIV cannot be transmitted through eating together, through swimming pools, sharing toilets, sharing utensils, telephones and clothing.

Despite the magnitude of the effects of the HIV and AIDS, the HIV infection is preventable, especially when individuals pay attention to the modes of transmission. To minimize the risks of being infected by the HIV one has to avoid the risk factors that facilitate the transmission of infection such as unsafe sexual activities and contact of blood or body fluids, which are infected. The prevention can be done through good and proper information, education, and communication in matters of human sexuality, health, and the HIV and AIDS. In this sense, understanding our sexuality, gender relation, reducing discrimination and other issues in our cultural and traditional systems help to prevent the spread of the HIV and AIDS.

---

69. Stine, *AIDS Update*, 179.
70. See Ibid., 179–180.

Impact and Challenges of the HIV and AIDS to Children

Many people have become infected by the HIV and AIDS. People have become sick and many of them have died from AIDS leaving their children helpless. This pandemic has brought many questions and challenges in all sectors of life: in economic, political, health, sociological, and religious sectors. The rise of the HIV and AIDS has raised many challenges because it is associated with sexual activities. It has released strong negative attitudes towards people such as prejudice, homophobia, and racism. It is a crisis that should be addressed and implemented by the Church but also in all sectors of life. According to Van Dyk, the UNICEF has the following words to say: "Neither words nor statistics can adequately capture the human tragedy of children grieving for dying or dead parents, stigmatized by society through association with HIV/Aids, plunged into economic crisis and insecurity by their parents' death, and struggling without services or support systems in impoverished communities."[71] The UNICEF's words above indicate that AIDS has caused many challenges in society. The illness and death of parents have caused many problems to children who have been left behind. The unspeakable problems which they face have caused fear, anxiety and depression, dropouts from school, resentment, and sadness to children. Hence, children grow up facing great risks of HIV, other infections (i.e., sexual), abuse, and exploitation.[72]

This pandemic has brought many negative factors in the lives of people; these factors include: fear, stigma, ostracism, poverty, grief, uncertainty, isolation, low self-esteem, anxiety, and death. These factors come as a result of the way society has misunderstood the whole issue of sexuality because of the HIV being basically a sexually transmitted organism. The myths, taboos, and some negative cultural beliefs have not judged rightly on the whole issue of the HIV and AIDS. Hence, issues of drug use, homosexuality, sin, poverty, blacks (Africans), women, and prostitution have been judged as the causes of infection without the knowledge of other ways such as heterosexual contacts and blood transfusions which can also infect anybody.[73]

Carr-Hill, Katabaro, Katahoire and Oulai wrote thus on the impact of HIV/AIDS and the need to respond on the issue:

---

71. Van Dyk, *HIV/AIDS Care*, 269.

72. UNICEF, UNAIDS, and PEPFAR, "Africa's Orphaned Generation."

73. Hunter (ed.), *Dictionary of Pastoral Care*, 17; cf. Shelp, DuBose & Sunderland, "AIDS and the Church," 1136.

> The rapid spread of HIV/AIDS in countries south of the Sahara over the past decade is no longer a health problem, but a major cause for the ongoing development crisis. Education is one of the many sectors that are being devastated by the spreading of the pandemic in those countries. In the absence of appropriate responses in this sector, the human resource infrastructure of these countries will be decimated by this epidemic and their economic output will continue to decline. Subsequently, the social costs of the pandemic will continue to rise.[74]

The above quotation implies that the whole society should take the issue of the HIV and AIDS seriously because it is a great threat and a crisis that has to be dealt with. The Church and counselors have to remember their responsibilities according to what the Scriptures have called them to do in this world. It is time for the Church and society as a whole to break the silence and begin telling stories of life and hope. Moreover, stories that are open to issues of sexuality, gender, and other cultural beliefs that are not good should be told. It is the time for telling stories that empower people who are downtrodden in society. It means that the Church has to open doors for all people to come in for love, acceptance, and affirmation of who they are.

In Sub-Saharan Africa, and Tanzania in particular, many women and children have been infected and affected by the HIV and AIDS. The infection is higher to women than to men. What is the problem that more women are infected than men? It is certainly because of what we have pointed out above on issues of gender inequality, cultural myths, and taboos in society. Women have no freedom over many issues that are being done in society, especially over their sexual lives. Therefore, something should be done to help women and young children educating them about HIV sex-related risks and encouraging safe sex practices.

The WCC warns about the impact of HIV infection that society faces. Some of these impacts are the increase in child and maternal mortality, decrease in life expectancy and economic growth and other effects. These effects have gone from various levels in society. They have affected from the high government level to local community's level, from one sector to another sector, from individual people and households to villages and towns. All these remain a challenge and a responsibility of the Church and society as a whole to take care of those infected and affected in order to preserve and keep the generation of young people and children not to fall into premature illnesses and deaths.

---

74. Carr-Hill, Katabaro, Katahoire & Oulai, *The Impact of HIV/AIDS*, 12.

The HIV and AIDS have infected, affected, and made children vulnerable because of the contexts they live in. The impacts of the HIV and AIDS to children have been increasing in our societies. Our communities have become more fragile despite the technology, scientific development, and the globalization system we have. The world has become not a better place to live in because of issues of health and relationship in this cosmos. Global warming, wars, discrimination, and poverty have affected human beings and especially our children and the generation to come.

Children who live with and are affected by the HIV and AIDS, and who are vulnerable to the HIV and AIDS suffer from discrimination, stigma, and psychosocial problems. They have been neglected from their rights to equal access to health care, treatment, education and other important social services. Moreover, these children suffer from trauma, anxiety, and isolation. Since they are becoming sexually active, they suffer the risk of exposure to the HIV. Poverty should also not be overlooked. It increases the risk of children becoming more vulnerable to the HIV infection.[75] Hence, children are the more vulnerable group which calls the attention of the Church and society as a whole.

The consequences of the lack of psychosocial support for children affected by AIDS can lead to secondary social problems such as child labor, child prostitution, child sexual abuse, stigmatization, discrimination, segregation, violence, teenage pregnancy, and street children. These problems lead to family disintegration, corrosion of culture, lack of parenting skills and mentors, destroyed social networks, lack of intergenerational mentoring, and transfer of life skills. Consequently, the dysfunctional society, which means the instability of economics, politics, (religion), and civil society emerges.[76]

The Church's responses to the whole issue of sexuality and particularly to the HIV and AIDS have been very slow and hardly in ways that are open and transparent. The Church has been far from openly teaching people about sexuality and health issues that would have prevented the further spread of the AIDS pandemic. Mageto, has called the Church as "a silent church = death"[77] Mageto puts well when he says that the Church should look for the courage of not staying silent on issues of the HIV and AIDS. It is very difficult and challenging to speak about issues surrounding the HIV and AIDS within the Church because of myths and taboos around it. The Church should look for any possible opportunity as its role to prevent and

---

75. Foster, Levine, and Williamson (eds.), *A Generation of Risk*, 137–139.
76. Ibid., 116; Sahin & McVicker, "The Use of Optimism," 1–2.
77. Mageto, "A Silent Church,"

take care of those who are vulnerable and at great risk of this pandemic. This means that the Church should be open and transparent on discussing issues related to human sexuality.[78]

The World Council of Churches (WCC) has also responded to the issue saying to churches that it is the responsibility of the Church not to remain silent because this fear of remaining silent is more dangerous than the HIV itself. The Church is supposed to be a place where we can acquire good information related to life and all its challenges. It is the place where open doors should be left for discussion and debate on issues related to human sexuality. In this case, the Church should avoid all kinds of prejudices and stigmatization, thinking that the HIV and AIDS is for some kind of people.

The Church's ministry is a compassionate one following Jesus Christ who is its founder. Christ invited and touched even those who were lepers and segregated or isolated in society. Hunter asserts that "the pastoral function relates to the church's role as a mediating and reconciling agency in the community."[79] The Church should see itself as a wounded one which has been affected and infected by the HIV and AIDS; therefore, it should seek ways of responding to it in a responsible way. It should stand in solidarity with vulnerable children to support them in the fight against the HIV and AIDS enemy.

Pastoral Care to Orphans and Vulnerable Children (OVC)

In discussing the challenges and impacts of the HIV and AIDS in the above section, we ended with the urge to the Church to fulfil its compassionate ministry to orphans and vulnerable children. In this section we turn to the way in which the compassionate ministry can be done by the Church—pastoral caring to orphans and vulnerable children. Despite the paradoxes, dilemmas, and complexities of languages and definitions of the terms used by different people in different areas about who is a child, orphan, AIDS orphan, vulnerable children and other words or phrases; it is good that in this particular study, we remain consistent with what we intend to use, that is, orphans and vulnerable children (OVC). However, we recognize the differences that other fields or organizations might be using as being genuine in regard to their contexts of use. Therefore, in this book, orphans and vulnerable children will mean those children under 18 years old who have been infected or affected by the HIV and AIDS, and have lost one or both parents. These children are also most vulnerable by AIDS; which means that they

---

78. Ibid., 292.

79. Hunter (ed.), *Dictionary of Pastoral Care*, 17.

are at great risk of being infected and affected by AIDS. Orphans are among the people who suffer most in society; they are very vulnerable to HIV and other ill treatments. The World Bank points out that these children "suffer the trauma of seeing their parents die of AIDS, often become "orphaned" several times over as new caretakers also become infected, fall victim to malnutrition and stunting, and risk becoming street children."[80] The most important thing in this study with OVC, therefore, is that we try to avoid any sense of misunderstanding of putting children under the labeling of stigmatization or victimization, which are unacceptable. Not all OVC are infected by the HIV; however, some are vulnerable to the HIV and AIDS and might be in greater risk of being affected and even infected by the HIV and AIDS. Why children? As Foster, Levine and Williamson put it, it is mostly because: "Children are generally powerless in society and have no political voice. But the silence about HIV/AIDS has now broken, and the number of orphans is too massive to ignore. It is essential to understand that loss of parents is only the most obvious impact of the epidemic on children, and that other vulnerabilities must be recognized and addressed as well."[81]. According to the statement above, children are understood to be vulnerable and powerless in many incidences in societies; they have been treated as half human beings. It is essential to understand that children are fully human beings and must be treated equally with respect and dignity. They must be treated according to their rights and needs.

The AIDS pandemic has created more than 15 million orphans worldwide. These are children under 18 years and have lost one or both parents because of AIDS. It is estimated that in Sub-Saharan Africa alone there are 12 million orphans, and the number is still increasing very rapidly.[82] This shows that OVC require support in every way possible. The UNICEF notes that "Neither words nor statistics can adequately capture the human tragedy of children grieving for dying or dead parents, stigmatized by society through association with HIV/Aids, plunged into economic crisis and insecurity by their parents' death, and struggling without services or support systems in impoverished communities."[83] We concur with the UNICEF's above statement. Children belong to the most vulnerable groups in various dangerous situations. However, it should be clear that children have the right to life, survival, equal treatment, respect, protection, participation,

80. World Bank, *Education and HIV/AIDS*, 16.

81. Foster, Levine, and Williamson (eds.), *A Generation at Risk*, 2; cf. Boss, "The Trauma and Complicated Grief"; Price, "Walking through the Dackness"; Jones, "A Theology of Hope."

82. Van Dyk, *HIV/AIDS Care*, 269.

83. Ibid., 343.

and development as is to grown up people. Children's needs which should be met are such as daily subsistence, protection, affection, understanding, participation, leisure, creation, identity, freedom and transcendence.[84]

As indicated in chapter two above, the number of OVC is alarming in Tanzania, and Mbeya region in particular. The government, churches, and other organizations have to take a serious action to respond to the problem of children. The foremost response is that all people should care for people who are affected and infected by the HIV and AIDS with unconditional love irrespective of age and gender. One of the Tanzanian presidents Jakaya Mrisho Kikwete once said: "*mtu akiugua anahitaji upendo wa hali ya juu na akitembelewa anapata faraja kubwa; hivyo, tunapaswa kuwatembelea na kushirikiana nao.*"[85] It means that "a person who is sick with HIV and AIDS requires greater love; and if the person is visited he or she will be much comforted; therefore, we are obliged to visit and collaborate with them." President Kikwete's words above indicate that the very important response is first to understand the psychological and emotional needs of OVC in our context. These psychological and emotional needs are important; however, thephysical needs such as food, clothing, health, and education as important as well. The WHO/UNICEF points out that "more guidance is needed to better understand and address the psychological and emotional needs of children orphaned by AIDS in culturally appropriate ways."[86]

Grief and loss in children is one of the factors which have to be understood. It is the issue that might affect children greatly if not responded appropriately. Children grow up with a sense of belongingness; however, when a loss happens they face loneliness, anxiety, and life seems to be unfair for them. Proper bereavement counseling process must take place for children who suffer from grief and loss. This bereavement counseling intervention helps to create proper growth that will allow the child to cope with life and its developmental stages. The ministry to children who are going through loss and grief must be available. Children must be helped to cope with grief.[87] Hence, one of the ways pastoral counselors may employ in ministering to children in crisis, especially in times of loss and grief, is the use of stories, journals, plays and arts.[88]

---

84. Ibid., 270–272.
85. Mwendapole, "Kikwete: Tusiwanyanyapae wenye UKIMWI."
86. Singhal and Howard (eds.), *The Children of Africa*, 86.
87. Lester, *Hope in Pastoral Counseling*, 90–92; cf. Boss, "The Trauma and Complicated Grief"; Price, "Walking through the Dackness"; Jones, "A Theology of Hope."
88. Lester, *Hope in Pastoral Counseling*.

Children, if provided open and non-threatening place, are capable of telling what they feel and can ask questions. They are able to show their true feelings and needs through plays and stories. Children are capable of expressing themselves whatever they feel, their sadness, anger, desperation, acting out, and can know how to control their emotional stances and feelings if are provided such opportunities, and if we are available to support them.[89] In Tanzania, it is very common to find that children affected by the HIV and AIDS are overloaded by many responsibilities. They are the ones who begin to take care of their ill parent/s. Also the older children are also the ones who take care of the younger ones.

We should emphasize more here that what children go through requires serious attention by the Church and society as a whole. The Church is responsible for making sure that children are being taken care of, whether through meeting them with their physical, spiritual, psychological and emotional needs or through any other way. Children have to find ways that will help them grow and mature to their fullness of life, the life which God has intended for them. Children require spiritual food, psychological needs, physical needs such as food, money, and clothing; they also require socializing with other people and particularly children in school, in games, in Church, and in society. Hence, these ways of dealing with issues surrounding their lives, such as grief, loss, anger, fear, and acting out are called coping mechanisms or resilience strategies.

These coping mechanisms come as results of personal awareness of understanding the life situation and how to live or intervene with it. As it is pointed out, "the individual showing resilience is not one who has a stable "resilient" trait, but one who demonstrates a positive outcome within a particular set of circumstances at a given time."[90] In regard to resilience, Singhal and Howard, point out thus: "Resilient children exhibit flexibility, communication skills, an ability to be reflective, a sense of independence and mastery, and a sense of purpose and future. The development of such skills is predictive of adaptation to later stressors. Resilience can be fostered by reducing risk factors, intervening to stop the occurrence of cumulative risk, and providing new opportunities for mastery."[91] Resilience, therefore, is a way of living a life of wholeness. It is a way of salvation from all the difficulties and challenges of life. It is not a way of running away from problems, but a way of dealing with issues in a way more creative, with more aware-

---

89. Singhal and Howard (eds.), *The Children of Africa*, 88–89; cf. Dyregrov, *Grief in Children*.

90. Singhal and Howard (eds.), *The Children of Africa*, 93.

91. Ibid., 94.

ness, and more responsibility. Facing the life squarely is a way of being open and transparent to issues of life.[92]

In this book, we decided to use narrative approach as one of the ways that can help children in finding out skills to solve problems they face in their own context. These skills or interventions lead children into coping with the issues they face as OVC. There are some good resources to empower children in the narrative approach if the Church uses it appropriately. Resilience to children can be found in applying narratives theologically. Therefore, it is the responsibility of the Church to be creative in opening up the use of narrative approaches such as stories, metaphors, journals, memory books, symbols, plays, music and arts with OVC in Tanzania, in Africa, and the world as a whole. Hopefully, these will help children grow up into the fullness of life, the life of wholeness.

Narrative Approaches

As pointed out above, the Church has to use narrative approaches to deal with predicaments facing OVC in the counseling and caring processes. What is narrative? The term 'narrative' is a word that has now become a popular with a wide range of understandings. It is a word or subject which is very wide and complex because it is used by different kinds of people in their various fields. From philosophy to psychology, from theology to sociology, from linguistics to anthropology, and from history to counseling, they all use the term 'narrative' in various ways and for various purposes.[93] Prominent theorists and founders in this field of narrative are such as Michael White and David Epston, Jill Freedman and Gene Combs, Gerald Monk, and Alice Morgan.[94] However, the literatures that will be used mostly in this subsection are from the social constructionists in the human science subjects. Speaking about narratives, we agree with White and Epston who say that people can organize and provide meaning to their experiences through their own stories. The story of the person explains some aspects in the life which that person experiences.[95] Therefore, stories are part of what people are and how they relate to each other and to the universe. In African

---

92. Denis (ed.), *Never too Small*.

93. Cf. McLeod, *An Introduction to Counseling*.

94. White and Epston, *Narrative Means to Therapeutic Ends*; Freedman and Combs, *Narrative Therapy*; Monk, et al. *Narrative Therapy in Practice*; and Morgan, *What is Narrative Therapy?*

95. White and Epston, *Narrative Means to Therapeutic Ends*, 12.

philosophy and context, for example, the person is a relational being who lives in relationship with the world and not in isolation.

It is argued that there are two ways of understanding the world. One of these ways is narrative knowing. Narrative knowing is a way of understanding the world through stories. Every corner of our lives is filled with stories. We all like to hear and tell our stories all time as we would like. McLeod testifies this by saying: "We structure, store and communicate our experiences through stories. We live in a culture that is saturated with stories: myths, novels, TV soaps, office gossip, family histories and so on."[96] Here McLeod confirms that storytelling is one important part of human life because it retells about his or her lived experiences and stores memories for future generations.

McLeod discusses the theory or idea of social constructionists or social scientists in regard to 'narratives.' This is also what we mainly follow throughout this book to be applied in pastoral counseling. Therefore, we summarize McLeod's understanding of narratives in the following points:

- "People live their lives within the dominant narratives or knowledge of their culture and family.
- Sometimes, there can be a significant mismatch between the dominant narrative and the actual life experience of the person, or the dominant narrative can construct a life that is impoverished or subjugated.
- One of the main tasks of a therapist is to help the client to *externalize* the problem, to see it as a story that exists outside of them.
- The therapist also works at *deconstructing* the dominant narrative, reducing its hold over the person.
- Another therapist task involves helping clients to identify *unique outcomes* or 'sparkling moments'—times when they have escaped the clutches of the dominant narrative.
- The therapist adopts a *not-knowing* stance in relation to the client: the client is the expert on his or her story and how to change it . . . at the completion of therapy the client is invited back as a 'consultant', to share knowledge for the benefit of future clients.
- A central aim of therapy is to assist people to *re-author* their story and to perform this new story within their community.
- Another aim of therapy is to help the person to complete important life transitions.

96. McLeod, *An Introduction to Counseling*, 144.

- Although much of the therapy is based on conversation and dialogue, written or *literary* communications such as letters and certificates are used because they provide the client a permanent and 'authoritative' version of the new story.

- Where possible, cultural resources, such as support groups or family networks, are enlisted to help the person consolidate and live a re-authored story, and to provide supportive audiences."[97]

Following the above points, 'narrative' is a postmodern[98] phenomenon used in different academic arenas by different theorists. Sometimes, it is a very complex and confusing subject. Scholars from different fields define the term in different ways. One scholar pointed out: "the concept of narrative has been used in quite different ways by representatives of competing theoretical approaches in counseling and psychotherapy."[99] This also means that there is richness on how to use the approach in a more free way as long as it works in a particular context.

Furthermore, in this book the term 'narratives' is used to refer to children's daily experiences and their stories. Narrative approach through children's experiences explains their life experiences in different forms of metaphor and story such as myths, dreams, fantasy, parables, proverbs, sayings, pictures, symbols, images, poetry, drawings and so on. Narrative is more than telling stories; it is about life's experience. It is about people and their feelings; it is about their dreams and how they see and understand the world.[100] Life stories (i.e., narratives) are different from folk stories, virtual stories, latent stories and untold stories. However, life stories can be accompanied and aided by other metaphors or imagery language such as poems, proverbs, riddles, songs and drawings. [101]

As pointed out above, the term 'narrative' has been used in different fields in the study of humanities particularly in postmodern times.[102] The

---

97. Ibid., 153–154.

98. For further discussion on postmodernism, see Finucane, "In Search of Pastoral Care," 185; Herman, Jahn and Ryan (eds.), *Routledge Encyclopedia*, 375; Graham, "Pastoral Theology"; Petta, "In Search of a Contextual Pastoral Theology," 195–207.

99. Ibid., 146.

100. Speedy, *Narrative Inquiry*, 6–7.

101. The distinction between a 'story' and a 'narrative' should be taken into consideration. For further discussion on the differences between these terms, see Kistner, "Reconciliation Unjustifiable, Justice Irreconcilable?" c.f., Speedy, *Narrative Inquiry*, 44–47.

102. Ryan, "Narrative."

Routledge Encyclopedia of Narrative expands the description of narrative by pointing out:

> Narrative is a particular mode of thinking, the mode that relates to the concrete and particular as opposed to the abstract and general . . .; narrative creates and transmits cultural traditions, and builds the values and beliefs that define cultural identities; narrative is a vehicle of dominant ideologies and an instrument of power. . .; . . . narrative is an instrument of self-creation; narrative is a repository of practical knowledge, especially in oral cultures . . .; narrative is a mold in which we shape and preserve memories; narrative, in its fictional form, widens our mental universe beyond the actual and the familiar and provides a playfield for thought experiments (Schaeffer); narrative is an inexhaustible and varied source of education and entertainment; narrative is a mirror in which we discover what it means to be human.

This definition is concretely related to what human beings conceive of themselves. Stories recreate people's values and human worth. They retell people's experiences of what it means to be human. Furthermore, in Herman, Jahn, and Ryan, narrative is "a fundamental way of organizing human experience and a tool for constructing models of reality."[103] Quoting from Paul Ricoeur, Herman, Jahn, and Ryan point out that "narrative allows human beings to come to terms with the temporality of their existence."[104]

In a simple explanation, the term narrative implies listening to and telling or retelling stories about people, events, experiences, and problems in lives. People in nature are narrative beings who live as a story to be told and being retold. People are always surrounded by stories. The way people communicate their experiences is through stories. In every corner the human being turns is about narratives, the TV, novels, newspapers, myths, family stories, work stories and so on; all are about stories. In other words stories are everywhere.

Let us summarize and interpret Daigneault's four assumptions on narrative therapy, which are worth noting:[105]

---

103. Herman, Jahn, and Ryan (eds.), *Routledge Encyclopedia*, 345.
104. Ibid.
105. According to Dunn, narrative therapy emerged in the 1980s from a joint work between an Australian Michael White and David Epston from New Zealand, and by 1980s, the perspective had spread in various places of United States, Europe and other places of the world (Dunn, Narrative Therapy, 8–9; Cf. Sanders, "An Exploration of Knowledge," 201–203; Besley, "Foulcouldian Influences").

> Narrative therapy is all about social construction whereby people can learn and experience life through the influence of the culture they live in.
>
> Narrative therapy is all about stories which make meaning in people's lives. Life itself is a story to tell and hear about how we relate to each other and the universe as a whole. Stories make us the way we are and the way we live.
>
> Narrative therapy is about stories that are life long process. We always make stories through experiences. We try to create stories according to what we experience in life to bring about purpose and meaning in life.
>
> People are not static beings; they can change their lives according the time and situation they are living in. The story of yesterday will not be the story of tomorrow. Human being is a creative being who live in discovering and creating new and different things in life. All this is part of what is narrative in the life of a person.[106]

The four points above cement on the importance of narratives as embodiment of human life. The human being is a representative of his or her own story which can be retold in his or her experiences. Narrative is retelling about what has influenced a human being in his or her life. This means that human beings are not static. They are sometimes influenced by their cultural and social environments, by time and space. All these make human beings who they are. Narratives (stories) and metaphors provide room for the person to celebrate the freedom of suggestions, but also the power of communicating in metaphors, which then results in change.

Freedman and Combs quoting from Mair write that "stories inform life. They hold us together and keep us apart. We inhabit great stories of our culture. We live through stories. We are lived by the stories of our race and place."[107] In the same way as others have mentioned before, Winslade and Monk asserts that, "we live our lives according to the stories we tell ourselves and the stories that others tell about us."[108] All these aspects are connected and must be integrated to make it more applicable in people's lives in whatever the ways or method one uses in the cause of helping people from their daily problems and challenges of life. Our emphasis on all the aspects from different scholars discussed above is accepting and trying to

---

106. Daigneault, "Narrative Means," 299–300.
107. Freedman and Combs, *Narrative Therapy*, 32.
108. Winslade and Monk, *Narrative Counseling*, 2.

integrate them to make them more viable and reliable in practical theology and more specifically in the pastoral counseling context.

For narrative theorists the motto shared and emphasized by most scholars about narrative therapy is this: "the problem is the problem, the person is not the problem." Morgan on this motto points out that narrative therapy is a non-threatening method. It looks on the value of the person and not as a blank person who does not know anything. It separates between the person and a problem. The person is an intelligent being who can not be overcome by the external pressure; therefore, the person is able of living a victorious life.[109] In his motto, Morgan sees a human being as a "living human document" that holds a meaningful story. We concur with her as she says that human beings must be interpreted because of the way they see and experience their lives and events. These interpretations should be done by the person to find a purpose and meaning in life. Stories are being made through all these events and experiences in life. These stories are what make people who they are. Stories look for the life of an individual or society that is meaningful and has a purpose as Morgan further says: "we give meanings to our experiences constantly as we live our lives."[110]

In narrative method counselors try to know people through their stories, how they organize, convey and how, when and what they tell. As they try to understand people's lives through the eye of narrative methods they should help people to break from the known (dominant) story to a new story (alternative) for good relationship and better hoped-future.[111] McLeod in her *Qualitative Research in Counseling and Psychotherapy* points out that, "the key idea in narrative analysis is that people largely make sense of their experience, and communicate their experience to others, in the form of stories" He continues to elaborate that, "the central idea in narrative analysis is that the stories told by informants or research participants can be treated as a primary source of data."[112] McLeod further points out that "narrative analysis is therefore an approach which combines a discursive emphasis on the construction of meaning through talk and language, alongside a humanistic image of the person as self-aware agent striving to achieve meaning, control and fulfillment in life."[113] Here McLeod points to the research potential of narratives as told by clients. Narratives yield primary data through record-

---

109. Morgan, *What is Narrative Therapy?* 2.

110. Ibid., 5; cf. Morgan, "Beginning to Use a Narrative Approach."

111. McLeod, *Qualitative Research*, 158–159; cf. Morgan, *What is Narrative Therapy?* 15.

112. McLeod, *Qualitative Research*, 104.

113. McLeod, *Qualitative Research*, 106.

ing the told stories. However, the aim of narrative therapy is "to participate in a conversation that continually loosens and opens up, rather than constricts and closes down. Through therapeutic conversation, fixed meanings and behavior...are given room, broadened, shifted, and changed."[114]

Boje says that "Narrative therapy places a great deal of importance on finding ways in which an audience can be invited to play a part in authenticating and strengthening the preferred stories that are emerging in therapy."[115] Boje further says, it is the work of a narrative therapist to help an individual to deconstruct the dominating story and find a way of reconstructing a new alternative story (externalizing story) that can bring about change and new meaning in the person's life. In this case, the individual is empowered by re-authoring the preferred story which ultimately leads the person to a life of wholeness.[116]

From the above discussions, it is obvious that narrative is a broad term which requires careful considerations and analyses. However, for the sake of this book, it suffices to summarize that narrative is a way of communication whereby people live to understand each other whether individually or in groups. Narrative is about language and how to relate to each other as people. Narrative is a process of understanding human beings in the way they relate to each other through events and experiences of life. Therefore, narrative approach is an effective way of understanding people and helping them from their daily problems and challenges. Narrative approach is the process for coping mechanisms and resilience, and for healing and wholeness. Narrative approach within the context of pastoral counseling is hoped to bring about meaningful interaction in people's lives.

Metaphors in Narrative Approach

After discussing the meaning and potential of narrative approach, we turn to the way in which metaphors can be used within the narrative approach. What is metaphor? Metaphor is defined as "a figure of speech in which a word or phrase is applied to something to which it is not literally applicable."[117] The *Microsoft Encarta Encyclopedia Standard* also defines it as a "word or group of words used to give particular emphasis to an idea or sentiment." However, the word metaphor originates from the Greek word *metapherein* which means 'to transfer'. It is pointed out that "Metaphor is thus a form of

114. Feedman and Combs, *Narrative Therapy*, 44.
115. Boje, "Narrative Therapy."
116. Ibid.
117. *Concise Oxford Dictionary.*

language, a means of communication that is expressive, creative, perhaps challenging, and powerful."[118]

The use of proper language is very much important in working with children in crisis. Communicating with children takes different paths of reaching the goals expected. One of the ways to communicate with children is through metaphors. Metaphors come in different forms and ways such as stories, narratives, tales, fables, myths, plays, arts, riddles, proverbs, poems, songs, and images. Metaphors are present in all these forms of art. Pearce said, "a metaphor is a story that allows people to bridge the gap between what is and what should be."[119] In this respect, metaphor is such an important tool for communication in this world as it has been discussed in the previous section. There is a great connection between narrative and metaphor because both talk about stories which come as metaphors to the person who experiences and confronts problems and issues of life.[120]

One of the prominent figures in the use of metaphor in therapy was Milton Erickson.[121] Ericksonian therapy, going further than the psychoanalytical model, emphasized more on the uniqueness of an individual in therapy (i.e., strategic therapy). He looks at the person's life in the present and the future and not on the past. For him, metaphor "is seen as an agent of change to propel the patient into the future, one that does not compel him to linger in the past."[122] Erickson understood and believed that every person, even a child is born with the capability and creativity to change the own lives. McFague further says: "From the time we are infants we construct our world through metaphor; that is, just as young children learn the meaning of the color red by finding the thread of similarity through many dissimilar objects (red ball, red apple, red cheeks), so we constantly ask when we do not know how to think about something, 'what is it like?' . . .metaphor is ordinary language. It is the way we think."[123] McFague's words above show that the human being is born whole, born with the capability different from that of other animals created by God.

Metaphor opens the door for communication that is more understandable, creative, and non-threatening. Metaphor is expected to be a way for understanding, healing, coping, and even creating room for a change in

---

118. Burns (ed.), *Healing with Stories*, 4.

119. Pearce, *Flash of Insight*, xiii.

120. Ibid., 1.

121. Haley, *Uncommon Therapy*.

122. Ibid., 31.

123. McFague, *Metaphorical Theology*, 15; c.f. Finucane, *In Search of Pastoral Care*, 216.

behavior (i.e., transformative).[124] Metaphors create room for the relationship that is not threatening and its goal is to "challenge, shock, and surprise to produce rapid change."[125] Hence, narrative and metaphor open a door for the inner story to come out, where dreams, wishes, fears, struggles, memories, and expectations are hidden.[126]

Children's life stories are full of metaphors. Biblical narratives are full of metaphors. Parables and allegories in the Gospels are full of metaphors. The life and surroundings are also full of metaphors. You can go nowhere without seeing the concept of metaphor in the life of people. We are surrounded by narratives that are full of metaphors. Most of the time people use language of imagery and symbols. Metaphors open doors for deeper vision and creativity. Finucane notes: "A narrative approach, appreciating the dynamics of metaphor, can rediscover the enchantment, awe and wonder, which is so much required for the pastoral care ministry. Metaphors empower meaning to be alive at the affective experiential level and also long after the 'facts' are forgotten."[127] In this case, metaphor is a tool for empowerment which leads the storyteller to rediscover the potentials highly required in pastoral ministry.

The use of metaphors in therapy, to children in particular, opens doors for new ideas and possibilities. Metaphors are communicable or interactive, interesting, and attractive. Metaphors open doors for imagination, for new opportunities, and possibilities for decision making and change.[128] Hence, Burns points out that "the use of story (storytelling metaphors) is a richer way of learning, permeates more the processes of thinking and remembering and empowers the listener to find his or her own conclusions."[129]

Ericksonian methodology depends on the clients' inner resources.[130] Erickson respects the clients' ability to change using the inner resources which the person has.[131] The therapeutic methods or techniques implied or used with metaphor in narrative approach are summarized as follows:

---

124. Pearce, *Flash of Insight*, 3.

125. Ibid., 8.

126. Morgan, What is Narrative Therapy? 5–6; cf. Morgan, "Beginning to Use a Narrative Approach."

127. Finucane, *In Search of Pastoral Care*, 222; cf. Morgan, *What is Narrative Therapy?*

128. Burns (ed.), *Healing with Stories*, 4–7.

129. Burns (ed.), *Healing with Stories*, 8.

130. It is not our goal to go deeper into the methodology of Ericksonian therapy in this book, but one can read more on Ericksonian methods in Pearce, *Flash of Insight*.

131. Pearce, *Flash of Insight*, 65.

SURVEYING NARRATIVE APPROACHES AND PRACTICAL THEOLOGY   103

- "Identification of the client's problem, its repetitive and self-defeating nature, and the focus on the expected result,
- The choice of visual, auditory, or kinesthetic modality for the delivery of the metaphor,
- The delivery of the metaphor, with special attention to cadence, tone, pauses, and details,
- Interspersal of focused words for the delivery of individualized symbolism ,
- Embedded of commands to focus the client's attention,
- Embedding additional metaphoric material for multiple-level communications
- Emphasis on delivery without explanation."[132]

The above points indicate that the ultimate goal of using metaphor is to understand human being's motives and experiences which bring about healing, hope, and transformation in that person's life. Despite the techniques which some people have implored in their therapy, we should understand that there are limitations of these techniques. However, despite the limitations which they may have, narratives and metaphors invite counselors to a more open, free, and wider perspective in its approach. Metaphors open doors for deeper meanings and for how we experience life.

Play and Art in Narrative Approach to Pastoral Counseling

After discussing the way metaphors are used, we should also explore about the use of plays and arts within the narrative approach.[133] Narratives and play approaches go hand in hand, especially to children who have been traumatized. Children can easily tell their stories through play. In other words, these two approaches are compatible to each other. They are two different approaches but can be used together in pastoral counseling with children in particular as was found in the field research. This is why we deal with these two approaches in pastoral counseling. It is also noted that, "all of

---

132. Pearce, *Flash of Insight*, 65.

133. The theoretical perspective of child-centred play therapy was developed by the Psychologist Virginia M. Axline (1911—1988) in the midst of the twentieth century. Being influenced by the Client-centered approach of Carl Rogers, Axline believed that the powerful tool for children to express their inner feelings was through interaction with the counselor in plays where children are allowed to explore their experiences through game materials (cf. Axline, *Play Therapy*).

play therapy is metaphorical work."[134] It is obvious that when people talk about narratives they talk about stories which can be played about. Narrative approach involves several factors or activities such as proverbs, stories, songs, and other aspects including games and play activities. Plays become very important when are combined with narrative activities, especially to children. Children like to tell their stories through plays. Telling stories of children who are vulnerable is very difficult; however, other media such as art and play becomes the means to speak out their own feelings and emotions. Therefore, let us look at some discussions of theorists in regard to play.

Play theorists assert that human beings are social beings and have been created in belongingness and connectedness with the universe. It is the assumption that points out that human beings live, think, value, feel and behave in certain lifestyles for a purpose. Schaefer and O'Connor quoting E. H. Erikson depict play as "a function of the ego, an attempt to synchronize the bodily and social processes with the self."[135] This implies that the person is always looking for a meaningful life that will bring about harmony and peace in the soul. Play usually plays that role in the person's life. Play tries to find a balance in the whole being of the person.

McMahon says: "play is not a mindless filling of time or a rest from work. It is a spontaneous and active process in which thinking, feeling and doing can flourish since they are separated from the fear of failure or disastrous consequences. The player is freed to be inventive and creative. Play is a way of assimilating new information and making it part of ourselves. . . ."[136] This is a good and broad understanding of what is play. This understanding leads people to appreciating the place of play in people's lives.

Particularly, when it comes to children, play becomes very important. Schaefer and O'Connor point out that "through play, children are assisted to expose and subsequently resolve their disturbing emotions, conflicts, or traumas."[137] Moreover, McMahon asserts that "Play is children's means of assimilating the world, making sense of their experience in order to make it part of themselves."[138] He continues to say that "by re-enacting and repeating events, often in a symbolic form, and by playing out their own feelings and phantasies, children come to terms with them and achieve a sense of mastery."[139] Therefore, it is obvious that play and activity are very important

---

134. Burns (ed.), *Healing with Stories*, 45.
135. Schaefer & O'Connor, *Handbook of Play Therapy*, 2.
136. McMahon, *The Handbook of Play Therapy*, 1.
137. Schaefer & O'Connor (eds.), *Handbook of Play Therapy*, 2.
138. Ibid., 2.
139. Ibid., 2–3.

for children and are natural media of communication. Hence, if play can be one of the media in communication, then this kind of communication can be done through narratives, which are the story telling of our lives.

It is pointed out that "play helps children make sense of their worlds and helps them to provide 'expression to their inner worlds'. Play is used symbolically by children to change 'what may be unmanageable in reality to manageable situations.'"[140] Playful metaphors are a way to help children cope and heal from difficult situations in their lives. Play is metaphoric in itself through which the child relates to what lies on him or her to the outside world. Therefore, play is a way of expression to what the child feels inside.[141]

Dyregrov provides ways of how children understand death and how adults can help them cope with the grief of death. He asserts that, "play gives children the opportunity to express themselves through action rather than words. . . at the same time a child is allowed to express aggressive fantasies (thought of revenge), guilt feelings, or other feelings that are difficult to put into words."[142] Play therapy is a method of helping children help themselves' it is "based upon the fact that play is the child's natural medium of self-expression."[143] Hence, through being a medium of self-expression, play becomes a therapeutic medium for children in difficult situations.

Theorists like D. Winnicott, A. Freud, M. Klein, V. Axline are the pioneers of this play therapy, especially with children.[144] Children's language and communication can be different from what pastoral counselors normally offer. Klein emphasizes the power of playing for children indicating that, "play is the child's most important medium of expression."[145] She further points out that "by means of play analysis we gain access to the child's most deeply repressed experiences and fixations and are thus able to exert a radical influence on its development."[146] Therefore, listening to their language and communication opens ways of understanding and healing. Wimberly clarifies that "Story-listening involves hearing the story of the person involved in life struggles. Being able to communicate that the person in need is cared for and understood is [sic!] a result of attending to the story of the person as he or she talks. . . . The emphasis must be on story listening to avoid the trap of shifting the focus away from the needs of the

---

140. Daigneault, "Narrative Means."
141. Burns (ed.), *Healing with Stories*, 49.
142. Dyregrov, *Grief in Children*, 106–107.
143. Axline, *Play Therapy*, 8.
144. Schaefer & O'Connor (eds.), *Handbook of Play Therapy*, 5–7.
145. Klein, *The Psycho-analysis of Children*, 30.
146. Ibid., 38.

person facing life struggles."[147] One significant way of reaching that end for children is through the narrative play process, where even words themselves can hardly express the depths of our inner being and its complexity.

Axline sets out eight principles for non-threatening play therapy:

- "The therapist must develop a warm, friendly relationship with a child, in which a good rapport is established as soon as possible
- The therapist accepts the child exactly as he or she is
- Permissiveness in the relationship, that means there should be a freedom of expression
- Recognizing the feelings of the child expressed is important
- Deep respect for the child's ability to solve his own problems, that means giving a child an opportunity to show his/her strengths
- Don't direct child's actions or conversations. A child should lead the way
- Don't hurry with a child, but be gradual
- Establish limitations that are necessary."[148]

The eight points listed above indicate that the use of media and activities in play therapy is important. However, the goals of using play are therefore:

- to help children tell their story
- to enable children project and express repressed feelings
- to enable children recognize issues repressed
- to enable children experience success and satisfaction
- to enable children gain a sense of mastery
- to enable children feel good about themselves

Involving play in counseling children helps them to communicate in ways that are non-threatening. Play facilitates communication that is not so traumatizing to the child, but builds up on good relationship with the child. Children like to use play to communicate their inner feelings and ideas. Counselors must keep in mind that the basis for coping and healing phenomenon to the child is not in the skills or techniques, but is in the

---

147. Wimberly, *African American Pastoral Care*, 6; cf. Doehring, *The Practice of Pastoral Care*, 35–45.

148. McMahon, *The Handbook of Play Therapy*, 29.

trusting relationship. It is said that "play therapy is a counseling relationship in which the child is allowed to communicate through toys and play."[149]

In pastoral counseling to children the maturity or growth of the child must be looked at holistically. As we pointed out above, the basic thing in the healing and growth of the person or the child is to have a good relationship. First of all the child must have a good relationship with oneself. That is how the child sees, feels, expresses, and hopes about oneself. The second is how the child relates to others. The question is how does the child see and think about others? The third is the relationship with the whole surrounding or environment. The question here is how does the child see and respond to issues around him or her? The fourth thing is about the child's relationship with God. The question is how does the child understand, trust, believe, and value God?[150] Pastoral counseling must pay attention to most of these characteristics of relationships in order to build a strong resilience, self-identity, and self-esteem in the child who has been traumatized. This trusting relationship comes as a result of proper use of play therapy and narrative approach in pastoral counseling. From the above understanding of play perspective, we can generalize that play comes in a variety of forms. It is a very general term which refers to games, music, arts, rituals, images and symbols, drawings and paintings; it even goes beyond what is physical, or what can be seen with naked eyes. Play is a kind of media which helps the person to communicate with the universe and its environment. Play is part of what we are. Our body mechanisms are always in activity and play. Therefore, playing is a natural reaction the human being has been created with.

When it comes to using art when counseling children, it is similar to what we discussed above in regard to play. To children, art comes naturally as a way of communication as we have seen with play above. Art is the way of expression which involves drawing, painting, singing, making images and symbols. Lester points out that, "Children are natural-born "artists," as any parent can confirm."[151] Children are creative beings who can express themselves more freely in arts with what is going on in the inner world, especially what they feel and experience. Children can tell their stories freely through art and play. Hence, both of these methods play and art, are very important in pastoral care with children, especially when used in combination. Pastoral counseling looks, explores, and examines approaches that are more applicable and are holistic in nature.

---

149. Coetsee, "Walking with Wounded Children," 128.
150. Ibid., 133–135.
151. Lester, *Hope in Pastoral Couseling*, 97.

Definitions of Terms used in Narrative Approaches

In discussing the use of narrative approach in caring and counseling of OVC, various terms are used. The following brief definitions of some of the terms used in this study are according to the *Cambridge Advanced Learner's Dictionary*. By the use of this dictionary, this part highlights what it means with the terms, and how they are going to be used in this book. It suffices to say that the definitions provided are not exhaustive, but just brief to enable readers understand the presented and discussed data in chapter five below. Moreover, not all terms used in the narrative approach have been defined here; and neither will all the terms be used in this book. Selectively, the terms defined here and used in our study are the following: stories, proverbs, riddles, methaphors, sayings, poems, songs, symbols, images, plays, arts, and games. .

Stories—A story is "a description, either true or imagined, of a connected series of events"; in other words a story is an account or report of some events. Everyone has a story, and we are the story because the lives we live and experience is a story by itself to tell and hear. This means that stories fill our lives as the water fills the lives of fish. Stories are too pervasive to our lives for us to be aware of them. Even children also have stories and love stories whether are fictions or non-fictions.

Proverbs:—a proverb is "a short sentence, etc., usually known by many people, stating something commonly experienced or giving advice." It is a short clever and wise saying, or catchphrase words. The synonyms of proverbs are such as aphorisms, epigrams, idioms, and sayings. The *Microsoft Encarta Encyclopedia Standard* writes on proverb as a "concise statement, in general use, expressing commonly held beliefs and received ideas. Most proverbs are rooted in folklore and have been preserved by oral tradition."[152] For example, the Bible has several proverbs such as 'An eye for an eye and a tooth for a tooth.' In the Tanzania context, proverbs are spoken and taught from home to school. Children learn proverbs from their grandparents, parents, and colleagues. In Tanzania, proverbs are part of life and a way of life.

Riddles:—a riddle is "a type of question which describes something in a difficult and confusing way, and which has a clever or amusing answer, often asked as a game." In Tanzania riddles go hand in hand with proverbs. They are also being spoken or learned since childhood until when they go to school. They teach children to be creative and thinkers about their lives.

Metaphors:—a metaphor is "an expression which describes a person or object in a literary way by referring to something that is considered to

---

152. *Microsoft Encarta Encyclopedia.*

possess similar characteristics to the person or object you are trying to describe." For example, "the mind is an ocean" or "the city is a jungle". It is said that "metaphor and simile are the most commonly used figures of speech in everyday language." Metaphors can be in a form of symbols, allusions, figurative language, idioms, and imageries.

Sayings:—a saying is "a well-known and wise statement, which often has a meaning that is different from the simple meanings of the words it contains." The synonyms of the sayings are such as aphorisms, adages, and proverbs.

Poems: a poem is "a piece of writing in which the words are arranged in separate lines, often ending in rhyme, and are chosen for their sound and for the images and ideas they suggest." The *Microsoft Encarta Encyclopedia Standard* defines poetry as a "form of imaginative literary expression that makes its effect by the sound and imagery of its language. Poetry is essentially rhythmic and usually metrical, and it frequently has a stanzaic structure. It is in these characteristics that the differences between poetry and other kinds of imaginative writing can be discerned."[153]

Songs:—a song is "usually short piece of music with words which are sung." A song is made up of verses and choruses. Verses and choruses of a song are made up of lyrics, i.e., the words that make up a song. A song can be sung by using symbols called music. Music, according to the *Webster's Collegiate Dictionary* (online edition), is "the science or art of ordering tones or sounds in succession, in combination, and in temporal relationships to produce a composition having unity and continuity." The voice of the music can be produced through human mouth, sounds of birds, animals, musical instruments, etc.

Symbols:—a symbol is "a sign, shape or object which is used to represent something else." For example, the heart symbolizes love, or the water symbolizes life. It is "something that is used to represent a quality or idea." Charon further defines symbols thus: "*Symbols are social objects used to represent (or stand for, 'take the place of') whatever people agree they shall represent.*"[154] Hence, symbols can be objects, words, colors or patterns; they stand for something else other than their basic idea and are used to communicate meaning depending on the preference of society concerned.[155]

Images:—an image (mental picture) is "a picture in your mind or an idea of how someone or something is." It is "the way that something or someone is thought of by other people." Therefore, image is the imagination

---

153. *Microsoft Encarta Encyclopedia.*
154. Charon, *Symbolic Interactionism*, 46 (emphasis original)
155. Mligo, *Symbolic Interactionism*, 23–24.

of the real thing formed in the mind and sometimes represented by real objects or drawings that can physically be seen by human beings.

Plays:—a play is an "activity that is not serious but done for enjoyment, especially when children enjoy themselves with toys and games." Landreth and Bratton assert that play forms the core of childrens means of expression and self-realization. They write: "Play is to the child what verbalization is to the adult. It is a medium for expressing feelings, exploring relationships, describing experiences, disclosing wishes, and self-fulfillment."[156]

Arts:—an art is "the making of objects, images, music, etc. that are beautiful or that express feelings."

Games:—a game is "an entertaining activity or sport, especially one played by children, or the equipment needed for such an activity."[157] An Example of them are the indoor games (i.e., board games, playing cards, computer games, etc.) and the outdoor games (i.e., football, hide-and-seek, netball, playing with marbles or baked clay, etc.). The *Microsoft Encarta Encyclopedia Standard* adds on children's games saying: "play is thus a learning process and a means of adapting to or coping with life situations."[158]

All the terms defined above are common to African people in the African context. As Healey and Sybertz say, it is their "unwritten Bible."[159] They are common in everyday speech. It is the way of conversation and communication. It is the way that is respectful to the African tradition and culture. It is the wisdom the fore-parents left for people and must be continued from one generation to another.

Narrative approach uses different kinds of languages and terminologies or definitions. This broad understanding of narratives helps the person to be more equipped with the richness of vocabulary and terminologies that helps the person to understand broadly on narratives. Narrative is a general term which in it the above terms are included or used. Hence, the above terms help the person to use them in presenting one's experience and how he or she understands the world. They are the ways of telling stories in different ways or methods.

Why is Narrative Approach Important for This Book?

After wrestling with the narrative approach in previous subsections, here we establish the rationale for using this approach in this study. Narratives

---

156. Landreth & Bratton, "Play Therapy," n.p.
157. *Microsoft Encarta Encyclopedia.*
158. Ibid.
159. Cf. Healey and Sybertz, *Towards an African Narrative Theology*, 28.

(stories) provide a sense of direction for life. Stories provide hope and identity. People live, formed, and are guided by stories. It is the way they communicate with God and their neighbors. Biblical stories, and especially the Gospel stories, provide new ways of direction as they practically integrate them with their own stories and life experiences. Hence, counselors, as narrative pastoral counselors, should try to participate in creating and interacting with telling and listening to stories of life.[160]

Narrative theorists assume that children can tell their stories more freely directly or indirectly through play. A good story is a story which is narrated and acted well. Geldard points out that "one very important way for the counselor to help the children change their view of themselves and find 'exceptions' is through the use of metaphors combined with some creative media such as art or play."[161] McMahon stresses that "play techniques, especially drawing and painting, and the use of stories and fantasies...help children to express their feelings, of profound anger as well as of sadness, and to begin to accept the irreversibility of death."[162] When people tell stories it is natural that our imaginations create a picture of the time and events. Stories are narrated in a form of play, symbols or images. Stories are not empty narratives with blank pictures. It is here where the researcher finds a connection of narrative approach with other therapeutic methods such as family systems, psychoanalysis, and play theories in counseling.

With suitable media and activities, "we believe that the most important part of any counseling process with a child is to help the child to tell their story."[163] Methods of observation, active listening, good questions, good relationships and appropriate media need to be of most important in working with children. These are the ways which children find easier to talk and tell their stories. Counselors have to find that kind of relationship where the situation of the child becomes easy for him or her to tell the story no matter how hard and hurtful the story is.[164] Counselors have to find ways and skills that are easy for children to tell their stories and accompany them in their journey of exploration by using proper media as it has been suggested above, such as play or any other type of arts.[165] Theologically, this means that narratives (stories) are the raw materials for—healthy relationship with ourselves, others, environment, and God. Robertson notes that a

---

160. Ibid., 22.
161. Geldard and Geldard, *Counseling Children*, 115.
162. McMahon, *The Handbook of Play*, 143.
163. Geldard and Geldard, *Counseling Children*, 42.
164. Ibid., 100.
165. Ibid., 49.

"story gives identity."[166] In summary, narrative approach is the way people live through their stories. Narrative approach helps us listen to stories of people in their struggling journey of life's situations. Therefore, stories of our lives (narratives) are very important in understanding who we are, how we relate to each other, and how we relate to the whole creation and with God.

Narrative Approach to Pastoral Counseling

There are many prominent on the use of narrative approach in counseling. However, few of them influenced our study including Gerkin, Capps, Louw, Dinkins and Healey and Sybertz.[167] There are other theologians who contribute greatly in this area of narrative use in pastoral counseling apart from the above-mentioned ones. Their works are respected their views are used and discussed in this study.

Narrative approach as expounded above can be applied in pastoral counseling. Pastoral theology borrows some techniques from narrative theology and in this case African narrative theology, more specifically African narratives in pastoral counseling. It is a kind of theology which goes and uses the basic knowledge of people in their daily lives. The traditional cultural lives of African people, bases on their way of life in stories, dreams, proverbs, riddles, myths, symbols, images, and songs. Therefore pastoral theology has to apply the 'theology from below' to respect African narrative ways of living; for story-telling plays a great role as a source of theological reflection in Africa.

Recently, theologians have also used the concept of narratives (stories) in analyzing biblical theology. There have been some discussions and arguments on how narratives are relevant to theology, especially the use of the concept of "narrative theology." The concept of 'narrative theology' has been debated for some time now, whether is relevant or not. It is pointed out that, "narrative theology is a current movement in theology gaining widespread attention."[168] Narratives have been important aspects in theology despite the criticisms from scholars who argue that since it is known that the phrase "narrative theology" is "the raw material for theology", it is just a

---

166. Robertson, "Storytelling in Pastoral Counseling," 41–43.

167. Gerkin, *The Living Human Document*; Capps, *Living Stories*; Louw, *A Pastoral Hermeneutics of Care*; Dinkins, *Narrative Pastoral Counseling*, and Healey, J and Sybertz, *Towards an African Narrative Theology*.

168. Robertson, "Storytelling in Pastoral Counseling," 33.

contradiction.[169] Therefore, it is our contention that narrative theology, with its components, is very important as ways to understand God and ourselves. Narrative therapy, as used in psychology, can be used in practical theology too. The caution is proposed as people use the term narrative in theology or in pastoral theology. The theology of story is very important for the pastoral counselors and is a valuable resource for counselors bearing in mind that stories are not beyond criticisms. Stories can be painful, and sometimes people can hardly know where to begin and where to end, and stories can be deceitful. Sometimes, narrative approach can be limited or deceived, making a "hermeneutics of suspicion" an important tool to apply.[170] Narrative approach is not only a matter of listening to stories, but also a matter of how to listen. Robertson recommends that "stories are told not just through straight narratives of events, but also through dreams, associations, pictures, or even fictional stories told about pictures."[171] Narratives (life stories) are important as are an appropriate medium which shows human self, identify, and experience. It is the way human beings discover the self and God. Discussing about the nature of revelation where God reveals God's self; it is further noted that history and memory are such important elements in the community or any society. Hence, history and memory make people who they are whether in Christianity as Christians or in the African culture as Africans. That becomes their identity as Christians or Africans.[172]

Narrative approach seeks to understand people in a non-judgmental respectful conversation as being played in various stages of life. "Therefore, to tell one's story may be an important step on the way towards the resolution of the problem, and the growth of the person beyond (or out of) the story" as Robertson puts it.[173] It is the way of transformation or wholeness of the person. It is what God intends to the created beings of becoming whole psychologically and healthy. It is the will of God. It is the responsibility of the pastoral counselor to be a curious listener and not as an expert or someone who knows things ahead of the client. The counselor and the client are both becoming "archeologists of hope" who try to reveal stories that are untold. Therefore, pastoral counseling, as in other fields in counseling, faces challenges in its practices.

One of the pioneers in the struggles of pastoral counseling profession is Charles Gerkin. He points out some of the challenges in pastoral care and

169. Ibid., 34.
170. Ibid., 41.
171. Ibid., 35.
172. Ibid., 37.
173. Robertson, "Storytelling in Pastoral Counseling," 38.

counseling that have lost its identity of Christian faith. He calls for more spirituality in what he calls new interpretation and meaning of human life. This is a model of hermeneutics in "the living human document," a hermeneutics which brings about healing and wholeness.[174] The above assumptions mean that the life of the person is a story in itself. It is the art or skill that every person is born with, that all people have the story and always bring it out in different ways as they commune and contact other people and the universe. Hence, people can tell their stories in so many different ways, through images, symbols, pictures, and plays, through verbal, non-verbal and action.

In his book, *The Living Human Document: Re-visioning Pastoral Counseling in a Hermeneutical Mode*, Gerkin points out:

> From very early in life, even as early as infancy, the developing self is presented with the necessity of making interpretations of what is experienced. Even before there is language this is the case. The "story" of an individual life begins with the earliest experience of being a self-separate from other selves. Drawing upon the images and language of culture as transmitted by parents and other significant figures, the self slowly develops a myth or story by which all experience is interpreted. From that mythic story new experience is anticipated and given meaning.[175]

The story of self or of an individual is what Gerkin calls the 'hermeneutical theory' of self where the pastoral counselor stands as an interpreter of the human life and experience in the light of Christian tradition. The pastoral counselor does all these with all the humility and respect towards an individual's narratives.[176] Gerkin further states, "Each of us has a story that is 'the story of my life.'"[177] This notion implies that the person is a story himself or herself. People live in stories where Gerkin quoting Hauerwas asserts that, a story as other narratives try to connect and reconnect with all the events and experiences people go through. Hence, narratives provide special intervention with problems and challenges of our daily lives. They are ways that enrich our minds and our humanity to live a life that is more meaningful.[178]

In general a story is divided and developed into four categories: setting or atmospheres, which "include not only time and place boundaries, but also the giveness of certain values or expected behaviors, violation of which

---

174. Gerkin, *The Living Human Document*.
175. Gerkin, *The Living Human Document*, 20.
176. Ibid.
177. Ibid., 112.
178. Ibid.

may be expected to bring guilt or blame."¹⁷⁹ *Plot* "embodies a sense of beginnings, a continuing story line, and a more or less problematic ending."¹⁸⁰ *Character* "refers both to the individual's own self-characterization and the characterizations assigned to significant persons in the life story. Characterization is the product of both imagination and behavioral profile."¹⁸¹ And *tone* "suggests the quality of stance or standpoint from which the narrative is related."¹⁸² Hence, the pastoral counselor using life stories must provide close attention to all four aspects of a story in counseling.

When people hear or tell stories, they discover who they are. Stories hold us and mold us. Stories are part of what people are, their wisdom, virtue, hope, and meaning is the result of how they tell or hear and understand stories. Wallace clarifies the point by saying "We live the life of faith in and through stories that testify that God is real, that growth is possible, that hope has meaning, that none of our suffering and none of our failures will ever finally destroy us, that nothing can separate us from the love of God."¹⁸³ Stories do not only make the meaning of our lives, but also show what value and honor is in our communities or in lives. Stories are the joining factor from one person to another, or from one community to another, and from past to present life. Stories create the identity of the person or community. Furthermore, stories bring about healing, meaning, hope, love, peace and harmony in communities.¹⁸⁴ The pastoral counselor is responsible to understand and interpret what is going on in the person's life. Conversation and dialogue are pastoral tools that help the pastoral minister to find meaning and purpose in someone's life. Therefore, listening carefully is an important factor for pastoral counselors; it is an act of will, being aware and sensitive to patient's needs such as values, trust, and other rights helps the process to healing and wholeness.¹⁸⁵

A pastor is looked as an interpreter of someone's life experience.¹⁸⁶ Gerkin continues to highlight that pastoral counseling is about understanding the person with what is going on in one's life and trying to find proper ways of conversing with the person in the light of the Gospel of Jesus Christ. Communication in all directions of our life is such an important tool in

179. Ibid., 113.
180. Ibid., 114.
181. Ibid.
182. Ibid., 115.
183. Wallace, "Storytelling, Doctrine and Spiritual Formation."
184. Ibid.
185. Boyd, "Pastoral Conversation," 347.
186. Gerkin, *The Living Human Document*, 34.

making life more meaningful.[187] Moreover, Capps in line with Gerkin argues that pastoral care and counseling in a congregational context should be done in the awareness and sensitivity of person's life story for the goal of developing new alternative story (externalizing story) of hope and healing. These stories have been in people's lives for many years and up to now. The stories are the same as people read in biblical narratives, especially in the Gospel accounts. Here Capps emphasizes on using arts that facilitates the power of suggestion, listening and understanding, identifying, and using a positive communication that will bring about new understanding and health relationship.[188]

Daniel J. Louw in his book, *A Pastoral Hermeneutics of Care and Encounter: A Theological Design for a Basic Theory, Anthropology, Method and Therapy* speaks about models which can help pastoral care to explain the meaning of life experience according to the Gospel. Louw is aware of the present challenges facing pastoral theology. The quest for spirituality and meaning of life in post modernism has filled people's minds. Postmodernism as a concept is a worldwide phenomenon which comes as a consequence of globalization even within the ministry of the Church in Tanzania. The longing of people in Tanzania in general can be looked holistically to suit the needs of people in times of crises. Louw therefore challenges pastoral ministry to change for the better. He looks at different models which have been used for a period of time for counseling in pastoral ministry and the Church to widen the horizon of its ministry for a change. It is from that dimension that he fills the gap which he thinks is missing ministry in the present time. Louw looks at a better interpretation of the Gospel which suits peoples longing and yearning in their social and cultural context of life.[189] It is in this understanding of Louw that the Church can better work with OVC, where children ultimately find ways of healing and coping.

One of the models which Louw uses is "interpretative story-telling, listening and assessing."[190] It is the model which is more suitable for children and adolescents. It is a model which involves plays in which the counselor can hear the story of the client. It is the model which helps children to tell their stories through playing. In playing children find ways to tell their repressed memories in a free and open space. The repressed feelings come out in consciousness; and through play media children are able to talk and

---

187. Ibid., 57.
188. Capps, *Living Stories*.
189. Louw, *A Pastoral Hermeneutics of Care*, 1–2.
190. Ibid., 15.

speak out their needs and feelings freely. Hence, for children, storytelling becomes a way of healing and coping.

We agree with Clinebell who also calls for transformation of pastoral counseling by challenging pastoral ministry "to develop and test new theotherapeutic methods which use the symbols, stories, archetypal images and other resources of our biblical, historical and liturgical heritage directly in counseling and growth facilitation,"[191] which are so relevant to the model we point to, a model centered on African view point.

When it comes to the African view of pastoral counseling people have to move away from the western world view of individualism (client-centered) and liberalism in their approach to Gospel and therapy; it should fit in our African context. Kiriswa adapts and integrates two models of therapy in counseling people living with the HIV and AIDS: the client-centered approach[192] and the cognitive approach[193] to suit his context.[194] Berinyuu also sees that African psychotherapy can be integrated with the western therapy despite the differences that might be present.[195] Therefore, this is the approach (i.e., integration of models) the pastoral counselors can adapt to make the pastoral counseling ministry effective according to the context of people, the African context in the case of this study.

When it comes to storytelling, Mucherera provides five issues in an African context of pastoral care, one of which being the use of narratives (stories). He writes, "narratives (stories) come naturally to most Africans. . .In some cases, the narratives may be presented in the form of a traditional fairy tale, story, or sometimes. . .proverbs or sayings."[196] People are the compilation of stories, stories that make them humans. People are all directed and guided by stories and live in a world full of stories, music, art, symbols, and plays. Through narratives people can communicate to each other and to God. God created human beings in a form of a story and our entire environment is surrounded by stories. Stories are means of communication with the

191. Clinebell, "Toward Envisioning the Future," 183.

192. Client-centered approach is that, "individuals have within themselves vast resources for self-understanding and for altering their self-concepts, behaviour and attitudes towards others." (Kiriswa, "Pastoral Care," 89–90) The founder of this psychological model of client-centered was the American psychologist Carl Rogers (1902–1987) developed in the 1940s—1950s as a response to the less personal or more clinical centred approach that dominated the field of counseling in that time.

193. Cognitive approach according to psychologist Ellis contends that the human being has the power to control his or her destiny by disputing his or her irrational beliefs (Kiriswa, "Pastoral Care," 90).

194. Kiriswa, "Pastoral Care," 89–91

195. Berinyuu, "An African Therapy," 20.

196. Mucherera, *Pastoral Care*, 172.

universe.[197] Therefore, as Dinkins says, "we dream in narrative, daydream in narrative, remember, anticipate, hope, despair, believe, doubt, plan, revise, criticize, construct, gossip, learn, hate, and love by narrative."[198]

However, Dinkins challenges pastoral counselors to engage in narrative conversations in their ministry. He sees that there is a great connection between biblical narratives and narrative counseling. Dinkins points out that, "the role of the narrative pastoral counselor is to create an environment in which people can tell their stories, feel their pain and their joy, and then discover their competencies and their faith in God who is the author and finisher of all our stories."[199] Developing a good relationship, as Dinkin challenges, is vital in narrative counseling. Good relationship promotes dialogue that creates good story, new meanings, and new alternatives.[200]

In summary, we have seen that narrative approach is practicable in pastoral counseling as an effective way in the pastoral ministry. However, the challenge is the way in which the narrative approach discussed in the above sections helps the authors of this book to apply it in their own context of OVC and the HIV and AIDS in Mbeya, Tanzania? What will this new research contribute to the existing scholarship field especially in practical theology? Is it about the new model/s, theories, instruments, or data which have been discovered? The following part indulges into a discussion of the way in which narrative approach will be helpful in the context of OVC and the HIV and AIDS at Mbeya Tanzania.

Narrative Approach in Pastoral Counseling to OVC

Narrative approach in pastoral counseling to OVC is very intact with an African understanding of sickness and healing. The approach is effective because of being very close to African ways of living. African ways of living are built upon stories, images and symbols. People live in groups (communities or villages); they work together when they are in meetings, farm works or any crises in villages. Therefore, the community based life which Africans exhibit enables them to tell stories to each other, have plays and arts to make life meaningful.

Bate rightly sees the need for inculturation in the whole process of healing in different cultural contexts. He says, "healing and illness are

---

197. Dinkins, *Narrative Pastoral Counseling*, 14–16.
198. Ibid., 17.
199. Ibid., 39.
200. Ibid., 33.

always affected by culture."[201] He continues, "In African traditional culture, healing is always about the restoring of human life."[202] In the case of the HIV and AIDS people should understand that this problem requires a solution probably of not curing it but of healing and coping with it. Most of the problems on this problem of the HIV and AIDS are not about the disease itself but about the social stigma, condemnation, and prejudices in societies. This kind of attitude towards PLWHA has created more problems such as hopelessness, desperation, shame, guilt, fear, and anxiety. These problems are what mostly have to be addressed and dealt with. Healing of these problems is more important than the healing the disease itself. Hence, there is a difference between healing and curing a particular disease. Healing is concerned with the whole totality of human health and his or her being, but cure is only dealt with scientifically, focusing on the germs that cause the disease.[203]

When it comes to healing, the African world view should also be put in perspective. This is because healing and health are not just physical aspects; they also have to do with mental, physical, spiritual, social and environmental harmony. The person is expected to be in peace with the whole creation; and this is what is known as wholeness in the person's being.[204] Mwaura further agrees with Milingo that "any healing ministry in Africa that does not take the African cosmology seriously is doomed to fail."[205] Therefore, Milingo emphasizes that "Pastoral care must liberate itself from its dominant middle-class, white, male orientation and become more inclusive in its understanding, concern and methods. It must become transcultural in its perspective, open to learning new ways of caring from and for the poor and powerless, ethnic minorities, women, and those in non-western cultures. On a shrinking planet, our circle of consciousness, and caring must become global."[206]

The above quotation emphasizes on the importance of every cultural heritage in this postmodern time. The Church, and particularly theologians, should avoid prejudiced minds. The Church should work together in order to destroy the common enemy which devours the world, the HIV and AIDS. As Africans or Westerners, people should all be transcultural in their perspectives on how to deal with different issues facing them. People can only eliminate or at least minimizes the risks of HIV if they work together as one world despite the differences they may have. Hence, one of the unifying

201. Bate "The mission to Heal," 72–73.
202. Ibid., 73.
203. Ibid., 78.
204. Mwaura, "Response," 66.
205. Ibid., 67.
206. Mucherera, *Pastoral Care*, 17.

instrument or object for the whole world has been the World Council of Churches (WCC). The WCC has been upfront in many issues that happen in this world such as fighting against injustices, wars, racism, and HIV/AIDS. The World Council of Churches (WCC) has been highlighting the HIV and AIDS issues since the 1980s. This ecumenical movement has been in the forefront in responding in the issue of the HIV and AIDS in different ways. Several publications have been launched to help different communities and people respond to the HIV and AIDS pandemic. The WCC established the *Ecumenical HIV/AIDS Initiative in Africa* (EHAIA), which works with the churches in sub-Saharan Africa to fight AIDS.

In response to the challenges of the HIV and AIDS, it is also important to notice the impact of deaths which leaves many children to suffering from psychosocial problems. One of these problems which the children suffer is grieving from the loss of their parent/s. In this time of grieving it is important for the Church or pastoral counselors to respond in proper ways in order to not harm or hurt the children more. Therefore, proper process of grieving for children must be carefully considered including the use of the narrative approach in the provision of pastoral counseling.[207]

The grieving process in the situation of OVC is very important. Several works have dealt with issues of grief in children, which must be consulted in the process.[208] Switzer says that "the whole family, including the children, must be led in grief counseling to a realignment of roles as a necessary adjustment to loss."[209] This is an important step and process as we work with children who have been affected by the HIV and AIDS. The death of children's parent/s causes the children to experience losses and griefs. This experience of children means that the Church or society as a whole should take some measures on how to work with such children and the psychosocial problems they have been experiencing.

The WCC is upfront in the struggle for making sure that the Church is a safe place for all people who are affected by the HIV and AIDS. These people include children living with the HIV and AIDS and orphans in particular. The WCC has published several documents and other media to affirm that the Church responds to the challenges of the HIV and AIDS. The Church has been called to be a healing community for every person. In one of the UNICEF's documents it is particularly stressed that a particular attention should be given to the conditions of infants and children infected

---

207. Cf. Boss, "The Trauma and Complicated Grief"; Price, "Walking through the Dackness"; Jones, "A Theology of Hope."

208. E.g., Switzer, *The Minister as Crisis*; Jackson, *Understanding Grief.*

209. Switzer, *The Minisster as Crisis Counselor, 154*; cf. Boss, "The Trauma and Complicated Grief"; Price, "Walking through the Dackness"; Jones, "A Theology of Hope."

and affected by the HIV/AIDS pandemic in terms of seeking suitable ways to build a supportive environment for these children to live.[210] It is further pointed out in *Facing AIDS* that the Church or society as a whole should create 'safe spaces' for people to be able to tell their own stories in their families and where they belong to the Church and society. This openness and freedom of people telling their own stories according to the events and experiences opens the door to healing and resilience, to an individual and communities as a whole. The Church has been called to bring such stories of good news (the gospel) to all people who face different kinds of problems and challenges of life. The gospel is about faith, hope, and love to all people who have been desperate and tired of this life in this world. The gospel should open the door to the alternative stories that are empowering.[211]

Another contribution of WCC is its focused on pastoral care and counseling to people living with the HIV and AIDS. The WCC emphasizes on issue of education so that every person acquires proper information about the HIV and AIDS including human sexuality and gender issues. According to Brunn, the WCC indicates the goal of AIDS counseling in twofold: to be an adequate space where the infected persons come to terms with their situations; and to promote common actions which enhance coping strategies for those who are infected and the affected by the pandemic, including the preventing or reducing strategies of the HIV-transmission.[212] These goals form a way forward even in this particular book. We try to look at ways and models that can accomplish this goal and be more effective in this ministry of pastoral counseling to OVC.

Narrative Pastoral Counseling to OVC: The Way to Resilience

This part discusses narrative pastoral counseling to OVC as their way of resilience. It is the responsibility of the Church to make sure that the OVC are being taken care of their needs and problems. The Church has to find ways to help such children who suffer from many problems. The children are overburdened by many things in their lives through which they require support from the Church and society as a whole. The loss of their parent/s, grief, fear, anxiety, despair, anger, and acting out are just some of the burdens they

---

210. UNICEF, "Caring for Children."
211. Igo, *Listerning with Love*, 3.
212. Brunn, "The World Council of Churches," 68; cf. Irinoye, "Couseling People," 182–183.

have to find ways of dealing with.[213] Shelter, food, medicine, clothing, and school fees add to their psychological and emotional problems. When the child misses school because of school fees or clothing, this child becomes angry and begins acting out.[214] Therefore, it is good for the Church to make sure that the response is psychological, spiritual and physical. Then, what does the Church has to do? It has to find some concrete strategies on how it should help OVC holistically.

Children are people like all the other people created by God. Whenever they experience loss, they must be provided a chance of grieving. They require to have an opportunity to grieve, and that the loss they experience are acknowledged. The process of grieving differs from one child to another. Some grieve through writing, and others through singing or talking to oneself. Some children grieve through playing games, arts, or through singing; and some grown up children can express their feelings orally by telling stories. All these ways help the child to stay in control over the ongoing life events.[215]

As it has been pointed out above, orphans and vulnerable children are people just like all others. If provided an opportunity and freedom to express their feelings and emotions, they can tell their stories and reveal their needs. One of the ways which we have found working with the OVC is the narrative approach. Narrative approach provides children to express their problems and needs in a non-threatening situation; it provides them an opportunity to see themselves as people who have their own identity and self-esteem. They find themselves to be respected by society; and therefore, healing and growth happen as a result of finding ways of coping with the entire situation they face in life. In such cases, narratives (stories) become "means of communication for those people whose voices are not often heard" such as children, especially OVC.[216]

Narrative approach by means of stories, proverbs, riddles, metaphors, plays and images is a natural way of life and experience to most African children. They have been in their lives for generation to generation as the result of their elders who passed their cultural practices orally to their children. Narratives (stories) work very well to African children since their early childhood. There is greater wisdom in telling stories, where people are being directed to the life of responsibility and of understanding the ways

213. Dyregrov, *Grief in Children*; cf. Boss, "The Trauma and Complicated Grief"; Price, "Walking through the Dackness"; Jones, "A Theology of Hope."

214. Ibid.; cf. Price, "Walking through the Daarkness."

215. Singhal & Howard (eds.), *The Children of Africa*, 96–97; cf. Boss, "The Trauma and Complicated Grief"; Price, "Walking through the Dackness"; Jones, "A Theology of Hope."

216. Cattanach, *The Story so far*, 7.

of life and in dealing with life issues, whether there is a crisis, disaster, calamity, illness, or any problem in society. Children know how to tell stories of their lives, the backgrounds of their families, and their lives in general. These children can tell stories in many ways, sometimes orally and through writing, drawing, painting, and sometimes through playing games. Through these media, the counselors have to learn how to counsel children about the HIV and AIDS by understanding the contexts of respective children. The counselor should understand the basic communication skills on how to interview the counselee who has been affected and infected by the HIV and AIDS. Moreover, the counselor should also understand how to counsel the child to cope in time of crisis such as loss, grief, guilt, shame, anxiety, low self-esteem, anger, denial, severe depression, and suicidal temptations. The basic skills which the counselor should have when counseling children are good interventions to ultimately build trust and good relationship. Sensitivity on how to attend the child is also very crucial in understanding that child. The counselor should respect the child as the person, direct eye contact with the child, and closeness to the child is another important skill the counselor should have. Active listening and asking good questions open up a way of deeper understanding about the child. Moreover, empathy, openness, and sincerity are also very important in helping the child build up resilience, hope, and balance in life.[217]

Children infected and affected by the HIV and AIDS in various ways should be helped by the counselor in different ways. First, the counselor has to keep in mind the child's age and developmental stage. Most children are not good in expressing their emotions and feelings through talking. Children require good guidance, leadership, and special ways of understanding and communicating with them. We concur with Van Dyk who provides us creative ways to communicate with children. In short, these creative ways are storytelling from the child, mutual storytelling where the client tells a story and also the counselor tells a story, which is a positive or an alternative story (externalizing story). Bibliotherapy is another way where the child is provided a book to read and explore the meaning he or she obtained from it. Dreams, 'what if' questions, three wishes, rating game, word association game, sentence completion, pros and cons, and non-verbal techniques are also good ways for the child to express his or her feelings.[218]

There is a social alienation and stigmatization to OVC in the Tanzanian society. Storytelling is one of the ways or interventions that is very

217. To read more about the HIV/AIDS counseling, which is not our main concentration here in this book, we recommend a book by Van Dyk *HIV/Aids Care and Counseling*, and an article by Irinoye "Counseling People affected by HIV and AIDS."

218. See Van Dyk, *HIV/AIDS Care*, 233.

important in working or counseling OVC. The pastoral counselors or the Church has to encourage OVC and those involved with them to see the problems as people outside of the child (the process of externalization). The AIDS orphans need to "experience their own identities and their problems as separate entities, rather than seeing their alienation and ostracism as being the result of characteristics inherent in their personalities."[219] The Church and society as a whole should open doors for OVC so that they continue to feel that they belong somewhere despite the loss they experience. Children would like to see the strong bond between them and the Church. They like to see that they are connected, remembered, respected, and comforted in all their stages of life as they grow into maturity. By the way of memory book or memory box where they can put some photos, family trees, history, and other information like stories or favorite things, the children's identity and self-esteem will reassure them that they stilln belong to their family members who have passed away.[220] Doing that becomes the way of enhancing resilience in children's lives.

Theologically, the narrative approach provides a sense of worthiness, forgiveness, grace, love, identity and hope in the lives of children. When children tell their stories in different forms such as plays, proverbs, songs, drawings, images, and symbols, they find themselves engaging in life that empowers, strengthens, and revives them. Narratives (stories) are media that join children's souls with the higher being, God. Dinkins says that narratives "are the primary means of communicating the Christian faith."[221] In another way we can say that narratives (stories) are one of the spiritual and psychological interventions for orphans and vulnerable children. Whenever children tell their stories, or sing, they express their deep feelings and needs. These interventions help children stay away from acting out, from anger, fear, sadness, low self-esteem, and other negative behaviors.[222] Storytelling, songs, proverbs, games, and other arts are ways of intervention for children who do not require any professionals to teach or use them in Tanzania; moreover, it is the intervention which is easy and a resource that is cheap to use in our African context. Singhal and Howard have correctly put it thus: "One has to only examine the centuries-old African tradition of storytelling, a frequently used method of healing for the people of the African diaspora

---

219. Singhal and Howard (eds.), *The Children of Africa*, 111; Daigneault, "Narrative Means," 299.

220. See Singhal and Howard (eds.), *The Children of Africa*, 98; Denis (ed.), "Sharing Family Stories."

221. Dinkins, *Narrative Pastoral Counseling*, 14.

222. Dyregrov, *Grief in Children*.

and one that could help the continent's children orphaned by AIDS cope with their grief and other psychological challenges."[223]

Additionally, Denis points out that "in traditional African societies, storytelling was an established practice. The children heard family stories from the mouths of their grandparents."[224] Singhal and Howard continue to say that "storytelling occupies a natural role in many African cultures and is therefore a potentially appropriate intervention strategy for AIDS orphans."[225] The above quotations mean that stories are important in the healing and coping mechanism of an individual or a group. Narratives (stories) are therefore one of the interventions for OVC.[226]

Narrative approach through storytelling, metaphors, proverbs, music, and arts is an intervention or a strategy found to be a non-threatening, respectful, and which children find themselves free and open to tell their stories. Stigma and social isolation, guilt, fear, and anger can be intervened through this approach. The approach allows for the freedom of the children to see that they are accepted, respected, and identified as normal people who do not have to be alienated, isolated, and discriminated. The Bible clearly speaks about love and compassion to children and those who are separated or rejected or looked down in society. Jesus regarded children with a very high esteem; in one instance, he told his disciples,

> Truly, I say to you, unless you turn and become like children, you will never enter the kingdom of heaven, whoever humbles himself like this child, he is the greatest in the kingdom of heaven. . . . Whoever receives one such child in my name receives me; but whoever causes one of these little ones who believe in me to sin, it would be better for him to have a great millstone fastened round his neck and to be drowned in the depth of the sea (Matthew 18:3–6; cf. Matthew19:14; 21:16 See also James 1:27).

Jesus' words above indicate that narrative approach is a two-way traffic; it is done in collaboration and relationship between the child and the counselor. It is in this relationship where healing happens. The approach or strategy itself cannot be meaningful if the love and good relationship misses between the child and the counselor. It is in this relationship where God the Holy Spirit stands in between as mediator, counselor, and reconciler. When we hear and tell and retell the stories, we re-author and find the alternative

---

223. Singhal and Howard (eds.), *The Children of Africa*, 108.
224. Denis, "Sharing Family Stories," 52.
225. Singhal and Howard (eds.), *The Children of Africa*, 109
226. Cf. Ibid.

story (externalizing story), the story that brings purpose and meaning to the lives of people.

Skills and Methods of Narrative Approach in Pastoral Counseling to OVC

Different skills and methods of narrative approach can be applied in pastoral counseling. As it has been noted above, the methods are not as important as relationship and understanding. All methods in narrative approach should lead people to an alternative story of hopeful future and wholeness, no matter which way people take to reach there. In order to lead to an alternative story, an open and sacred space is vital for fruitful conversation with children. This method allows a space for good relationship. Hence, this method invites the Holy Spirit to be between the counselor and the client. The power and guidance of the Holy Spirit allows time for both counselor and client to feel comfortable to tell and listen to stories freely. The questioning should be in time and place. Both the counselor and client should be able to play their stories in a safe ground.

Methods like observation, active listening, good questioning, good relationships, and appropriate media should be put into consideration by pastoral counselors for children. Narrative approach is more than logical analysis where you take step by step in techniques in analyzing things. Narrative approach is to "expect the unexpected," entering in a conversation with children with the "not knowing" attitude. The pastoral counselor, in this uncertain conversation, uses open-ended questions to find more of the story told and retold for a hopeful alternative future story. Hence, observing, listening and telling stories require skills of attention, empathy, and non-judgmental attitude.

The method or process of narrative approach in pastoral counseling is not much with the techniques or formulas of some series of 'abc' methods. The most important step in working with OVC in pastoral counseling using narrative approach is the space that is open to positive relationship and communication. In summary, the narrative process, according to Dinkins and Elliot, should include the following aspects:[227]

- Building a good relationship
- Telling and listening to stories
- Asking good questions (i.e., when, how and what)

---

227. Dinkins, *Narrative Pastoral Counseling*; Elliot, Using Narrative.

- Active and creative listening
- Using proper media (i.e., games, play, and art methods etc.)
- Having the 'not-knowing' mindset or approach
- Externalizing the problem
- Naming the problem
- Deconstructive listening
- Reconstructive conversations
- Re-storying
- Closure or referral, and
- Confidentiality (ethics) and boundaries

The narrative process has also been summarized in what others have called by Landman as the "MEET" process. MEET stands for Mapping, Externalizing, Empowering, and Thickening an alternative story. This MEET is explained in the following process:

1. Mapping: the counselor and patient map the latter's problem-saturated story
2. Externalizing: the counselor follows the patient in externalizing the problem
3. Empowering: the counselor and patient empower each other to deconstruct the problem
4. Thickening an alternative story: the counselor and patient become co-authors in recreating the patient's story of hope and thickening this story with inside and outside witnesses.[228]

We agree with this process of MEET because it fulfills the focus of counseling children discussed at great length in the previous paragraphs—to provide the child with a safe space to tell and retell his or her story as a means for resilience. However, this method should not be taken as a formula of doing narrative counseling processes to children. The process is not an ABC formula. One has to work through the process in a natural way as it flows from the child and being reflected in the counselor. At this situation, one just has to be attentive and sensitive to see what goes on and take the process not in a rigid way; otherwise, it might harm the positive relationship.

McLeod in his *Qualitative Research in Counseling and Psychotherapy* points out that "the key idea in narrative research is that people largely make

228. Landman, "Doing Narrative Counseling," 119.

sense of their experience, and communicate their experience to others, in the form of stories."[229] He continues to elaborate that "the central idea in narrative analysis is that the stories told by informants or research participants can be treated as a primary source of data."[230] Finally, narrative analysis is a way which stresses on the way of making meaning through language or conversation we always have in life.[231]

The book, *Research in Practice: Applied Methods for the Socials Sciences* points out that narrative analysis methods "are based on the assumption that all people construct and live a narrative for their lives."[232] The aim of the narrative approach is "to participate in a conversation that continually loosens and opens up, rather than constricts and closes down. Through therapeutic conversation, fixed meanings and behavior. . .are given room, broadened, shifted, and changed."[233] Following these quotations, several scholars use the narrative method because of its power of healing in counseling.

The narrative theory shows that "people make meaning in their lives through the stories that they construct and the stories that they tell."[234] Through narrative theory the growth of the whole being is assumed and hopefully met. Narratives are universal; they are found everywhere and are the oldest forms of human communication. Quoting from Barthes and Jenkins, Daigneault states: "Narrative is present in myth, legend, fable, tale, novella, epic, history, tragedy, drama, comedy, mime, painting . . . stained glass windows, cinema, comics, news item, conversation. Moreover, under this almost infinite diversity of forms, narrative is present in every age, in every place, in every society; it begins withthe very history of mankind [sic] and there nowhere is nor has been a people without narrative . . . it issimply there, like life itself."[235] The universality of narrative pointed out by Barthes and Jenkins above indicates that narrative communication is part and parcel of human existence.

Moreover, narrative is a way of understanding the way people think and live lives. This kind of thinking and the way people experience life and other events depends on different situations and environments or the cultures they live in. This environment or culture is what creates the value and

229. McLeod, *Qualitative Research*, 104.

230. Ibid.

231. Cf. Ibid., 106.

232. TerreBlanche, Durrheim, and Painter (eds.), *Research in Practice*, 464.

233. Feedman and Combs, "Sexuality," 44.

234. Daigneault, "Narrative Means," 299; cf. Engedal, "The Theological Foundation," 53–56

235. Daigneault, "Narrative Means," 141; cf., Ganzevoort, "Narrative Approaches"; Rescoe & Madoc, "Critical Social Work."

belief system of every individual or society. Narrative is a method or an instrument in which people can know themselves and others. Self-identity and self-awareness can all be created in the realm of narratives. Therefore, narrative is a way to know each other in a more meaningful way as human beings with *utu*. Narratives direct to what is empowering and healing in human's relationships.[236]

In a simple explanation, the term narrative implies listening to and telling or retelling stories about people and the problems in their lives. In nature, people are narrative beings who live as stories to be told and being retold. In the same way as others have mentioned before, Winslade and Monk state well when they say that "we live our lives according to the stories we tell ourselves and the stories that others tell about us."[237] For narrative theorists the motto which they share and emphasize about narrative therapy is this: "the problem is the problem, the person is not the problem." Morgan, for examples, points out that what is more important with narrative therapy is because it is not judgmental and considers the importance of humanity (*utu*); it sees the person as worthy, creative, intelligent, and competent with his or her belief systems that can help the person to live a life of freedom and victory over the challenges of life. In summary, we can conclude that narrative theory is a way people live through their stories to find purpose and meaning for their lives.[238]

Conclusion

The chapter has surveyed various literatures concerning the the narrative approach to/in pastoral counseling to OVC in Tanzania. Different studies have been done to see how other scholars have written on the mentioned matter. Different scholarly perspectives on narratives from different fields have been discussed and analyzed to accommodate the objectives we laid down for this study. Different subjects related to this study such as theologies (different types of theologies), narratives, human sexuality, HIV and AIDS, and particularly the context of orphans and vulnerable children have also been discussed and analyzed. Therefore, this chapter is hoped to enrich the following academic discussion about the use of narrative approaches in practical theology and how they should be more effective in ministering or working with OVC in the African context and the Tanzanian context in particular.

---

236. Ryan, "Narrative."
237. Winslade and Monk, *Narrative Counseling*, 2.
238. Morgan, *What is Narrative Therapy?* 2.

CHAPTER 4

Conducting Empirical Research

"Interviewing can inform us about the nature of social life. We can learn about the work of occupations and how people fashion careers, about cultures and the values they sponsor, and about the challenges people confront as they live their lives. We can learn also, through interviewing about people's interior experiences. . . . We can learn the meanings to them of their relationships, their families their work, and their selves. We can learn about all the experiences, from joy through grief, that together constitute the human condition."

WEISS IN ELLIOT, USING NARRATIVE IN
SOCIAL RESEARCH, 19

Introduction

THIS CHAPTER IS ABOUT the methods which we used for data collection in the field research. It helps the reader to see the ways in which the objectives of the research are met. Methodology is all about how to use different scientific instruments and procedures in collecting and analyzing the required data. Therefore, this chapter is like a road map or direction to show how we went about gathering data and analyzing them to fulfill the research objectives. This particular research relies on qualitative procedures. The methodology we used focuses particularly on this type of research and the objectives we laid before. Hence, the methodology used in this study fits well within the field of practical theology in pastoral counseling to OVC in the African context, and Tanzania in particular.

This study is an integral one because we use different research designs or methodologies which are similar as in the process they are supporting one another. These methodologies are ethnographic research (case studies), participant research (PAR), and life history methodology.[1] In conducting this type of research one has to be a participant (insider), because the conducting of research is broad in its approach.

Research Design

Research design is defined as "a plan or blueprint of how you intend conducting the research."[2] The design of research in this book is qualitative empirical *case study* which aims at providing "an in-depth description of a small number (less than 50) of cases."[3] The type of study in this research is 'exploratory' through case studies. According to TerreBlanche, Durrheim, and Painter, whom we concur with, exploratory research tries to investigate an area which has not been done by other researchers. This way is a free investigation which is more open and adaptable.[4]

Case studies are studies which try to investigate particular individuals or groups in details. It is the method which studies individuals or groups intensively through description and information about those individuals who have been chosen.[5] This kind of investigation uses observation where the thesis statement is made with the assumptions already in mind. It is a kind of research which detail investigation is being done for collecting the data and other clue information along the way. This research design or type shows our way to and try addressing research objectives and questions. Heitink observes well when he says that explorative research is about forming of an idea or assumption which later becomes a hypothesis or rather a "thesis statement."[6] Explorative research emphasizes on the explanation and interpretation of themes, concepts, and ideas that emerge out of the interaction between the counselor and the counselee. Hence, explorative research results in developing or creating models applicable to practical theology in particular.

TerreBlanche, Durrheim, and Painter point out that, "qualitative research can be used not only for exploratory purposes, but also to formulate

---

1. See Mouton, *How to Succeed*, 149–152, 172; cf. Mouton, "Autumn School on Research."
2. Mouton, *How to Succeed*, 55.
3. Ibid., 149.
4. Terre Blanche, Durrheim, and Painter (eds.), *Research in Practice*, 44.
5. Ibid., 460–461.
6. Heitink, *Practical Theology*, 230.

rich descriptions and explanations of human phenomena."⁷ Some of the characteristics of qualitative research are its flexibility in its open approach, especially when it comes to interviews and observations. There is freedom of descriptions and interpretations of themes that emerge in the process of counseling or communication between the researcher and participants. In this case, qualitative research emphasizes on the importance of context in which the research is undertaken; and the process is rather exploratory in nature and the whole process is wider than single events as it is in quantitative research.⁸

The theoretical approach used by this research is a social construction where the human being becomes an interpretive being using phenomenological and ethnographic methods such as case studies. The mode of reasoning in this type of empirical research is more of 'inductive' where specific narrative methods are found, explained and evaluated into more general understandings.⁹ In our research, key ideas, concepts or principles of narrative method are used when describing or interpreting issues surrounding OVC in the pastoral counseling context. As we worked with OVC in Mbeya these concepts and ideas emerged in the process of interactions, interviews, observations and other processes used in research. Hence, these ideas and themes are discussed and interpreted for the purpose of reaching out the research objectives of the study laid down before.

As we discuss about the theoretical framework of our study, we agree with Kotzé and Kotzé who state that, "We are committed to research that will not only contribute to the transformation of our society through care with the marginalized and disadvantaged, but also address cultural discourses and societal practices that promote injustices."¹⁰ It is true as the above statement asserts that we must be part of the change we desire for our society particularly to bring justice to the over-trodden ones. This assertion means that as we work with children who are marginalized and are at great risk of becoming vulnerable to the HIV and AIDS, poverty, and other sicknesses commitment is highly required. The African context should promote a theology which longs to liberate and empower such people who are marginalized. It is a theology that begins from the bottom up (i.e., contextual theology).

Researchers, co-researchers, research participants, and people we work with (i.e., academicians, pastors, leaders in different sectors, social workers, teachers, caregivers, children, parents, etc.) should work together

---

7. Terre Blanche, Durrheim, and Painter (eds.), *Research in Practice*, 45.
8. Dreyer, "Doing Empirical Research."
9. Mouton, *How to Succeed*, 149–150.
10. Kotzé & Kotzé (eds.), *Telling Narratives*, viii.

for the benefit of individuals and community as a whole. This type of working together is what social scientists have called it as the participatory action research (PAR) in "which therapists collaborate with people in challenging oppressive discourses and negotiating ways of living in an ethical and ecologically accountable way."[11] One South African academic C.J. Hugo[12] of UNISA used to tell the story of a chicken and a pig, where the chicken contributed eggs and the pig itself was involved by giving its meat by being killed. Hugo's story emphasized the question of involvement of the researcher in the research process. In this kind of participatory research we had to be involved and not just contribute.

Participatory action research (PAR) "aims to produce knowledge in an active partnership with those affected by that knowledge, for the . . . purpose of improving their social, educational, and material conditions."[13] We continue to emphasize that PAR aims at empowering and establishing good relationships with people we work with. Furthermore, PAR attempts to make a social change and transformation. It is all about open relationships with participants that facilitate the improvement on individuals and the community as a whole.[14]

The logic of a study in this research design (i.e., case study) falls on three categories as explained by Mouton. The first is the logic of contextualization where the cases are explored in great depth instead of generalizing. The mode of reasoning in contextualization (individuation) bases on the uniqueness and specificity of the case study. The second logic of reasoning is discovery versus validation. Discovery (exploratory case studies) aims at explaining and interpreting the thesis statement and the objectives of the research. The third logic is a synchronic versus diachronic. The mode of reason on synchronic study is over a period of time. Hence, the study is interested in looking at the person in the way change occurs over a period of time not just at a given period of time. It is a process of historical development over a period of time, life histories.[15]

---

11. Ibid., 8.

12. Mwenisongole's Conversation with Dr. C.J. Hugo of UNISA, Pretoria, 06/04/2010.

13. TerreBlanche, Durrheim, and Painter (eds.), *Research in Practice*, 430.

14. Ibid., 437–439.

15. Mouton, *How to Succeed*.

Methods of Research

As pointed out above, the research methodological approach is *qualitative* which tends "to keep field notes as [researchers] participate in the field work."[16] Qualitative approach to research looks at ways to understand people in very natural ways. It is a way which tries to describe and analyze the way people live from their natural habitations. It emphasizes on how to do things through mostly using language instead of numbers or quantity. This research approach is about the quality of how people live in their lives. It looks at ideas, theories, themes, concepts and more other ways to understand people for better improvement of their lives.[17] In this kind of participatory research you try to become an insider. Therefore, the methodological approach in this qualitative social research as we relate to the world is being an insider.[18]

In TerreBlanche, Durrheim, and Painter, it is pointed out that "qualitative researchers collect data in the form of written or spoken language, or in the form of observations that are recorded in language and analyze the data by identifying and categorizing themes."[19] They continue to say that "qualitative methods allow the researcher to study selected issues in depth, openness, and detail as they identify and attempt to understand the categories of information that emerge from the data."[20] Mouton explains four domains of research methods: Methods of selection cases, methods of measurement, methods of data-collection and methods of data analysis.[21] These domains are the ones going to be explained below (interviews, observations, and samplings).

In this research, we used interviews as one of our methods for the data collection process. Qualitative research using interviews is very important in the use of narratives as Weiss says being quoted in Elliot. Weiss contends that interviews are important because they

> can inform us about the nature of social life. We can learn about the work of occupations and how people fashion careers, cultures and the values they sponsor, and about the challenges people confront as they live their lives. We can learn also, through

16. Mouton, *How to Succeed*, 107.
17. Ibid., 161.
18. The concepts or stances of being an outsider, insider or the participant in research methodology are elaborated in one of the lectures of Mouton. For further reading see Mouton, "Autumn School on Research."
19. TerreBlanche, Durrheim, and Painter (eds.), *Research in Practice*, 47.
20. Ibid.
21. Mouton, "Autumn School on Research."

interviewing about people's interior experiences. . . . We can learn the meanings to them of their relationships, their families their work, and their selves. We can learn about all the experiences, from joy through grief, that together constitute thehuman condition.[22]

Following Weiss's words, it is our aim that the case studies support the thesis statement set out before. The information from individuals and groups was taken through audio tapes and note-taking. These tapes and notes were finally analyzed thematically as we will see in the following chapter.

In this book some case studies of children about twenty four (24) were recorded in details as they told their stories and as we observed them as participant observers. In-depth descriptions of the cases were accomplished. These cases were taken from the conversation counseling sessions, whether one in one session or sometimes in groups. We also used audio tapes and notes to write what they thought and said to be helpful and interesting to them and what we saw to be helpful in our interaction and conversation. This way of doing means that these cases were used to verify the objectives and thesis statement.

Another method we used was the focus group activities, where ten or fewer children were selected randomly for discussion and having activities on themes which emerged during case studies, activities or as we observed issues surrounding children in relation to their caregivers, volunteers, and teachers at home, school and at the *Amani* Orphanage Center. In this method, themes or issues were picked up, explored, discussed, activities conducted, and interpreted to find alternative meanings and purposes for the better development of the child physically and spiritually.[23]

Population, Samples and Sampling Techniques

Sampling is defined as "the selection of research participants from an entire population, and involves decisions about which people, settings, events, behaviors, and/or social processes to observe."[24] By sampling we mean the representatives of some particular people from which the researcher aims to draw a conclusion. How one selects the representatives depends on the focus of the aim of the research question/s. The sampling procedure may be random or non-random; this procedure means that sampling can be

---

22. Elliot, *Using Narrative*, 19.
23. Bloor, et al., *Focus Groups*.
24. TerreBlanche, Durrheim, and Painter (eds.), *Research in Practice*, 49.

convenient, random, and purposive.[25] The number of participants depends on the nature of research itself or whether the aims have been reached and satisfied. Sampling should make sure that the intended goal and objectives of the research are reached. Qualitative research is concerned much with the in-depth analysis not much with statistical accuracy but with descriptions in the form of words, images, pictures, etc. Qualitative research aims at understanding things in a naturalistic settings or contexts even in the minimal selection of the representatives (sample population).

In this research, the sample consisted of children of age 12 to 17. We worked with more than 50 children at the Faith Based Organization (FBO) known as *Amani* Orphanage Center in Mbeya Tanzania. The children of both genders of that age (12–17 years) were selected randomly to participate in research. Much of the data were collected during the personal contact with each child. Moreover, the number of children and their ages were selected randomly depending on the more manageable sample for the types of qualitative work we did, and for the depth of interview information we obtained. However, we knew that in various life circumstances during the fieldwork the 50 number of children would eventually decrease.

The type of children the *Amani* Orphanage Center has, are known as orphans and most vulnerable children. As also discussed in chapter two above, orphans are children who have lost either one parent or both. Most of these children very rarely have support from their other family members. They may become orphans because of their parent/s death from the HIV and AIDS or from other causes such as accidents, sicknesses, and other natural deaths. The most vulnerable children, in the sense of this research, are children who are at great risk of becoming vulnerable to other circumstances of life such has the risk of becoming infected or affected by the HIV and AIDS, becoming street children, becoming child laborers, and becoming victims of rape and drug abuses. Other vulnerable situations facing these children are poverty and sicknesses (diseases).

Children in this research were picked randomly from the ages we mentioned above, both males and females. They came from different ethnic groups such as Nyakyusa, Safwa, Kinga, and Wanji. They were also from different religious faiths such as Christians (i.e., Roman Catholics, Lutherans, Moravians, Tanzania Assemblies of God and others). This means that *Amani* Orphanage Center does not segregate the needy children because of their ethnic or religious backgrounds.

25. Ibid., 50.

Instruments for Data Collection

TerreBlanche, Durrheim, and Painter state that "data are the basic material with which researchers work."[26] In our research, data were collected through in-depth interviews and focus group activities. The data were collected in order to verify the meaning which we aimed to achieve after the analysis and interpretation of those data collected. Therefore, in order to fulfill this purpose, data were valid and reliable despite the difficulties or differences and challenges that sometimes arose out of these methods.

This book took the profile of each child which was kept from the beginning of the research to the end paying attention to their family history circumstances, school development, age, and gender. Interviews with adults, caregivers/guardians, and pastors took place in the center's office or at the child's home. Those interviews intended to find the historical background of the organization, the child, family history, success, and failures of ministry in the organizations. TerreBlanche, Durrheim, and Painter point out that interviewing "gives us an opportunity to get to know people quite intimately, so that we can really understand how they think and feel."[27] Therefore, it is important to make sure that good planning for interviews are conducted in a manner that is ethically acceptable. That means questions and arguments must be piloted before you embark on interviewing the children, especially the most vulnerable ones. Good planning for interviews is very crucial for several reasons including timing and privacy, what to ask and not what to ask, when to speak and when not to speak, and other considerations. During interviews it is good to keep notes as you continue observing and conversing; these notes are known as 'process notes'.[28]

Eighteen (18) in-depth case studies of 24 individual children were used in the research process to verify the applicability of the narrative approach in pastoral counseling.[29] McLeod asserts that narrative case studies rely on the use of qualitative techniques to elicit and analyze descriptive accounts. Ultimately, narrative case studies are concerned with making sense of stories people tell about aspects of their experience.[30] It is also described by Mouton as "an in-depth description of a small numbers (less than 50)

---

26. Ibid., 51.
27. Ibid., 297; cf. Corbetta, *Social Research*, 264–283.
28. TerreBlanche, Durrheim, and Painter (eds.), *Research in Practice*, 299–300.
29. In these 18 cases, some of the children came from one family. They were siblings in one household. We categorized these children who came from the same family as one case study.
30. McLeod, *Doing Counselling*, 101.

of cases."[31] Moreover, Kothari points out that, "case study is essentially an intensive investigation of the particular unit under consideration."[32] Therefore, in our study, we carefully observed and analyzed the case histories of OVC to find out the assumptions that were made.

Extensive use of written and oral testimony was done throughout the study of children's lives. The written testimonies were obtained from stories they selected to write, letters, stories, proverbs, sayings, songs, poems, symbols, images, and other drawings they wanted to draw or paint. These works were done at their own time at homes and then shared with us during sessions. Stories and other works done by children were documented through note-takings as scribed session notes. We used their memory books and story-books to gather the information we required, however, with their own permissions or of their guardians. Other documents, such as letters, journals and other kinds of metaphors, arts and games were used for the goal of understanding their resilient stage and to find out the value of their lives (the meaning systems of their lives). All these activities were done out of religious or faith contexts to see the applicability of narratives in the context of Church or other faith communities in Mbeya, Tanzania.

The vastness of the oral testimony was collected in a series of life history interviews with each child, with caregivers/guardians, and with other related adults like pastors who were involved with children. The aims of this collection of life stories were to:

- establish the basic chronology of significant episodes in the life of the child,
- supplement and cross-check the child's own account, and
- elaborate in-depth about people, places, and events of the child's life.

Open-ended interviews with children generally vary from different subjects on daily life experiences to make the child more comfortable and easy to talk. These were done to individual children and in focus group discussions and activities. The topics were about domestic duties and chores, games, leisure-time activities, church activities, and school activities. The unstructured open-ended questions for interviews characterized by their flexibility and freedom of questioning were used.[33] Hence, much of the time was also spent in participant observations of children in their activities and interactions with friends, caregivers, and other related adults in different

31. Mouton, *How to Succeed*, 149.

32. Kothari, *Research Methodology*, 113.

33. Kothari, *Research Methodology*, 98; cf. Bless & Higson-Smith, *Fundamentals of Social Research*, 105.

circumstances or contexts which also had to be noticed and recorded for a fair judgment and interpretation.[34] Notes were also taken throughout the research process by their own informed consent.

Data Analysis and Presentation

In the book, *Research in Practice: Applied Methods for the Social Sciences*, TerreBlanche, Durrheim, and Painter point out that "qualitative researchers want to make sense of feelings, experiences, social situations, or phenomena as they occur in the real world, and therefore want to study them in their natural setting."[35] The aim of qualitative research points to contextual interpretation so as to understand human beings in their natural settings. This conception of knowledge (epistemology) one has to be inside and not outside of the field research.[36] Qualitative research in our study looked at how to collect data in context, to look at the situation of orphans and vulnerable children in Mbeya, Tanzania. Hence, collecting data in this context was very important for our research to remain naturalistic in its setting.

On data analysis, careful consideration should be emphasized on designing a study. The aim of data analysis "is to transform information (data) into an answer to the original research question."[37] Our study concerned with qualitative techniques as we considered the data analysis process. Themes, concepts, and ideas were identified in the process of analyzing and interpreting. Data analysis helped us understand different components of data that were collected in the sphere of personal relationships. These data were measured in different ways to see whether they were reliable and viable in our study. Then, data were analyzed and interpreted to find out the results in relation to the thesis statement or objectives. Interpretation of the data was a way of relating the results of the data to the existing premises or methods which we laid down for the book. The interpretation also supported the data which were gathered with the theory of narrative we suggested. Data results and interpretation helped to see whether the methods used were viable or reliable.[38]

During the research process, we kept good record of pastoral counseling sessions with special emphasis on narrative approach in pastoral counseling context. The interviews with children were conducted in the

34. Bless and Higson-Smith, *Fundamentals of Social Research*, 104.
35. TerreBlanche, Durrheim & Painter eds., *Research in Practice*, 287.
36. Mouton, "Autumn School on Research."
37. TerreBlanche, Durrheim & Painter eds., *Research in Practice*, 52.
38. Cf. Mouton, *How to Succeed*, 108–109.

center's office or sometimes in the outdoors when there was a fine weather. To evaluate the narrative approach in pastoral counseling, we depended on feedbacks from caregivers and pastors, whether there were changes or any impact in the lives of children as we engaged in conversation and interaction with each other. We also used our own observations to see whether we could use the narrative approach in the context of the Church situated center. Theologically, we analyzed the contribution and impacts of narratives in the lives of OVC in Tanzania. Hence, data analysis through qualitative analytical methods and content analysis of the key themes or concepts, we examined the results from the interviews and observation methods we used. To evaluate the effectiveness of the narrative approach in pastoral counseling context, we depended on the feedback from children themselves whether there were changes or any impacts on their lives.[39] The interviews and content analyses were examined to interpret themes that verified children's resilience for their situation of who they were. We used content analysis to assess and interpret the data and results of the interviews.

Ethics in Research

It was very crucial to consider the ethical guidelines as we embarked in a field research especially with children who were most vulnerable. With this vulnerability in mind, in our research we were able to work in the manner that was acceptable, respectable, benefitable, justifiable, sensitive, non-threatening, and without harming or hurting anyone involved in the research process. It should be clearly understood that research ethics are there to protect research participants from physical social and psychological harm. As TerreBlanche, Durrheim, and Painter have pointed out, research ethics "should be a fundamental concern of all social science researchers in planning, designing, implementing, and reporting research with human participants."[40]

Therefore, in order to safeguard the required dignity of the vulnerable children, we sought consent from the third party. Oliver elaborates clearly about this strategy when he writes: "The strategy of obtaining third party consent may be relevant where school pupils are to be research participants. While it may be feasible to explain the research in outline to the children, the fully informed consent would be obtained from parents or guardians, teachers or other relevant professionals."[41] Moreover, the confidentiality

---

39. Denis, "Sharing Family Stories," 31.
40. TerreBlanche, Durrheim, and Painter (eds.), *Research in Practice*, 61.
41. Oliver, *Student's Guide to Research Ethics*, 37.

of information provided by the center and by children in particular was considered as part of the agreement before the commencement of research. It was good to treat others' information in a manner that was respectful. Confidentiality was encouraged, especially in focus group sessions and with particular individuals. The taped interviews and data from other documents were securely locked in a cabinet, and were finally completely destroyed after the completion of the research. Moreover, we used the instruments supplied by the Center and by the children after their permissions and only for the research work we were doing. The purpose of the research was clearly explained to the participants prior to the commencement of research for them to understand the goal of the research before providing the consent to participate.[42] Therefore, it is our conviction that we attempted hard to secure the necessary ethical procedures to mitigate possible psychological, mental, social and physical harms to research participants.

Conclusion

This chapter concerned about empirical research, research design, methodology, and methods that were used in the process of collecting data, analyzing, and interpreting them. It has been clearly stated in this chapter that we employed case study design within the qualitative approach to conducting research using interview as a method of data collection. This methodological chapter was the road map of the whole study showing the way, process, and direction of research and report writing. Using the methodological perspective stated in this chapter, the research was hoped to be scientifically valid and reliable.

Furthermore, the research used the methods that were fit to this study under the practical theology field. Proper and careful consideration of the methods was our upfront to make the written report scientific and applicable in various fields in the human science subjects, especially those which used qualitative research methods. Hence, this chapter takes us to the next chapter which concerns about the results of the data collected, the analysis of the data, and the interpretation of those data.

---

42. Oliver, *The Student's Guide to Research*; Israel & Hay, *Research Ethics*; Loue, *Textbook of Research Ethics*.

CHAPTER 5

Making Sense of Obtained Research Data

"CT [Child Theology] calls us to revisit our understanding of Scripture, our dogmatic truths, our church history, and our faith and church practices by placing a child in the midst of all of our theological reflections. A key question in this regard is: How do children influence what we are seeing and hearing?"

—Grobbelaar, Child Theology, 11.

Introduction

THE AIM OF ANY research is to obtain data to be used as evidence to argue a case. In order for the data to perform this important function, they have to be processed. Processing means making sense of them; and it involves the process of organizing, analyzing, interpreting and discussing them. Without making sense of the obtained data, they remain a heap of useless research information. This chapter discusses the processed results of research undertaken in the field in Mbeya, Tanzania. As pointed out in the previous chapter, data were collected through qualitative methods: semi-structured interviews, unstructured interviews, and focus group discussions and activities. These data were recorded by note-taking or what research theorists call "process notes."[1] These data and results were analyzed and interpreted to fulfill the objectives and aims of research study.

Van der Merwe and Gobodo-Madikizela, as quoted in Streets, describe about the trauma experience of the suffering person and how it is reversed through narratives thus: "Narrating one's life is about finding structure,

---

1. TerreBlanche, Durrheim, and Painter (eds.), *Research in Practice*, 302.

coherence and meaning in life. Trauma, in contrast, is about the shattering of life's narrative structure, about a loss of meaning–the traumatized person has 'lost the plot'. A fundamental issue concerning trauma is the regaining of meaning after trauma, the rewriting of one's life narrative to incorporate the traumatic loss in the new narrative."[2] The regaining of new meaning from the narrated stories was the main concern in our interaction with OVC in this study.

In the following sections we use interview schedule results with case studies to discuss the personal life stories of children. We observe and interpret them therapeutically to see what goes on or what children did in sessions (i.e., using metaphors, playing games, telling stories, writing their memory books, drawings and paintings). As participant action researchers (PAR), we used their stories which they heard or learned and which were related to their life stories to reconstruct their lived experiences. Telling and hearing stories was by itself a healing phenomenon. Furthermore, we explored and assessed therapeutically the stories and metaphors which children heard or told themselves. This was our therapeutic involvement[3] with children on how we helped them to find a relationship that would ultimately help them grow into maturity and holistic being. At the end we provide our own reflections and general assessments.

Interview Schedule Results

Speaking about the importance of stories to human beings, both children and adults, Coetsee and Grobbelaar echoed: "Children—and adults—love stories. Maybe because we are created in the image of 'a storytelling' God."[4] They further add:

> Storytelling can be seen as a special form of play, where the mind is 'at play' even when the body is inactive. Stories create a world of imagination and therefore a world less threatening for the child or adult who struggles to face the harsh reality of his own world. "The remarkable thing is that because of this distance between the world of stories and the real world, the child can come closer to his true emotional world when listening to stories. Therefore stories have the power to change his world of

---

2. Streets, "Love: A Philosophy of Pastoral Care," 5.

3. More than being researchers and pastors in the field, we also worked as pastoral counselors in the organization (*Amani* Orphanage Center) which was a Faith Based Organization (FBO) under the MCTSWP.

4. Coetsee & Grobbelaar, "A Church Where Children are Welcome," 813.

feelings and beliefs. Because he can identify with the heroes in the stories, he can start living a new life in his imagination, from where it can be transferred to his real life."[5]

As we stated in the above section, in order to enter into the world of children and their stories, we used the interview method. Interviewing is one of the methods used to collect data in qualitative research, and in our case, in the form of narratives (stories) from children's lived experiences. The method provides an opportunity for people to interact in a more naturalistic way. TerreBlanche, Durrheim, and Painter point out that "it (interviews) gives us an opportunity to get to know people quite intimately, so that we can really understand how they think and feel." [6] In order for it to facilitate knowing people, our interview schedule was planned in such a way that it provided us the opportunity to understand children intimately about what they thought and felt. It was a two-way traffic where researchers and participants collaborated in the field to build the relationship that resulted into knowing one another better. Interviews were conversations we told to each other about who we were. The open-ended questions were ways to the conversation. Hence, this kind of conversation is free, easy and non-threatening.

In the following pages interviews and observations were analyzed and interpreted in in-depth case studies of 18 case studies which comprised of twenty four children. These eighteen case studies cover different and various themes or issues (i.e., sexual, physical, and verbal abuse, child labor, sickness, domestic violence, poverty, segregation, homeless, loss, grief, shame and guilt) related to children's experiences, feelings and other circumstances with people who were involved with them, such as caregivers. The themes and issues related to OVC illustrate the importance of narratives in pastoral counseling context for the well-being and the resilience of children. It was seen in the analyses that surely, there was a big contribution of narratives in practical theology in particular as we saw in children's cases. The theological themes or concepts that imaged from cases of children were such as the following: hope, sin, forgiveness, grace, love, reconciliation, salvation, spirituality and many more others.[7]

The case studies illustrated and pointed out the significance of narrative approach in practical theology and particular pastoral counseling. The children's biographical information was elaborated; children's feelings, life circumstances, stories, metaphors, and other experiences were discussed and analyzed in details. These details of information proved the effectiveness

5. Ibid.
6. TerreBlanche, Durrheim, and Painter (eds.), *Research in Practice*, 297.
7. Cf. Moore, Gomez-Garibello, Bosacki, & Talwar, "Children's Spiritual Lives."

of narrative approach to OVC as a means which churches or faith based organizations and society in general could apply for the betterment of OVC from their issues of life and how to cope with such issues. Hence, through stories, metaphors, arts, and games children were able to find resilient life and cope with the difficulties of life. They were able to grow into fullness of life, the life of wholeness.

The following case studies and information on children's biography, stories, metaphors, memory book, pictures and drawings were reached out through different methods. The process of collecting data and intervention with children in the research took us more than one year. The methods we used to record data were such as notes-taking (process notes) during the observations, interviews and counseling sessions. We were guided by semi-structured or rather unstructured open-ended questions. We also used tape-recording of their stories, gaving them homework, visiting their homes, doing some group discussions, conducting individual conversations, and carrying out small classes where they were provided topic/s to write, discuss, play (drama), act, draw or paint. They sometimes used their memory books which they were guided on how to use them. This was done under the careful supervision and guidance considering also the relevant ethical procedures and norms. Hence, in the presentation of cases below, a particular pattern is followed in all the 18 cases: first, we introduce the child and state our observation and interpretations about that child. Second, we present the dominant story of the child and the dominant experiences written in their memory books. Third, we relate the dominant story of the child with a therapeutic story from the Bible in order to make the child reach to his or her self-realization and move out of their existing situations.[8]

Case Number 1: Raphael

Background

We begin the cases of children with case number one, the case of Raphael. Raphael was born at Babati in Manyara region, the northern part of Tanzania. Raphael had four brothers and two sisters. He was 17 years old. His mother-tongue was Bena from Njombe district in the then Iringa region (now Njombe Region). Raphael's mother died soon after his birth. Raphael's mother died mysteriously and the cause of her death was unknown to them, especially to Raphael and Emmanuel his brother. Raphael and his brother Emmanuel (19 years old), whom they stayed together, did not know the

---

8. Wimberly, *Using Scripture in Pastoral Counseling*.

cause of their mother's death. In 2001 Raphael's father also died from a great pain and breeding from his chest problem followed by a car accident. Raphael's father was working in small industries here and there. Raphael's parents left behind seven children. Raphael was the last-born child in his family. At the moment, he was studying in Form One at Itezi Secondary School in Mbeya. Some of his brothers and sisters were scattered around the country. It was only him and his brother Emmanuel who lived in the house. Very occasionally, their sister (27 years old) helped to take care of them with small things whenever she was available and for whatever she could afford. Secilia also did not have any stable job to earn some income to support her brothers.

Our Observation and Interpretation

Most of the time, Raphael and his brother Emmanuel were at home by themselves. They mainly had some support from the Church for food, clothing, and school fees. Most of their supports were from the Moravian Church in Tanzania, the South West Province, under the department of women and children, especially through the *Amani* Orphanage Center. Economically, life was very difficult for them. Their elder brothers seemed to have abandoned them; they had very little concern about them!

Raphael liked to play a lot, especially football. Moreover, he also liked to study and draw pictures. His school development was good according to his teachers at school and volunteers at the organization. The living environment and condition of Raphael and his brother Emmanuel was not good in a standard that we could call a good standard of life. When we visited the child in the area where Raphael and his brother Emmanuel lived, we found that they did not even have enough space for sleeping, sitting, and cooking. The house they lived in was left with their deceased parents. The house by itself was not that bad, but was very small for them and other three children they lived with. These other children belonged to Raphael's sisters. Raphael said that sometimes they slept without having any food to eat.

We also observed that Raphael was usually happy when was out playing with his friends or when was at the center; but when he was at home with his brother alone, one could see that he felt differently. He showed sadness in his face. He stayed quiet and very calm and cold. He seldom spoke and whenever he spoke it was about his house problems of not having enough food or clothing. Raphael had a good dream for his future. He was very optimistic about his future life. He hoped that after acquiring enough education, he would work as traffic police. This was one of his positive ideas (strengths) he had for his life. This story was very clear in his memory book.

Raphael belonged to the Lutheran church at Uyole in Mbeya, and one of his drawings he liked to draw was his church building and the pastor of his church. Raphael believed in Christianity but was also influenced by traditional beliefs, especially of traditional healers and of witchcraft practitioners or witches. These showed that Raphael had both fear and hope in his life. He believed and trusted in God's grace to provide him with their needs and problems. Despite the hope and faith he had, Raphael as a normal human being was also uncertain about his future life; there was a worry and fear which surrounded him. Below we look closely at one of the stories he wrote in his memory book.

Raphael's Story

Raphael's story written in his memory book goes like this: "Once upon a time there was a grandmother who was a witch. There was another person by the name of Mboza who had a friend named Amina. One day Mboza and Amina went to a well to fetch some water, while fetching water, Mboza's necklace fell in the water of the well and they could not take it out and decided to leave. On the way, Mboza asked Amina to escort her to look for the necklace at the well; but Amina did not agree. Mboza went back alone, and when she was at the well she found her necklace above the water and she tried to take it out, but suddenly she found the hand of the grandmother holding her. The old woman grabbed her and pulled her down in the well and Mboza was drawn. Then the old woman took Mboza and put her in the drum and she began going through the streets in the village saying, 'I am a singer' and the people were telling her 'then sing for us,' and she commanded Mboza in the drum saying to her 'sing' and Mboza began singing, 'I am a child Mboza, my necklace fell and I also fell in the well waah!.'

Then Mboza's mother heard about that old woman and began to ask herself about her. One day Mboza's mother called the old woman and told her, 'let us go and sing for me at home.' The old woman agreed and went with her at home and she was invited for food to eat. Mboza's mother asked the old woman to take her drum and put it inside the house in a different room and she also agreed. Later on, Mboza's mother decided to snick inside the room where the drum had been put. She entered into that room and decided to open the drum to see what was inside the drum. When she opened the drum, she found that she was her daughter Mboza, who was lost several weeks back. Then Mboza's mother took Mboza out of the drum and in return she put back some bees inside of that drum.

When the time came for that old woman to leave, she also asked about her drum to be given back to her so that she did not forget to go with it. So the old woman left with her drum full of bees inside. On her way back she met other people and as usual she invited people saying, "you know I am a singer;" and the people said, "good then sing for us and we will provide you some nice local beer to drink to the full." Then she began to sing saying to the drum, "Mboza sing," but it was quiet, again she said, "Mboza sing," but it was quiet again. In anger, the old woman tore out the drum and the bees came out furiously and began stinging the old woman and people who were around. The old woman was bitten until death. At the end, Raphael wrote, "the story teaches us that we should not be wicked and be like the witches who always want to harm others."

Raphael's Memory Book

In Raphael's memory book he wrote his autobiography. He wrote about his family, his mother, father, and his brothers and sisters. He also wrote about the pains and struggles he went through. He described that life in his family was very troublesome as he put in Swahili metaphor, "*balaa tupu!*" which means "it is all about trouble after trouble." This happened when his father decided to marry another woman after the death of Raphael's mother. Raphael explains that his stepmother became very ruddy to children, especially when their father was away from his home for his job.

One of the sad true stories he wrote concerned about his stepmother quarrelling with his sister. Raphael explained that it was at no reason the stepmother did not like his sister and her baby. She was ruddy even to the baby which did not know anything about the family. She even dared to say, "even if your child dies, I will not cry at all." Raphael said that it was the incident which he said that he himself was hurt very much and which he could not forget! Raphael continued to write that the next day after the quarrelling between his stepmother and his sister about the baby, the baby died. And the stepmother said, "My dream has been fulfilled".

Raphael continued to tell his story that after the funeral more problems came to their sides. The stepmother began refusing to provide them food especially when their father was away in his traveling. Raphael wrote that, one day when the father was away, the stepmother sent Raphael to the meat shop to buy meat, and the mother was left alone at home. When Raphael returned he found that his stepmother had gone. When his father came back, he found that she had gone, taking all her clothing, the license of the car, and the money. Then Raphael's father decided to sell the house and buy another one at Uyole. Later, in the following years, Raphael's father traveled and stayed for a long time without coming back home to his children. When he came back in 2001 he stayed for a while with them; he became very weak and finally died.

Concerning his stepmother, Raphael seemed to be very angry with her and at the same time very sad to be without any parents. He complained that they had all left him. To his stepmother he wrote that she should not dare to come back for she will see the fire and would explain what made the snake to come out of its pit. In Swahili sayings, Raphael wrote, "*Cha moto atakiona na ataeleza kilichomtoa nyoka pangoni*." Other things which Raphael included in his memory book were his favorite proverbs, stories, and dreams for his future. He drew some pictures such as a picture of a policeman, which is his dream. He also drew some motor vehicles, which he seemed to be interested in.

In his favorite proverbs, which we think related to his stories and his background, was the proverb which said in Swahili, "*Akupendaye kwa dhiki ndiye rafiki wa kweli*," which means, "the one who loves you when you are in hardships is a friend indeed." Also the other one in his memory book too went like this, "*Kikulacho ki-nguoni mwako*," which means, "the thing which devours you is in your own clothing." This proverb means that most of the time people who are your enemies are not far from yourself. The enemies are usually around or close to us.

Therapeutic Intervention

Raphael's life story and his general stories and metaphors about his surroundings above present issues or problems he experienced. The issue of his parents' separation and their deaths was one of those big problems he faced. There was a loss and grief surrounding his stories. Fear and uncertainty of life was also a problem to Raphael. As the result of these problems, Raphael struggled with his life. He lost a sense of direction, because there was no figure of a parent to guide his life. The life for Raphael was uncertain with full of anger and fear because of the mysterious life he lived where there was no one around him to care, protect, support, and guide. Sadness and fear of life of being alone without parents was an issue. The support was very little for him and his brother.

For Raphael, talking about his family was very difficult especially at the beginning of our counseling sessions. It took time until when he became open to talk without any force through his own initiatives and with our positive attitude towards them of not being judgmental and harsh, Raphael's feelings were open through different media such as through his memory book, pictures, his stories and proverbs. However, one of the most important skills in this kind of intervention with children is building up a good relationship. This good relationship by itself is a healing phenomenon for children who are affected by so many things that happen in their lives. Playing, metaphors and using things which the child likes to do is such a good place to start in building a good relationship. These are things which children like. We believe that we as researchers must be involved with children's activities and not only participating or volunteering.

One of the methods we used to work with them, especially Raphael, was picking up from what interested him, which we thought was most helpful for his resilience and healing. This was the stories, music, and pictures he liked to draw. We gave him freedom and opportunity to do whatever he liked but with a little bit of guidance so that we found the ways of helping him to cope with his situation of fear and sadness. At another point he drew a picture of the person showing his feelings of happiness. This came as a result of the narrative approach which we used with them. Children like to draw pictures and out of them they can be free to talk about their drawings. For Raphael happiness was the result of love and the ability of loving one another whereby people could be able to work together in unity and solidarity. The symbol of love and happiness for him was the heart. Raphael explained that if people could love each other, they would be happy. Being happy for Raphael was something very precious than material things and riches.

We explored more on his proverb which he wrote saying "*Akupendaye kwa dhiki, ndiye rafiki wa kweli.*" Together with him we tried to externalize the problems of sadness, anger, fear, uncertainty, low self-esteem through picturing and telling stories. One of the good examples we used with Raphael to gain an alternative story was about his own proverb which he used. The proverb says, "*Akupendaye kwa dhiki, ndiye rafiki wa kweli*, which means that "the one who likes you even in times of hardships is a friend indeed." Raphael knew that there are some people who seem to be friends only when everything goes well and smooth to you. But when you face difficulties and troubles the same people who seemed to be friends start running away from you. They keep distance as if they do not know you. This is hypocrisy and is not a true love or friendship. Raphael experienced such life where friends even his own relatives deserted him especially in the time of need. From that proverb we picked up something to share with him. We used the gospel story which ultimately helped Raphael to accept who he was and continued to live a life which was focused, the life of faith and hope. The goal was to live a life full of hope, joy and good dreams for the future. The alternative story we introduced goes like this:

> Once upon a time there was a wise old man who lived many years of which no one had ever lived. This wise man saw and experienced many things in his life; but he continued to live a life of hope to a dream he had since his childhood. He experienced hardships and every kind of problems in his life. Many of his people rejected him. But he knew that there was only one person who would always love him. He continued to live a life that was focused. This wise man had some friends who liked him and tried to follow him, despite the problems they had, the wise man loved his friends and he wanted them to live to their dreams until when they fulfilled the mission which they have been provided. He assured his friends that they should always live in hope, joy, and life of goals despite all the problems they experienced in life; they should not despair.

The story is our creation from the Gospel of John 16: 33, where the wise teacher, Jesus, encourages his disciples to remain firm in worldly troubles. Jesus is a model for his disciples to follow in the life to come. The gospels explain clearly that in this world there are different kinds of hardships even to followers of Christ. This alternative story also indicates that abandonment can even be exerted by those people who are very close such as relatives and friends. However, Jesus promises that he will always direct, guide us, protect us, and always be in our side even in the midst of hardships (John 16:33). However, by the way of being open to tell and share our stories and by using the African proverbs and riddles we were able to empower Raphael by thickening his stories of fear and sadness. Together we became the co-authors in making the sad or fear stories more hopefully with the faith in Christ Jesus who is the source of all powers and good things he has stored for his people. The story Raphael wrote above seems to be full of fear of the wicked circumstances which happen in peoples lives. Through the positive relationship that came up as the result of the positive alternative stories, Raphael was able to find peace, courage, and continued to live a life full of hope and good dreams for his future.

Raphael showed faith and hope through his future dreams and proverbs. He indicated this in his empowerment words, "*Mvumilivu hula mbivu,*" which means that "the person who endures hardships will eat ripe fruits." This is a very positive outcome, which calls people to be patient with the hardships of life no matter what, as the Bible testifies, the one who will endure to the end will be saved and eat of the tree of life (Matthew 24:13;

cf. Revelation 2: 7b). There are benefits in being patient, working hard, and persevering hardships in life. Even without comment or explanation it is obvious that Raphael knew the way forward for him. That is why he took the wisdom of the people by writing in his memory book that, "*Mvumilivu hula mbivu*," which means that "if you are patient enough you will eat the ripe fruits." Raphael knew that to be patient and persevering in life even in times of hardships would ultimately fulfill his dreams and goals of becoming who he wanted to become.

Case Number 2: Bertha and Sylivia

Background

The second case was that of Bertha and Sylivia. Bertha was 14 years old. Bertha's family was originally from Iringa region. Their home language was Wanji. Bertha's parents had seven children, three of them died while very young, one died while was only two years old, and the other two children died at stillbirth. Only four children were left. Bertha was the sixth child and had her little sister, the last one in the family whose name was Sylvia aged 12 years old. At the moment, they were four children in their family. Bertha was the third child and her little sister Sylivia was the last born child. Their sister was married and their brother was also away living independently. Therefore, it was only Bertha and Sylivia who lived with their mother.

Bertha was born being physically very well. She also grew up without any major health problems. Bertha's father died in 2000 after being sick for a long time, about three months or more, as they did not remember very well how long it took. Bertha's mother was not physically very well; most of the time she became sick. She worked as a small business woman in the Uyole market at Mbeya where she sold firewood; however, she was also involved in small scale farming during the rain seasons. She was the only support for these two children, Bertha and Sylivia, despite her low income from selling firewoods and small faming activities.

Bertha's family condition was not very good. They lived in a very hard situation due to low economic condition . Sometimes they did not even have food to eat. To skip a meal was just a regular routine for this family. They sometimes had to beg food or money so that they could buy necessary things or be able to go to hospital when were sick. Sometimes, they did not even have money to pay for opening the hospital file. Though Bertha's family had some relatives, they almost had nothing to support other people apart from their own families alone.

Bertha's family went to church. They belonged to the Apostolic Church at Uyole Mbeya, where they were involved in different activities of the congregation. Bertha told the authors of this book that her prayers and dreams for the future were that she acquired good education and passed her exams well and went to the university or college where she could study and eventually become a traffic police. In this way, she could live a good life and help others be happy. The dream of Sylvia for her future after acquiring a good education was to become a nurse.Bertha's other interests included memorizing biblical verses, playing with her friends, doing house chores, and doing physical exercises. Some of the biblical verses she had in her memory book were, "Honor your father and your mother, that your days may be long in the land which the LORD your God gives you" (Exodus 20:12) and "The Lord is my shepherd, I shall not want; he makes me lie down in green pastures." (Psalms 23:1)

Our Observation and Interpretation

The verses she wrote seemed to be important to her because they showed her that it was good to continue honoring her mother no matter what circumstances they were going through. The hope was found in the next verse which showed that God was their guide and their sustainer who could not forsake them and would always provide something for them (Psalms 23:1). These children seemed to live their lives in the hope they found as Christians, and stood up for the biblical promises they read and memorized, hoping that God would be faithful to promises for the dreams they had in life.

Bertha liked to have both parents; unfortunately, she only had the mother and she looked worried and unease. Bertha told the authors that she liked to be close to her mother so that she could be able to help her whenever she had the need or faced any problems. Bertha learned from school and from the *Amani* Orphanage Center that, "*Asiyesikia la mkuu, huvunjika guu,*" which means that, "the one who does not listen to his or her superior ones will break his or her leg, i.e., he or she will be destroyed." She also wrote this proverb in her memory book, "*Asiyefunzwa na mamaye, hufunzwa na ulimwengu,*" which means that "the one who is not taught by his or her mother, the world will teach him or her"[9] In the above description, Bertha seems to be very close to her mother. Both Bertha and Sylvia like to help their mother with different activities such as house chores, even whenever they have the time they help their mother selling firewood at the market, fetching water and firewood from the mountains.

9. Cf. Ndossi, "The Significance of the Female Perspective," 39.

For various reasons Bertha and Sylvia did not do very well in school. This would be because of their mother's frequent illnesses; many chores at home were in their hands in such a way that they did not have enough time to study and do their homeworks. They faced economic problems which restrained them from going to extra lesson in the evenings; and furthermore, they did not have electricity in their house. And for that reason they could not study at night; however, sometimes they went to their friends who had electricity at the neighborhood. Naturally and generally, Bertha and Sylvia were intelligent and could do much better if had good support and favorable environments and facilities for their education. Bertha's personality, as we saw her at home and at the *Amani* Orphanage Center, seemed to be very quiet unlike her little sister Sylvia. Bertha was not very talkative and naughty like Sylvia. Most of the time Bertha liked to tell stories by writing down in her memory book, but not in public. She was good in writing down her stories but not in speaking, especially in front of people.

Bertha's Story

Bertha wrote the following story in her memory book, which we think teaches something in her life. The story goes like this: "Long time ago there was a mother, father, and a child. One day the father became angry and went to hit the mother, and the mother became angry too and decided to bit the child. The child also became angry and went to hit the dog, and the dog became angry and went to beat the cat, and the cat became angry and went out to eat the rat, and the rat became angry and went out to eat the maize in the store. Then the whole family entered into trouble because it did not have any food to eat, because the rat ate everything in the store."

What did this story teach Bertha? Bertha said the story teaches that "we should not hold on to anger for a long time!"

Therapeutic Intervention

The problem of Bertha or Sylvia was not themselves. As we mapped together of what was the problem, we found that the problem was anger, sadness, and loneliness. It was anger because life seemed to be unfair to her family and especially to her parents. Loneliness faced them because there seemed to be no one to help and support them from their daily problems, especially when their mother became sick, and only children remained who could not afford to keep her from her problems, especially when it came to financial needs. However, as we continually visited her house, we realized that she was HIV positive. She was troubled frequently with other related diseases to the HIV and AIDS. Afterwards she became very free and open to talk with us different issues and stories about her family. All these stories made Bertha and Sylivia sad, angry, and lonely. They required a psychosocial support in order to cope with those difficulties and problems they faced in their lives. Having visits was one of the healing phenomena which encouraged people who were HIV positive and were affected by the HIV and AIDS.

Visiting the home of Bertha and Sylivia, also their mother, was so empowering for them. We noticed that children's self-esteem grew up as a result of frequent visit to their house and talking to them different things relating to life, both spiritual and physical life. The loneliness became an issue which could be dealt with through story-telling and keeping themselves busy with homework and other home activities. Keeping themselves busy was another way of reducing unnecessary anger and sadness. Bertha and her sister Sylivia had good relationships with their friends in the neighborhood. They also liked to play different games at home and at the *Amani* Orphanage Center. These activities were encouraged by the center especially in the approach of narrative counseling with children. Those activities helped children to cope with their problems and kept them focused with their future dreams of success and prosperity; however, more important were their lives of content, of wholeness, and of making them what God wanted them to be.

Bertha's mother was very much connected to their New Apostolic Church at Uyole Mbeya. This seemed to be very helpful to their lives. The faith and hope they had were because of the connectedness they had through this local church. Bertha and Sylivia were also very interested in studying the Bible and following their precepts so that they remained good Christian girls. They tried to memorize biblical verses in their hearts, which seemed to them as an important part in their spiritual life. The connectedness was very important to Bertha and Sylivia. Loneliness and low self-esteem could be defeated through the connection with God, with good people, and with the community around them. Friendship and relationship was very important for them. In one of her poems, Bertha wrote:

Urafiki kitu bora, ndugu nisikilizeni
Tuudumishe ubora, na uzalendo nchini
Daima tu watu ubora, unyama tuuacheni
Tudumishe urafiki, kwani ni kitu adimu.

This poem explains that friendship is something precious. We should keep it, and should be precious too; we have to keep friendship because it is so scarce. As the Swahili proverb says, "*Urafiki ni bora kuliko marijani,*" which means that "friendship is better than precious jewels" or friendship is better than anything good we posses such as the precious material things."

Our intervention through the story of Bertha tried to explore more on the issue of anger as was expressed in her story. The Swahili people tend to say, "*Hasira ni hasara*," which means, "anger is loss" or with another meaning, "anger does not profit anything." In anger we can not do anything constructive or profitable. Bertha and her sister lived in the principle of love. They tried their level best to love one another and did their best not to be angry or have anger at anyone else. How did they do that? It was through skills they learned at the center and through stories. Positive relationships among themselves was one of the basis for maintaining the principle of love; and this positive relationship came as a result of being able to play together while telling and listening to each others' stories.

There is also a verse in the Bible which says, "Be angry but do not sin; do not let the sun go down on your anger, and give no opportunity to the devil." (Ephesians 4:26) We should deal with our anger wisely. Anger is part of our human emotions, but the anger should not control us. In anger we should not loose our sense of humanity and our self-worth. In anger we should remember self-control. Children should always remember what Christ taught. Telling our stories is a healing phenomenon by itself. Some of the issues in the family are very difficult to talk about such as issues of sex and AIDS. The problem can be recognized by everyone in the family; but there will be no one to talk about it. Shame, guilt, ignorance, *Unyanyapaa* (stigma), and taboo can be one of the reasons of people's silence. In thsese circumstances, narrative approach welcomes people with simple and easy skills, freedom and non-threatening skills to open up for positive stories that empower and heal the broken relationships between them and God, and between them and their surroundings.

Case Number 3: Emmy

Background

The third case concerns Emmy. Emmy was 17 years old, studying at Pankumbi Secondary School in Form one. She was the second born child among four children of her family. However, the first child died while Emmy was two years old; Emmy was then the oldest in her family and only three children were left. Emmy lived with her little sister Happy in their grandmother's house, the one who took care of them. Her father died after becoming sick for a short time in 2002. The cause of his death was not known. Her mother still lived and involved herself in selling charcoal and other small businesses. Emmy's grandmother took care of other three children from her relatives, such as the children of Emmy's young father (uncle). She also lived with her son whose wife also died. Emmy's grandmother was a small farmer, an activity from which she obtained her needs to support her family. This was the circumstance which Emmy lived with her grandmother.

Our Observation and Interpretation

Generally, Emmy's life was not as bad as other children at the *Amani* Orphanage Center. However, she also required a great deal of support psychologically and for other physical needs because her family was too big to care them all, especially when it came to school tuition fees. The loss of father and grandfather affected her in the way she felt about herself and the way she understood the world.[10] Emmy grew up in a good background with many relatives and friends around her. Despite the good backgound she came from, she still faced some minor problems in her childhood, such as a leg injury while playing in school at standard five. She also had some skin infections with a bad headache while in standard four. Emmy still remembered these events, incidents, and experiences. Furthermore, Emmy told her story as a girl who liked to help her relatives to do some chores at home. She conceived of her family as being good, peaceful, and whose members understood each other.

At school, Emmy was a school leader who liked her teachers and students especially good students. Emmy was a social person who liked to talk to different people. She had several friends at school and at home. For Emmy, friends were those people close to her and were willing to help each other, comfort, and respect each other, especially in the time of need or problems. Emmy had different gifts or talents and hobbies in her life. She liked to read books, do physical exercises, play different games, watch and listen to church choirs, drawing pictures, reading the Bible, and studying further to the point where her dream was to become a school teacher. She hoped and prayed that her dream became true.

One of Emmy's favorite verses in the Bible was from the book of Ephesians 6: 1–3, which says, "Children, obey your parents in the Lord, for this is the right thing to do. 'Honor your father and mother. . .' (this is the first commandment with a promise), 'that it may be well with you and that you may live long on the earth.'" Emmy liked to live a descent life. In this case

---

10. Cf. Boss, "The Trauma and Complicated Grief"; Price, "Walking through the Dackness"; Jones, "A Theology of Hope."

she liked to learn more about spiritual life, a life with good knowledge on how to live well, knowledge about the HIV and AIDS, sexuality, and a life of success and prosperity. Emmy longed and was so passionate to have good relationship with people, especially those close and important to her. These people were such as her grandmother the one whom she lived with, her aunt who was a teacher at Chimala area, and her mother who required much support from Emmy, not only in physical needs, but also in psychosocial needs.

Therapeutic Intervention

As we continued to visit and talk to Emmy, we observed and found that she required some guidance to her life. Desperately, Emmy seemed to be lost in confusion of her life control in moral life. She started troubling her relatives, especially her grandmother, the one she stayed with. According to her friends and relatives, Emmy seemed to be involved with young men and even some adults in sexual relationships. She sometimes came back home very late. In this case, in her condition of confusion and insecurity, Emmy required more support and counseling. When we asked about her knowledge of the HIV and AIDS, she admitted of knowing very little about it.

However, Emmy was very closer to her grandparents than her parents. She began living with her grandparents since was standard two. Her father died when she was just standard four. Her grandfather died when she was standard six. She seemed to be closer to her grandparents than to her parents. Even when we asked about her feelings she had most of the time, she said it was just sorrow and sadness about her late grandfather who died while she was standard six. It was the one she remembered most, but not much about her father. When we also asked about the person who was very close and important to her life, Emmy mentioned that it was her grandmother whom she lived with since her childhood.

We worked with Emmy for almost a year trying to help tell her stories and write her memory book, which by itself was the healing process to wholeness. In that circumstance, we were Emmy's "companion on the journey." Emmy was an intelligent girl; she liked school and liked to study. She also had good connections with many people including her relatives. She was a social person. That personality helped to cope with her situation of sadness, especially after the death of her father and her grandfather whom she liked a lot.

We worked with Emmy so that we might learn to deal with life situation together. Some of the things we discussed together were about the knowledge of the HIV and AIDS and issues relating to sexuality. This was not easy at the beginning; however, as days went by, Emmy became more open and free to talk about different issues relating to her family and friends. In her memory book she wrote about her family history and about herself. She wrote what she liked and what she did not like in her life. We also learned further about the basics of the HIV and AIDS so that we know our responsibility of what to do and not to do. At the end of our counseling sessions Emmy was able to mention the ways which could transmit the HIV and how to protect herself from acquiring the viruses.

Emmy learned a lot in the process of our pastoral counseling using narratives through stories, metaphors, and pictures or images. These helped her to be happy no matter what was the circumstance. Despite the loss and grief she went through, Emmy learned to be happy through laughing. Laughing was very helpful to her as she was with friends. She liked to laugh. And she laughed with a good reason and with a good heart and intention. And she was careful when laughing not to hurt others. This means that Emmy accepted the reality of the loss that took place in her life.[11]

Emmy and us together found that the Bible was full of narratives (stories), which also made us laugh and be happy. Laughing was a good medicine for the heart that was sorrowful and sad. The Bible text says, "Rejoice in the Lord always; again I say, Rejoice." (Philippians 4:4). In the book of Proverbs we also read that, "A cheerful heart is a good medicine, but a downcast spirit dies up the bones." (Proverbs 17:22) The biblical texts were used to reinforce stories or themes which children themselves liked. Hence, they were very helpful because they were said in the context which was similar to the Tanzanian context.

As our relationship grew further, Emmy could know how to separate between herself and sadness; she understood that she was not the problem. She knew to respect herself as a person and a girl who was good and intelligent and who could control her feelings in circumstances she might be in. Through narratives, stories, and images or arts she could cope with different situations of her life. Her eyes looked at the Lord Jesus to guide her in new ways and new opportunities for her life. She looked at stories of hope and faith and not at stories that were destructive and not empowering. Emmy's journey as she explained her grief process was a positive experience which she found meaning out of these tragic experiences at the end of the journey. Understanding death is always a mystery for a human being. However, life must continue and remain as God intended it to be. The life of integrity and

---

11. Cf. Boss, "The Trauma and Complicated Grief"; Price, "Walking through the Dackness"; Jones, "A Theology of Hope."

reassurance must remain in touch with the person in grief. Emy believed in the Swahili saying which says, "*Maisha ni safari ndefu, iliyojaa taabu,*" which means, "life is a long journey full of troubles."

Case number 4: The Family of Ipyana, Agnes, Neema, and Nuru

Background

The fourth case involved the family of the above-named children. In this family, four children were seen; these were Ipyana (14 years old), Agnes (16 years old), Nuru (16 years old) and Neema (12 years old). Nuru Paulo was not from the same siblings like Agnes, Ipyana, and Neema. Nuru was a cousin to them. She began living with her aunt, Agnes, Ipyana and Neema's mother since 2003. Nuru's father died in 2003 from unknown sickness; he was suffering from legs problem from which they could not find what the real problem was. Nuru's mother, according to Nuru's story, deserted Nuru and ran to Dar es Salaam where she seemed to live there. According to Nuru's story, Nuru did not know much about her mother and what she was doing in Dar es Salaam. Hence, her aunt Veronica was the only person she knew and could run to for help of anything she might have.

In this family, the mother was the one who took care of these four children. She was involved in small businesses in the market at Uyole Mbeya, such as selling bananas. Veronica's husband died on 6th July 1999. His death was so sudden and the cause of his death was not known. The total number of children in this family was seven, including Nuru. However, the older ones were not living with their mother; they were grown up and lived independently. Therefore, only these four children lived with their mother and all of them were being helped by the *Amani* Orphanage Center. Agnes, Ipyana and Neema belonged to the Moravian Church at Uyole Mbeya. Nuru belonged to the Tanzania Assemblies of God at Uyole Mbeya. Originally, this family came from Rungwe district in Mbeya region. They belonged to the Nyakyusa ethnic group.

Ipyana went to Itezi primary school. He completed standard seven in the year 2007. Agnes was in Form one at Hayombo secondary school in 2007. She was 17 years old. She described herself as a quiet girl and that she was very close to relatives such as her grandmother, aunt, uncle, and her brothers and sisters. Agnes began primary education in 2000 at Mabonde primary school in Rungwe district. Then she moved to Uyole in Mbeya urban district where she continued with her primary education at

Itezi primary school located at Uyole. Neema was 12 years old in 2007 and was baptized when was one year old. She grew up in Kyela district being physically good. She began her primary education in 2002 at Nsalaga primary school in Uyole Mbeya. She liked to study and attend church services regularly. She liked to sing in Sunday school and being a choir conductor. Neema had several friends at home and at school. She also missed her father and other close relatives who passed away such as her grandparents, uncle, and aunt.

Our Observation and Interpretation

Veronica's condition was not very stable. She became sick frequently. At the same time, she took care of her mother who was mentally sick for a long time; but in November 2007, the grandmother of these children passed away. The life of this family was not very good because of the extreme poverty they were in. The business of their mother was not very promising due to instability of the market and other huddles of life, such as her frequent illnesses. The family could only afford for some food to survive and other minor expenses. When it came to school fees for children and medical expenses, they could not afford to pay for all of them.

Ipyana was physically strong and healthy. He was very talkative and sometimes very delinquent; however, his delinquency was underneath. He did not want people, especially those who were older to him, to know what he was doing except his age mats. To these he could do whatever he liked. As one observed him, Ipyana seemed to be very shy and very embarrassed as one looked at him. He also liked to sing, play, and act in drama, especially at his church in Sunday schools. However, he also did not want to show his talents very openly. When asked about his feelings toward his father's death and his openness to talk about his father, it was obvious that he was not willing to talk about his father's death. At the same time, which was very positive for him was that he had a good connection and relationship with other people around him who were able to support him, talk to him, and obtain any psychosocial needs he wanted, especially his friends.

Agnes was physically well and her health condition seemed to be good. Her school progress was also good. She liked to study and do other activities at home and at school. She also liked to do physical exercises and play different games. Agnes also liked to sing. She especially sang with a youth choir at her church. Agnes was a descent girl who was quiet and did not like quarreling with other people. She had several friends who were very close to her. She also liked to help her mother from small businesses such as selling whatever her mother had at the market.

Still, Agnes had the remembrance of her father who passed away and all the troubles she had on her primary education because of the hard situation they had financially. They could not even afford to buy small things for school or pay school fees. She also remembered her grandparents who passed away. This remembrance sometimes made her sad. However, Agnes had some good hopes and dreams for her future life. Her hope was becoming a traffic police. In this case, she wanted to study hard up to university level where she could specialize in studying about internal affairs, safety, and traffic rules so that she became a traffic police. In one of the writings in her memory book, especially her proverbs, she wrote, "*Mtaka cha uvunguni, sharti ainame,*" which means, "the one who desires something which is underneath, he or she must bend down." This indicated that Agness was willing to work hard to fulfill her dreams no matter what hindrance faced her.

Neema was a charming girl, very talkative unlike her sister Agnes. She was a God fearing girl, well-disciplined, and tried to honor all people. Physically, Neema had skin problems. This problem began when she was still very little; however, it became worse when she stayed with her sister at Uyole Mbeya. This skin problem happened since then and was a problem in her body. These rushes and scars in her body itched a lot ending up making sores and making her uncomfortable. The center tried to take care of her by taking her to some skin specialists at the Hospitals in the city of Mbeya hoping that she would recover soon, and be a healthier girl. Despite the problem Neema had, she still liked school. Neema had great expectations and hopes for her future life. When she grew up and obtained good education, her dream was to become a lawyer. In one of her proverbs she said, "*Mchumia juani, hulia kivulini,*" which means, "the one, who harvests in a sun, eventually eats under the shade." From this proverb, Neema understood that good life must be earned with hardships.

Neema understood her life condition and of her family. She knew that she required working hard, which was the only way to success. She liked to know how her mother did her businesses and sometimes went to the market to help her mother in selling some bananas and tomatoes. In the other place, another favorite proverb she had went like this, "*Asiyefunzwa na mamaye, hufunzwa na ulimwengu,*" which means, "the one who is not taught by his or her mother, the world will teach him or her" She explained that respect to her mother allowed her to learn many things from her, otherwise she said that if not from her mother she would learn from other people, which was not expected of her. The world provided different expectations and perspectives of life.[12] Despite all the difficulties Neema went through, she still held on hope for the future. Her faith and love in Jesus was what held her up. Her favorite drawings were flowers. In one of her flowers, underneath it, she wrote the verse from Psalms 23:1, which says, "The Lord is my shepherd; I shall not want; he makes me lie down in green pastures." It is the verse which for her brought hopes and comfort in times of need and difficulties.

Agnes's Story

In her memory book Agnes had the following story: "Once upon a time there was a child who was going to his sister. On the way, he met the hyena; and the hyena desired the clothing of that child. The hyena told the child, 'let me try your clothing' and the child gave the hyena the clothing to try. The hyena told him, 'I will give them back to you just after a little walk.' When they reached the place where the hyena promised to return the clothing, the hyena told the child again that he would give him just ahead after a little walk, and they continued to walk until they reached the place which the hyena promised to return the clothing and he could not return them.

The child reached to his sister and his sister did not receive him; and instead, she received the hyena because he wore good clothing of that child. The child remained silent and quiet and he was left in the place where chicken were kept and the food provided was not good for him, but the hyena was received with good food and a better place to stay and sleep. The other day they were told to go in the farm to chase birds which were eating rice in the farm. The child chased the birds, but the hyena did not; the hyena just ate and not worked. The hyena told the child, "eat there and I will be eating here." They chased birds until the sun went down, the time they had to go back to eat and sleep. The child's sister continued to serve the hyena very well; but the child was treated very poorly eating and sleeping in the chicken cage.

One day, the husband of the child's sister noticed that the one who was treated poorly was her real brother in-law. The child's sister did not agree and accept it; she told her husband that he wanted to chase away her little brother. Her husband replied to her saying that if you want to believe me, when they go to the farm tomorrow we should also follow them behind without them noticing us. The other day, as it was usual, they went to the rice farm to watch for birds. The child's sister and her husband followed them behind. When they reached at the farm they found that the hyena was

---

12. Cf. Ndossi, "The Significance of the Female Perspective," 39–40.

eating the rice instead of chasing birds; and the one who was denied to be her little brother was busy chasing birds away. The child's sister believed that she was wrong. Then they returned home, and she prepared a good food for that child in the chicken cage; and then, she dug a deep pit and on top of that hole put a mattress and gave the hyena some food to eat on that place. When the hyena was eating on that mattress, he suddenly fell down into the pit. While falling down the hyena proudly said that it was good that he tortured their relative." Agnes wrote that the story teaches us "we should think before acting," as one of the Swahili sayings which says, "*Fikiri kabla ya kutenda.*" This means that we should not treat or judge people the way they look like. We must first carefully consider them as they are.

Neema's Story

On her part, Neema wrote the following story: "Once upon a time there were three friends, the Hare, the Hyena, and a Wild Dog. They were very good friends. They were all good hunters. When they were hunting, they would all share the food. One day all the three friends decided to kill their mothers and all agreed to do so. So the wild dog and the hyena went and killed their mothers. The Hare also went home but he did not kill his mother. The Hare just smeared the sword with blood so that his friends would know that he killed his mother, and his friends believed. The Hare hid his mother in the room and whenever they went out for hunting he would deceive his friends that he lived himself at home; but it was a lie, the Hare took some potion of the food to his mother in the hiding room.

This was his routine; every day, he deceived his friends that he was going to the toilet to relieve himself, but was not true. He was going to provide his mother some food to eat. Whenever he went to the hiding room he knocked and sang to his mother saying "open, open, it is *Kavunje vunje, vunjenje, kavunje vunje;*" and his mother asked "who are you?" The Hare said again, "*Kavunje vunje, vunjenje, kavunje,*" then his mother opened the door and ate the food brought by the Hare. And this continued for a while until the Hare's friends became suspicious of him.

One day after some hunting, the Hare did the same thing kidding his friends that he was going to toilet. When he was going to provide some food to his mother, they decided to follow him behind and to see what the Hare was doing. Another day the hyena went to the hiding place where Hare's mother was hiding. The Hyena tried to imitate what the Hare was doing, knocking the door and singing like the Hare. The Hare's mother opened the door thinking that it was her son. The Hyena jumped in and killed the Hare's mother and ran out and closed the door behind.

When the time for the Hare to go to the house to provide the food to his mother arrived, the Hare did the same; unfortunately, this time he found that it was quiet. He knocked for a while; still it was quiet. His mother was already dead, killed by the hyena. The Hare broke the door and went in and found that his mother was dead; the head had been cut off. The Hare cried, cried, and cried a lot without no one to comfort him. And that was the end of their good friendship." Neema wrote in her memory book that this story teaches her and others that we "should not be liars like the Hare," as the Swahili saying goes, "*Njia ya mwongo fupi*" which means, "the path of a liar is short."

Therapeutic Intervention

This family seemed to have good relationship with each other. Despite the problems they faced, they were together and not separated. They all worked as a team and helped one another as much as they could no matter their hard economic situations. Despite the vulnerabilities which children were in, still they knew how to cope with most of the difficulties they were in.

What we did together, as a family and individually, was to help them be open to who they were. Guilt and shame were part of the family problems. This seemed to originate from their family background. They also seemed to have some beliefs in witchcraft because of the mysterious death of their father and other relatives, the illnesses in the family, and other problems. They found and thought that there must be a cause for those problems. This was the mapping process we did—to find out where was the problem with these children and the family as a whole.

Ipyana was so open at the beginning to talk about his family problems, but others were not until later in the process of counseling through narratives, stories, metaphors, and memory book in which they were more open to tell their stories and stories of their family. Frequent visits were also very important to this family; it became a healing process itself. Because through visits they were assured of who they were, as important, loved, and respected. In this way, they managed to cope with bad thoughts of witchcraft, of fear, and sometimes of anger and sadness.

The belief in witchcraft dominates our culture especially in this side of Tanzania. Because of envy, jealousy, and other unreasonable aspects, witches prefer to torture others through their evil deeds of magic. Neema, in one of her proverbs, wrote, "*Mkuki kwa nguruwe, kwa binadamu mchungu*" which means, "spearing the pig seems to be all right, but to the human being is so painful." Neema explains that there are people who like to torture other people without any reason, but when it comes to them it seems to be hurting more. This Swahili proverb is similar to the golden rule which is found in the Bible saying, "So whatever you wish that men would do to you, do so to them; for this is the law and prophets." (Matthew 7:12) The text was used to strengthen the story she told in order to create room for an alternative story of hope and encouragement for her healing and coping.

Things that have been so empowering to these children were writing the memory book and drawing pictures which obviously showed hope, love and peace in their future life. Singing Christian songs was also very empowering for them. The assurance of forgiveness and the victory which they showed was something which we tried together to cement it, forgetting the dominating stories which were negative and depressing. The focus of the narratives was to those stories and metaphors or things that brought about alternative stories, the stories of hope, faith, love and success.

Case number 5: Augustino

Background

The fifth case was that of Augustino. Augustino was 13 years old. In 2007, he was in standard Four at Chemchemi primary school located at Uyole in Mbeya. He was a Kinga by tribe (originally from the neighboring region of Njombe). He was the last born of five children in his family. Augustino was a member of the Lutheran church at Uyole in Mbeya. He lived with his sister in-law who was involved in small businesses such as selling tomatoes at the Uyole market in Mbeya. She was married to Kyachi, Augustino's brother. Agustino's parents died. His mother died in 2005 after becoming sick for a couple of months. Then, his father also died in 2006. According to Augustino's story which he acquired from his relatives, it was believed that his father was bewitched by Augustino's grandfather.

Our Observation and Interpretation

Augustino told a sad story about his life to be very difficult because of his sister who tortured him very much. According to Augustino's story, his sister beated him and sometimes denied him food and also denied to buy clothing for him even though she had money to buy for him. The house which Augustino stayed in was very poor. It was very tiny and dirty. There were lots of rats inside and the arrangement of the house was very shabby. During rain seasons the house became wet. The floor was muddy and dirty. The clothings were not clean as if nobody took care of the house. The house looked like it had been deserted for a long time. Generally, the house environment was very poor for people to live in.

We visited Augustino more than twice. Unfortunately, there was no chance of meeting his sister who took care of him and his little sisters. These little sisters belong to his sister. The entire story we heard from Augustino was from him and the neighbors. Augustino's sister did not care much what the children would eat; or even if they were sick, she did not care. Augustino and his little sisters suffered from malnutrition and other sicknesses most of the time. They also suffered from physical abuse, which disturbed their thinking capability, emotional, and psychological stances. At the first meeting with these children Augustino and his sisters especially the youngest, we found that she was very sick because of malnutrition and skin diseases. According to the neighbor who lived in the same compound, the child was actually in the dying stage, and her mother did not care much about her child. Actually, these children required much support from food, health, and all psychosocial needs which they hardly got.

Therapeutic Intervention

Augustino was very weak and sad because of the situation he faced. He was affected physically and psychologically. He could not even concentrate with his school. He was overburdened by the works at home since he was the oldest among the children he lived with. He had many things to take care of; actually it was more than enough. At the same time they missed the basic and necessary needs for their lives. Augustino's brother and the sister-in-law, who were the caregivers, did not actually stay at home most of their time. These children obtained support mostly from neighbors and friends.

Our visits to this family were very important and helpful. It was so sad to see those children living into that condition which was very poor and abusive to children. Further intervention and support was required to help the children get rid of the situation they lived. Otherwise, the school progress and other psychosocial progress would not be seen and instead the children would grow weak and psychologically damaged.

To help these children, we tried to be very friendly and close to them. Building positive relationship with them was the basis for healing and wholeness. Good relationship opened the door for them to tell stories about their lives more freely. Augustino's little sister (Happy) became very friendly to us and was very open to tell many things about their lives and the difficulties they faced. Through their daily activities at home, we also found the way of talking to them different stories that would empower them and change the attitude of who they were and how they felt about life, the life of weaknesses and sadness. We tried together to show that they were very important children in society no matter what difficulties they were going through. We tried to help them keep distance from the problem they faced because they were themselves not part of the problem. The real problem was the problems that faced them, not the children. In reality, the problems are always out there and that problems are not them. This was the process known as externalization in the narrative approach.[13] According to Dunn, "Externalizing means that the person gives voice to, or personifies, the problems they are up against; therefore giving the problem a separate identity from the person. . . . The ability to see the problem as not a part of the person is a way to give distance from the problem saturated story that the person may be experiencing, and allow people to develop a greater understanding of the problem and of themselves outside of the problem."[14]

We tried to find out together the things they were familiar with so that they could try to cope with the difficulties of life and be happy. For example, the house was full of rats that were very troublesome, even to the point of chewing their feet at night. Through these rats we found the story that the rats could be overcome. The rats were not something to be scared of; they were foolish and could not win over people. People were more important and clever than the rats. This story of a rat and a rabbit goes like this: "Once upon a time there were two friends, a rat and a rabbit. The rabbit was very clever and intelligent, but the rat was delinquent and foolish. One day they decided to go and visit their friend in the neighboring village in which they had to cross the river. When they reached at the river they decided to take the boat in order to cross to the neighboring village. The boat was made by the cassava roots.

The journey was very long and they started to feel hungry. At the middle of the river while crossing the river, the rat began complaining about his hunger that he could not withstand. He told his friend that he was starving. The rat noticed that the boat was made of cassava. Then secretly the rat decided to start chewing the cassava roots little by little until the boat had some holes in it. The rabbit noticed it and became very angry at the rat and told him, "don't you know that if you continue eating our boat will sink; and we will drown?" However, the rat did not pay any attention to the words of

13. Daigneault, "Narrative Means," 299.
14. Dunn, "Narrative Therapy," 11.

the rabbit, and secretly continued to chew the boat and the water began to fill the boat. The rabbit tried to talk to the rabbit but without any success, he tried to warn about the danger that would happen if he continued to eat the boat but still he could not listen.

What happened next was that the boat began to sink because of the water which filled it. Then the rabbit told the rat that they should jump out of the boat and start swimming towards the bank of the river because the boat would drown them if they continued to stay in it. The rat did not accept the advice of the rabbit. The rabbit jumped into the water and began swimming until he reached the bank of the river where they were going. Then the boat began to sink the rat tried to hold on it, but the boat continued to sink down, and the rat began swimming but he could not because he did not know how to swim like the rabbit. The rabbit tried his best to talk to the rat that he should swim hard to the bank of the river, still he could not. The rat became tired because he did not know how to swim and finally was drowned in the river. And that was the end of the story, the rat died foolishly because of his stupidity and delinquency."

This story teaches us that we should be clever and intelligent like the rabbit and not foolish like the rat. We should hear the advice of other people who understand life perhaps more than what we think we know. In Swahili we have the saying which says, "*Asiyesikia la mkuu huvunjika guu*," which means, "the one who does not listen to the advice of grown up people will break his or her leg." In other word, this means that the person who does not listen to what people say will be destroyed. For Augustino and his sisters this story helped them to identify themselves with the rabbit which was clever and intelligent, but not with the foolish rat. The rabbit became a hero for them to identify with. From that day they decided to deal with the rats by destroying them by being clean and looking for a cat that chased the rats away. Moreover they found the rats' poison that would ultimately kill the rats, which were very destructive for their own clothing and health in general. The rats became no more a threat to them. Augustino and his little sister were not afraid anymore of the rats; they were courageous enough to fight against them. The story empowered them to deny the defeat against the foolishness of the rats. Again they accepted the saying which said, "*Asiyesikia la mkuu, huvunjika guu.*"

Augustino and his sisters faced other difficulties which also required support and help. *Amani* Orphanage Center and other people tried to help them in a continuing counseling and giving them their physical needs like clothing, food, medicine, and some money for small needs at home and for their school needs. It was our hope that these children would ultimately cope with their lives and be able to live a life that was worthwhile and a life that was empowering for their lives physically, spiritually, and academically.

The most important thing we tried to work with these children as active participants was to build a health relationship. Pastoral counseling is not only about using tough and complicated skills that are too clinical; it is also about positive relationships. This good relationship can be gained through simple and easy skills especially when working with children. This good relationship includes being able to be with them, walk with them, listen carefully, and play with them. Coetsee shows succinctly that if we want to help the child who is emotionally wounded, it is very important *to walk with* a wounded child for healing and wholeness.[15]

Case Number 6: Tumaini P.

Background

Case number six was that of Tumaini. Tumaini was 14 years old in 2007. She was in standard six at Nsalaga primary school. She was a Nyakyusa by tribe. She was a Christian attending the Tanzania Assemblies of God church, who recently decided to switch to the Lutheran church at Uyole because of the company she had found herself in. Tumaini's parents died. Her mother died in 2001 and her father died in 1997. The causes of their death were not openly known; but it was believed that they were bewitched. Tumaini's guardian, who was her uncle (young father), told the authors the story of his family that they had a curse in their family from their own relatives, who because of greedy of inheritance of properties in the family, her uncle's grandfather casted a curse on children by bewitching children, and one after another in the family had been dying since then. Tumaini's father was also one of the children who died because of the beliefs they had about witchcraft in the family.

Tumaini grew up at Usangu in Mbeya rural district and some of her relatives still lived there, such as her two sisters who lived with their uncle and grandmother. Tumaini was reared in Usangu with her uncle until when she was standard five when she moved to Uyole to live with her uncle (young father) in 2006. Tumaini lived with her uncle who was just a peasant and a builder/contractor, married, but separated and had married another woman. She was the one the uncle lived with her then. Bruno tried to support Tumaini in every possible ways; but he also required support from the

---

15. Coetsee, Walking with Wounded Children."

Amani Orphanage Center. Tumaini benefited also from the Center in various ways in which the center was capable of doing.

Our Observation and Interpretation

Tumaini's life at her uncle's family was sometimes very difficult for her. Coping with new environment, new family, and new school was a big change for her. At one time Tumaini tried to run away from her uncle to go back to Usangu where she grew up, but she later returned back. The problem was that she stole some rice from a neighbor and was afraid to be beaten by her uncle and being scolded by people and friends. Tumaini's life circumstances were very difficult. Her study performance at school dropped down. At home, she worked a lot and did not even have a chance to study and play with her friends. She always fetched water or cut grass for the cows, or took care of little children such as bathing and feeding them. Tumaini's story was difficult to comprehend. According to stories we obtained from neighbors, Tumaini's life was very critical. It was said that Tumaini's uncle tortured Tumaini a lot; such tortures included giving her hard works which were not proportional to her age. He also used physical and verbal abuse against Tumaini whenever she failed doing what he commanded her to do. Through these circumstances Tumaini lost a sense of direction and self-esteem.

Physically, Tumaini was a strong and energetic child. When was with her friends at the center she was very prayerful and charming. But, when was at home or alone, she seemed to look sad, uncomfortable, worriful, insecure, and unconfident. In her memory book Tumaini wrote a poem which she called it, "A Sad Song," which went like this:

> Where did I lost my parents
> I have lost my mother then my father
> Yes, they all have left me
> Alone am left
> My relatives also have left me
> My aunt and my uncle have left me
> My grandparents have left me!

It is the poem which shows or pictures her sadness and murmurings about her life. She also wrote:

> This child goes to school
> He's very sad
> Because he has no one to educate her/him

> If he goes to secondary school
> Who will educate her/him?
> She/he does not have any real answer!

This poem also indicated sadness in her soul because there was no one to take care of her education when she went for further education. With this poem she also drew a picture of this sad girl who was going to school without any hope for the future of her education. Another Poem she wrote went like this:

> This child is very sad
> I don't know why?
> Because she has climbed on top of the bus
> And she does not have a bus fare to pay
> The owner of the bus, has told her to climb on top of the bus
> The owner of the bus, does not care
> The owner of the bus says it is up to you if you fall down!

This poem also indicated how Tumaini longed to visit her relatives at Usangu. She sometimes went to board a bus without a fare to pay in the bus. So she wrote out of her own experience. It showed how some poor people like her suffered when were being mistreated with people who owned buses, when they failed to pay the bus fare. Tumaini was very sad with the kind of life she lived.

Therapeutic Intervention

Tumaini was an intelligent girl. She was very energetic and determined. As one looked at Tumaini, she was physically very healthy. She liked school and was socially active; she liked to play with her friends. However, sometimes Tumaini was very shy, which was normal according to her age. Tumaini passed her life with difficult situations. She changed people she has been living with, the school, friends, and environments. These transitions contributed to dropping down of her school progress and her relationships with relatives and friends.

Tumaini also felt sad because of what happened in her life, the death of her parents, and the general situation she passed through, such as difficulties to meet her daily needs and other psychological problems. For example, her uncle filled the mind of Tumaini with stories he talked to them especially about the curses and witchcraft in their family. Therefore, sometimes children were filled with feelings of fear and anxiety for their lives. Some of Tumaini's feelings were expressed clearly in the poems she wrote above.

We spent sometime together discussing and telling stories about life. Tumaini was very open to talk about her life with us. Therefore, it was easy to create other alternative stories that would help her cope with the situation she experienced. Stories of success and hope were emphasized. For example, we sometimes imaginarily decided to dream for the future life of success and joy. So, what we did together was to think of positive things. We thought of Bible stories which they usually studied at the Center. One of the memory verses they learned and which we talked about was from the book of Jeremiah 29:11, which says: "'For I know the plans I have for you,' says the Lord. "'They are plans for good and not for disaster, to give you a future and a hope.'" The story of a young Jeremiah became a real mirror for Tumaini who was questioning about her life and her future life. The story of Jeremiah became like her life's story and wanted the story to be the map for her life.

The problems of sadness, fear, and uncertainty which faced Tumaini were identified and talked about separately. These problems were analyzed to see the influence or impact they had on her. All these processes had the goal of externalizing the problems in order to move toward the relationships that would be healing, empowering, and finding meaning in the face of problems. The question that came was on how to move or reach to that goal. It was finding where the person was strong and could have control over, looking at skills or qualities and support the person must have. For example Tumaini was good in writing poems, she was also good in telling stories, and was a social person. Therefore, we talked with her issues or problems focusing on her strengths.

Eventually, Tumaini learnt that life was a struggle which sometimes could seem to be unfair and full of wickedness. Moreover, she learned that God was in control of every situation and no matter what were the circumstance; God had good plans for her. Tumaini then started trusting God no matter what she was going through; she continued to live with hope and in dreams of success to her future life. In that case, she promised to study hard and do all what was necessary and pleasing to God in order to ultimately fulfill her dream of becoming a successful business woman one day. Those new stories and dreams became positive alternative stories for her life and became a roadmap for her life that followed.

Case Number 7: Kenny

Background

The case number seven concerned Kenny. Kenny was 12 years old in 2007 who expected to be 13 soon and was standard five at Nsalaga primary school. He was Safwa by tribe, and a Christian believer of the Tanzania Assemblies of God church at Uyole Mbeya. Kenny's parents died a tragic death. His father died in 2000 from a fire burnt which was caused by a fuel inside the house. His mother died in 2003 from skin infections in Swahili known as "*Mkanda wa Jeshi*," which literally means the "army's belt." Sometimes the symptoms of this kind of disease relate to those of the HIV infections.

Since the death of Kenny's parents, his paternal grandparents reared and took care of him. Kenny was the only child in his family. His younger sister died. Most of Kenny's support was from his grandparents; but he also obtained some support from his relatives such as his aunt and his uncle. His grandmother complained in her stories that the side of Kenny's mother (maternal side) rejected and deserted their son Kenny by not taking care of him, even not providing some support and other basic needs. They even did not want to visit him, since the death of his parents.

Our Observation and Interpretation

The school progress of Kenny was very good. Most of the time Kenny held good positions in his class during exams; he was also very intelligent and smart. He liked to study and was very creative and inquisitive. He liked to learn and listen from his older ones. Generally, Kenny was a disciplined child.

One of the dreams of Kenny for his life was acquiring good education hoping to work as an accountant in the bank; however, he also liked to be a civil engineer. All these jobs attracted Kenny because he saw people around him working and thought them to be good jobs. Kenny was very close to his grandmother. He was the one he could talk to her for anything he had in his mind. She was the one whom Kenny could go and express his feelings, needs, hurts, and the need for support at home. It seemed that they were very close to each other.

Kenny's life condition was not generally worse. The house environment was good and clean. He acquired the basic needs for his life from his grandparents and other relatives. He had a good place to sleep, enough food, and clothing. His health condition was generally good; however, he sometimes suffered from stomachache; which was yet to find its cause. This was the physical problem he had most of the time. The other thing he suffered from was his feelings about the death of his parents and his young sister Anastazia. For him, it was difficult to establish a coping mechanism for these problems. However, at the same time, Kenny tried to forget about his relatives' deaths. Kenny's interests and hobby was playing different games like football, reading different books, and working in the garden. He was also interested in Bible stories and memorizing its verses, and listening to and telling stories. The following is one of the stories he had in his memory book.

Kenny's Story

"Once upon a time there were two hunters who went for hunting to the village they did not know. They asked one old man to take them to the forest for hunting. When they reached at the forest, they succeeded to shoot a buffalo and decided to provide the head of the buffalo to the old man. The other day they succeeded to kill an elephant and did not provide the old man the head; instead, they changed their rule and decided to provide the whole meat to the old man. However, the old man refused to receive the whole meat because he knew that the head of the elephant was worth than the whole meat.

The old man decided to open the case to the chief of that village. The chief said to the hunters "you did a mistake from the beginning when you gave the old man the head of the buffalo; so you have to provide him the same thing now, the head of the elephant." The old man was so happy for the decision of the chief and through obtaining that head of the elephant, he managed to build a good house which was made of gold and became very rich."

Kenny said that the above story teaches us perseverance, and the Swahili proverb says that, "*Mvumilivu hula mbivu,*" which means, "the person who endures in life will eat ripe fruits." He also wrote that human beings prefer to live in a way they used to living. In Swahili there is a saying which says, "*Mazoea hujenga tabia,*" which means that "behavior is being built by what we tend to do daily" or "watch your habits, and they become character." When things change it becomes a challenge to many people and becomes difficult in coping with new changes. Change is always difficult and sometimes people must be ready for any risks.

Therapeutic Intervention

Kenny was a boy with great expectations and good dreams for his future life. Despite all the difficulties of life that he faced, he knew and believed that one day those troubles of his sickness and grief over his parents would be over and he would be able to cope with life in responsible ways and live a prosperous life. Kenny also believed in a life that was descent and disciplined. He tried to follow what his caregivers and what he learned from the Bible to be the good guide for his life. Obeying God and his caregivers was something very important in his life and was something he put in front of him.

Sadness, grief, and sorrows of life for Kenny was not something to be denied or repressed down, but dealing with them openly and finding ways of coping with them. He had a Swahili proverb which said that, "*Mfichaficha maladhi, kilio kitamfichua,*" which means, "the one who hides his or her illnesses and sicknesses, the mourning will reveal him or her" Kenny through conversation and stories came to understands that talking the issues over and openly was one of the best ways in healing from all the bad feelings in life; it was a way of acquiring things over and starting afresh with life that God intended for every individual.

Finding alternative stories, the stories of hope are the work of narratives. The dominating stories of sadness, grief, and sorrows are translated and recreated to the stories that empower and finally brings healing and wholeness in the life of the person. Working with Kenny was not so difficult because he was so open to talk about his stories; therefore, the work of mapping the saturated problem was easy. Through his memory book and his stories of life, we were able to thicken the alternative stories together with different ways of narratives such as proverbs, biblical stories, and other folk stories.

For example, one of the things which made Kenny sad and feel lonely was the death of his relatives. For him he thought the good ways of not feeling that way was by forgetting about them. However, that way was not easy for him; he kept remembering them. The more he tried to forget them, the more he kept remembering them. Therefore, together we tried to look for another alternative way of dealing with the problem. Forgetting was not a solution for him for not feeling down or sad. Then we tried to change the dominating story of forgetting the death of his relatives to an alternative story of trying to remember them positively. To keep the memory or to remember people who passed away was not a bad thing. First, we started talking about his relatives who died and the good things he might remember about them. Through his memory book, he also wrote some of the history about the family. We also encouraged Kenny to keep the memory through images, pictures or photos of their deceased relatives. That way helped Kenny to honor and remember his deceased relatives in positive ways. Kenny kept a good memory of his parents and his sister.

The story of the two hunters which Kenny told was used to identify his worries about life. Through that story Kenny had a lesson of being patient with life and being courageous with all the challenges he faced in life. Kenny was able to identify with that man in the story who was patient and courageous to wait for the right time to obtain what was right for him. Kenny promised himself to keep his hopes and dreams in working and in fulfilling his passion. He did not want to concentrate on negative thoughts and things that could ruin his dreams of being a successful man any more. Kenny's dream was to become someone with good knowledge of life before God and society as a whole so that he could serve them responsibly.

Case Number 8: Eva

Background

The case number eight concerned about Eva. Eva was 12 years old. She was standard four at Nsalaga Primary school. She was a Wanji by tribe and a Christian belonging to the Lutheran church at Uyole in Mbeya. Eva lived with her young mother. Her parents died while she was very young, with only six months old. They both died in one year with some months apart. They died in 1996. Eva had no good remembrance of them, since she was still a baby. They both died sudden deaths from stomachache. Eva's guardian mother was married and the life condition of the family was poor, but not that worse.

Our Observation and Interpretation

Eva still required support from physical, academic, social, and psychological needs and problems. She sometimes showed a sign of sadness and worry. The authors visited her at home several times to see her progress and the life she lived with her caregivers. The positive side of Eva was that she was upfront in volunteering several things at her church and at the *Amani* Orphanage Center. She was open to learn and do different activities when asked by her teachers or counselors. She was also upfront in singing or leading prayers and expressing or addressing something to people on behalf of other children such as thanking people who came with gifts for the children and for all who came to visit the *Amani* Orphanage Center. Generally, she was not a girl who felt shy. She was courageous and bold enough even to stand up in front of people. Generally, Eeva was a charming girl whenever in a good mood. She liked to talk, play, sing, and act in drama. These virtues became some of the ways to cope with difficult situation whenever she felt down. Her major coping mechanism for her situation of being orphan was to be socially associated with her friends and other close relatives who were a good support for her psychological and physical well being.

Eva's Story

Once upon a time there was a certain hunter and an old man. One day the hunter decided to go to the forest for hunting. In the forest, he succeeded to shoot an antelope; but, unfortunately, he did not have a knife for skinning the antelope. The hunter decided to go to see the old man and borrow a knife from him, and promised to share some meat with the old man if he would give him the knife. When he took the knife from the old man, he skinned the antelope and returned the knife to the old man. At the end, he did not want to share the meat with the old man. He told the old man that the meat was only enough for him and his family. The old man told the hunter that "*Ahadi ni deni*" which means that "the promise is a debt." The hunter continued to insist that the meat was only enough for him and his family only. The old man told the hunter once again that "promise is a debt. If you do not want to share with me the meat, you will remember me!" When the hunter decided to go away carrying his hunting, he heard a voice from behind saying "you will remember me!" When he looked back to see who was saying, he could not see anything. When he reached home, he heard again heard the voice saying, "You will remember me!" The hunter took the calabash of the honey to go to see the old man so that he could ask him for forgiveness. At the end he understood his mistake done to the old man, and the honey in the calabash was something precious and important for a real and true repentance. In that way the old man was able to forgive him. But the forgiveness became more costly than the meat he could have given him instead of the honey."

Eva wrote in her memory that from the above story we learn "the need to fulfil our pledges." The Swahili proverb says "*Ahadi ni deni*," which means that "promise is the debt." This means that when we promise anything to someone we should keep our promise. And when we discover that we have not kept the promise, we should find a solution quickly instead of staying quiet; otherwise, the curse and other bad things can continue following our lives. And this is very costly. The lesson of the story is very important to children as it was to Eva in her life in the way she lived with her relatives and friends. She understood the importance of words in our lives and the power they have in our lives now and in future. We also learned from the scripture that it taught the same thing. The Bible text says, we should not be quick in saying, but quick in listening, that we should avoid empty words which are meaningless (James 1:19).

Therapeutic intervention

Eva was a social child. She was not shy, and was upfront in different things and activities. She was upfront in working with different activities in the *Amani* Orphanage Center. She was upfront in discussions and in Bible study. She was upfront in answering and volunteering with questions and homework provided by her facilitators, volunteers, and teachers when asked to do so. Moreover, Eva respected her caregivers. She was a girl who wanted to please her caregivers. In the family of her caregivers she was the oldest. Therefore, she was responsible for many things in the family. Sometimes these activities became a burden for her. Her caregivers were sometimes out from early in the morning and came back home very late in the evening. Eva was the one who had to make sure that the young children at home obtained their food and were clean; and she had to make sure she did all the house chores.

The consequences of her busy work were that her school progress was not very good. She sometimes missed doing her homework from school subjects. Also, according to her age the works were too much for her. She did not even have enough time to play with her mates. The many works she did also made her feel sad. Eva knew about her feelings and she said that she did not have any choice. Her life was like that since her childhood and her caregivers were like her biological parents. She tried her level best to please them and fulfill all that would make the caregivers happy with her.

When we met and talked together on how she was dreaming and planning about her future life, we tried to change the story of her sadness and worry to be a story of joy and successful life. In order to help Eva improve her school performance and her life in general we also talked to her caregivers to find ways that would provide Eve the chance to study and do her school homework well. The caregivers agreed to shift the work between themselves to make sure that one of them was at home during the noon time, so that Eva did not trouble herself to cook for her two cousins. This worked well and since then Eva improved and finished her homework and eventually her health changed.

According to her story, Eva wanted to be a successful woman when she grew up. She wanted to be a nurse who would be able to help other people, especially children who became sick. We talked about the good promises, the positive promises that would change her story of worry and sadness. We promised each other to stand in the promise which says in Swahili, "*Ukitaka cha uvunguni, sharti uiname,*" which means, "if you want something which is underneath, you must bend down." Working hard was the way to a successful life. Successful life was not a short cut way; it required perseverance and hard work as another Swahili proverb said, "*Mchumia juani ulia kivulini,*" which also means, "the one who works out in the sun will finally eat under the shade."

Another healing which we found working with Eva was through playing. In the playing we found that the body kept itself busy; and also we found enjoying and laughing. We also found other related stories from the friends which kept them alive. Playing kept the person more creative because the mind became active and refreshed the whole body. Playing was not only about making the person strong and active but playing made the person happier and joyous. The Bible also recognized the power of healing through joy and happiness. Proverbs 17:22 says, "A cheerful heart is good medicine, but a downcast spirit dries up the bones." Therefore, we found that sometimes in the middle of our conversation, laughing, playing, and enjoying ourselves with life made us healthier and whole.

The narrative approach helped Eva to develop different ways of resilience. Resilience from sadness and worry of her life were suppressed through the stories and her memory book she had learned to write and remember. As an actor too, in the drama they perform at the church or at the center, she learned to act in a way that enabled her to dismiss the bad inner feelings which could be destructive and hurtful to her life. The Center also encouraged those activities which kept the child away from thinking too much about his or her family problems. Drama and stories helped her towards creating positive imaginations of who she longed to be in her life. Through those dramas and stories, she could be able to act in a way that her self-esteem, boldness, and peace of mind were recreated and thickened in her mindset.

For example, one of the dramas she acted was about the story of Esther in the Bible. Esther, who was a foreigner in the land they were taken as captives, did not reject her background and her people, though was promoted in a position where she became a queen. Esther was in a position where she could obtain anything and where she could be safe and live a life she liked. However, Esther after hearing about the doom which was going to face his people, the Jews, she was able to stand up for her rights. Despite all the opposition and risks she faced, Esther did not fear the result of claiming her rights or speaking for her people and even being open of who she was and the faith in her God. Hence, Esther stood for her rights and spoke what was true in her heart (Esther 7–9). Eventually, Eva took the story of Ester as her model where she would be able to stand up for her people and for her rights as a girl. Despite all the struggles and conflicts she experienced or oppositions she faced, she would continue trusting God who helped Esther to rescue her people from destruction. Eva believed that one day her dreams and wishes would ultimately be fulfilled and come true.

Case Number 9: Lucy and Joshua

Background

Case number nine concerned Lucy and Joshua. Lucy was 15 years old in 2007. Her childhood was good and healthier. She began primary education at Sinde primary school in Mbeya urban district. In 2005 they moved to Uyole where she continued with her primary education at Nsalaga. Lucy remembered one of her life time when she became sick from a bad wound which did not heal quickly for a period of time. She said that she was very close to death because of that wound and everybody in her family was confused. She further explained that after becoming well from that wound, she again became sick from lung problems. Lucy's both parents died. Her mother died in December 2006 in the age of only 31 years old. Her father passed away in March 2007 being 42 years old. They did not know the causes of their deaths. Lucy's parents were blessed with six children, but unfortunately only two children were left: that is, Lucy and her young brother Joshua (14 years old) who was also attended by the authors of this book. Lucy was the first born child and Joshua was the second born. However, from the third child to the sixth child all died while were still very young. Lucy's condition and her progress were very good by the time of this study. Her health was good, and her school progress was also good. Lucy and her young brother Joshua lived with their maternal grandmother who was their guardian and a very close relative to supports them in whatever they required. Lucy's grandmother was a hard worker. She could work in the farm and also keep some animals such as chicken and pigs.

Our Observation and Interpretation

Lucy liked different things in her life. She liked to play different games, some domestic works like cookery, and animal husbandry. She liked to study and be a good child towards her relatives and other people. She also liked to know and follow her clan traditions and customs. Lucy learned that wherever there was a goal or need in her life there was a way out. In

Swahili proverbs, Lucy wrote in her memory book that, "*Penye nia, pana njia,*" which means, "wherever there is a goal, then there is a way." She also wrote, "*Mtoto umleavyo, ndivyo akuavyo,*" which means, "the way you rear the child, it is the way he or she will grow up." These proverbs and more others direct people to be responsible and pursue what is good in life.

Lucy's dreams and her passion after acquiring good education and skills of life was to pursue something that would make her a traffic police. Lucy's feelings about her parents' death were still the disturbing feelings for her. It was very difficult for her to talk about it. When asked what she did about her parents' death in order to cope or let it go of her grief, she said that being with her friends, playing, singing, and talking to her grandmother helped her to forget or let go of her feelings of pain, sadness, and grief. Lucy learned to focus on her dreams which she had for her future life. These were the dreams of becoming a successful woman in the business which would help her and her relatives to live a life of joy and happiness. Focusing the thoughts in what was positive and empowering was the narrative approach in pastoral counseling especially with children. The children who lost their parents, lost their identity, and their self-esteem had to be helped to regain new and empowering alternative stories that would increase their confidence and hope for the life that was worth living.

Therapeutic Intervention

Lucy and her young brother Joshua were left behind with their parents unexpectedly. They went through difficult psychological emotions. The story and the history of their parents' death were unclear to them. It seemed that they lost a sense of direction and uncertainty about life. Concerning their parents' death, there were many suspicions and rumors going on within the society they belonged. They heard different stories from people that their parents died from AIDS; but others said that they were bewitched, and still others said it was a curse from their past generations because of breaking customs and traditions in their society.

Children were brought to *Amani* Orphanage Center by their father shortly before he passed away. It seemed that he knew that he would die soon; this was because it was only after one week when he brought the children to the center and finally died. Fortunately the children were accepted at the center and lived with their grandmother since then. Therefore, they moved from their father's house and went to live with their grandmother about four kilometers from where they were living before.

Using narrative approach in helping these two children from their psychological and social problems, we recalled stories that they heard from people about their parents' death as pointed out above. Their social and school developments were sometimes not very good because of all the feelings they went through, i.e., the movements and grieving over their parents' deaths. Visiting children and talking to them was one of the therapeutic interventions we used for their resilience. At the Center, we also continued working with them through stories that empowered them; we introduced stories that dismissed the hopeless stories they heard from people, especially those which instigated the fear of curses and witchcraft in their family.

We tried to empower children through singing hymns that encouraged them to remain strong in Christ no matter what the circumstances were. We played and drew pictures and images that kept us focusing on what was joyous, hopeful, and successful. This was the way of thickening the alternative stories that were different from what filled their minds with bad and depressing thoughts. One of the songs they used to sing was the following:

> *Baba na mama waweza kuniacha* (Father and mother can leave me)
> *Lakini Yesu hawezi kuniacha.* (But Jesus will never leave me)
> *Ndugu, rafiki waweza kuniacha* (Relatives and friends may leave me)
> *Lakini Yesu hawezi kuniacha!* (But Jesus will never leave me!)

Another song went like this:

> Orphans, have neither mother and mother, nor clothing and food
> Where shall they go, where shall they eat, oh orphans.
>> God the father help orphans
>> They should come out of streets and garbages
>> They should come out of tunnels!
>> They should come out of cruelty.
>
> Orphans should be helped to have food, clothing and live a descent life
> They should be out of abuse and maltreatment.
>> Oh God the father help those orphans
>> God the father help those who are orphans[16]

These songs and stories became coping strategies which led them to personal insight of who they were before God who never left them nor forsook them. They remembered some of the heros in the Bible who were not even scared of curse and witchcraft, such as Paul who was a Pharisee but disregarded his background and intelligence because of Christ he knew. He was

---

16. This song is translated from Swahili language.

not afraid of being witched and being thrown away with his people (the Jews) because of mingling with Gentiles.

Lucy and Joshua learned that life was difficult; however, if one had a goal in life he or she could focus on the goal and struggle to reach to the goal. Stories of Joseph in the Bible were a good example for them to follow. Joseph had dreams that pictured the success of his life in the future, despite all difficulties he went through in his life. Joseph was almost the last child in the family. No one paid attention to him. He was like a useless boy. However, deep inside he had big dreams which God put in him. Despite the challenges he obtained from his brothers and parents, he kept on dreaming and telling them of all he dreamt about. Joseph passed through difficulties even to the point of death; however, at the end we see his victory in the midst of difficulties. His dreams became something to hold on and not despair; and at the end of all struggles he went through, he became a successful man in Pharaoh's kingdom in Egypt and to his family (Genesis 37). Therefore, this story of Joseph from the Bible became their alternative story to hold on to make their lives successful.

Case Number 10: Gregory

Background

The tenth case was of Gregory. Gregory was 15 years old in 2007. He was born at Uyole in Mbeya and completed standard seven in the year 2007 at Nyigamba primary school. He was Safwa by tribe belonging to the Roman Catholic Church. In his family, they were born five children and Gregory was the last born (the 5th child) of the family. His three older brothers were independent. Gregory and his brother Oswald lived by themselves at the house which their parents left when they died. Their mother died in 2003 from what in Swahili was known as *"chembe ya moyo"* which was like a heart problem. Her sickness was for a very short time. In the following year, after their mother's death, their father also became sick for a very short time. In 2004 their father also died from diabetic related infections. Therefore, up to that moment Gregory and his brother Oswald lived by themselves, and did not depend on anyone, except from minor supports from the rooms they rented and also from the *Amani* Orphanage Center.

Our Observation and Interpretation

Gregory's progress at home, school, and at *Amani* Orphanage Center was not bad. He did well at home, school, and at *Amani* Orphanage Center. He and his brother understood their situation and the condition they were in. They did not complain much or become sad whenever they missed anything. We sometimes found that they did not even have money for grinding maize to obtain flour for food whose cost was at least 500 Tanzanian shillings only by then. It seemed that Gregory's ways of dealing with issues surrounding him was to know that there was people and community around him for care, support, and comfort. This seemed to be the good way of letting go of all the problems in their family with his brother Oswald.

Oswald, Gregory's brother was troubled by the disease known in Swahili as "*kifafa*," (i.e., epilepsy). It was the condition which he felt like being shocked by something, and trembled and shook and finally fell down, which caused him to have many sores in his head. Oswald and his brother Gregory did not know the origin of his sickness; however, he used some medicines recommended by doctors. According to his brother Gregory, the medicines did not help much. He occasionally, at least once a month, fell down and hurted his face. This sickness caused him to lag behind especially when it came to his school progress. Therefore, Gregory was the person who cared for his brother most of the time.

During counseling sessions, we observed that Gregory was talented with listening and compassion to people especially who were like him—those children who were in difficult situation. He was very attentive and sensitive to issues that troubled people such as sicknesses, poverty, and injustices. The narrative approach helped Gregory to acquire skills of knowing how to listen and tell stories and memories we have in life. Sharing our memories and stories became a healing process for Gregory and other children at *Amani* Orphanage Center. Gregory recalled of the story which his grandmother used to tell them. The grandmother told them that respect to people started when one also knew how to be attentive and listened to other people's needs and stories. His grandmother used to tell him that people required heeding what was heard from relatives who were older than them. Her grandmother used also to tell the story of Martha and her sister Mary that was found in the Bible in which Mary selected a good portion of sitting down and listening to the words which came out of Jesus' mouth. Jesus commended Mary that she chose the right portion of listening to him rather than becoming busy with other things. There were things that were more important than that of physical needs and these were spiritual needs (Luke 10:38–42).

Therapeutic intervention

Fortunately, Gregory and Oswald were at least very easy working with them when it came to pastoral counseling. The problem with Oswald was his illness because the epilepsy caused him to speak in staggering and muttering way; he couldnot speak very well. Generally, these two children were very open to talk about their issues with their teachers and counselors. They were very cooperative. One of the approaches or methods that were very easy for them to work with was through drawings and talking about the drawings. They liked drawing pictures and images that showed what they wished in life. We also discovered that talking to the child was as important as listening to him or her. Together we looked at new ways of thinking and behaving so that the person might grow healthy. It was always good to remember that most of the time the child talks through play and listens through stories.[17] Play and art can be a good way for the child to tell the story.

For example, at one occasion, Gregory drew an image of the moon which in it he also drew some trees, people, and other creatures such as insects and animals. For him, the image meant a life he wished, and that life was a life full of justice and harmony. As we shared his story, Gregory was tired of life existing in society he lived, a life full of illnesses, crimes, poverty, injustice, and other misfortunes in life. One of the dreams Gregory had was to become a lawyer who would be involved in helping his society to the life he wished, the life of peace, harmony, and prosperity. He liked to become the person to fight for peace and justice in society.

Together with Gregory we entered and created a world of imagination which he created through play and drawings. For Gregory grief was not a big deal to deal with, but the future of his life and his brother. Gregory's imagination was seen in his play and drawings in which we clearly saw his intention and goals for his future life. In another occasion, he was able to create a world of fantasy with which he hoped and prayed that God would be able to help him and become the person with bright future, the person whom people honored because of his service to society especially on bringing peace and justice in the world. One of the stories which Gregory liked was about David the king and Nathan the prophet concerning the issue of Uriah and his wife Bathsheba (1 Samuel 11 and 12). It was clear that David did not do what was right before God, Uriah, and society. From this story Gregory learnt that it was good to do what was right and just. The verse which was transforming to David and which also became a memory verse to Gregory was, "I will instruct you and teach you the way you should go; I

---

17. Coetsee, "Walking with Wounded Children," 151.

will counsel you with my eye upon you" (Psalms 32:8). Another translation says that, "I will instruct thee and teach thee in the way which thou shalt go: I will guide thee with mine eye" (KJV). Gregory saw Nathan the prophet as a hero and model to follow in facing people of authority, especially those in government positions. Nathan was not afraid to confront the king; he was able to talk the truth in a very simple way, where the message could be understood. Nathan used a story to deliver the message to the king in which it would be easy for the King to know what he did and be responsible for his action.

We also learned from the Swahili proverb which said, "*Uzuri wa mkakasi, ndani kipande cha mti*," which means, "the sweetness of a pineapple, inside it there is a piece of log." This proverb has many implications. David sleeping with Bathsheba was so sweet at the beginning but the end of it was so bitter. His family felt the consequences of his action and the whole society felt the bitterness of his action. The proverb was itself a healing to Gregory because its message was so real, clear and simple.

When we talked about the issue of sexuality and AIDS, the children learned that people tended to look at things on the surface instead of going deep to see the in and out of the things young people were doing. Sex before marriage for young people became something they liked to do without any pre-caution or understanding its consequences. They did sex without any caution and the result of it was teenage pregnances, sexually transmitted diseases, and HIV infections. Moreover, they learned from what the Swahili people said that "*Uzuri wa mkakasi, ndani kipande cha mti*" and also that "*Fikiri kabla ya kutenda*" which means that "think before you act," because as Swahili people say, "*Majuto ni mjukuu*," which means that "you will start mourning when it is too late!" All these sayings and proverbs were very important in teaching and counseling children who were in this age (teenagers of between 13 to 17 years old). The wisdom of the proverbs helped them to live a life of reality and not of taboos and destructive customs and traditions particularly those related to issues of sexuality.

Case Number 11: Devotha

Background

The eleventh case was that of Devotha. Devotha was 14 years old by 2007 and was the fourth child and the last born of four children in her family. Her family originated from Njombe region. They were Kinga by tribe coming from Makete district in Njombe region. Devotha's parents died in the same year with just two months apart from each other. Devotha's father died in June 1998 from bad stabbing pains (*vichomi* in Swahili). Her mother died in August 1998 due to birth complications. The family was privileged with four children, Suzana, Sheyo, Tobias, and Devotha. They all belonged to the Roman Catholic Church at Uyole.

The four children from this family lived together at the house which their parents left when they died. These children did not depend on anyone, but on themselves. They struggle by themselves to make sure they survive in the midst of life challenges and difficulties. These children, especially the two elder ones Suzana and Sheyo, did not have an opportunity to continue with their secondary education. Suzana (21 years old by 2007) involved in small cultivations for vegetables. The family had a small farm which they cultivated for planting maize for food. Devotha's brother Sheyo (19 years old in 2007) collected stones for selling to house builders (contractors) during dry seasons despite the farm work. This work helped him and his relatives to buy some of their house needs. Tobias (16 years old in 2007) completed his primary education in 2007. His sister Suzana explained to the authors of this book that they worried that they would not be able to help and support Tobias go to a secondary school, if he passed the national examination. Devotha was standard six at Nsalaga primary school. She liked to go to school and study hard. She also liked to play different games such as netball.

Our Observation and Interpretation

Devotha was very close to her grandmother who did not live far away from their house. Devotha went to visit her grandmother several times where she also helped her to do some chores and other works she had. She went to her grandmother especially on week ends. This seemed to help Devotha a lot from her psychosocial needs and problems she had. Generally, her behavior and personality was good. She felt happy and joyful, but still required some more support, comfort, and encouragement from society. The environment she lived was very tempting and vulnerable especially when it came to issues of sexuality. Devotha required guidance and support in order to stand up for her life.

Therapeutic Intervention

It was through good relationship, conversation and the stories we shared that helped Devotha to live a life of hope and love despite the difficulties of life they had in their family. The life situation of this family where Devotha belonged was very poor and had very little support from outside. Physical needs had to be met first in order that their lives might feel somehow comfortable. The *Amani Orphanage* Center tried its best to meet the necessary needs for these children. *Amani* Orphanage Center helped children by providing them clothing, food, school materials and other small needs.

Talking about issues relating to her parents' death was difficult for her. The authors' questions were the following: "How can we help the child develop a new and healthy values system? How can we help her be free and talk and listen? Therefore, writing and drawing in her memory book helped us to find ways of talking to her. The fear and grief from her parents death was clearly expressed in songs and poems she recited in her memory book. At one point she wrote and sang:

> *Baba na mama waweza kuniacha* (Father and mother may leave me)
> *Kaka na dada waweza kuniacha* (Brother and sister may leave me)
> *Lakini Yesu hawezi kuniacha x2* (But Jesus can never leave me)
> *Ndugu, rafiki waweza kuniacha* (Relatives and friends may leave me)
> *Na wote pia waweza kuniacha* (And all people may also leave me)
> *Lakini Yesu hawezi kuniacha x2* (But Jesus can never leave me)

This song, in a form of poem, says that my father and my mother may leave me alone, my brother and my sister may also leave me alone, but Jesus can never leave me alone. Relatives and friends may also leave me and all people may also leave me, but Jesus can never leave me alone. Therefore, it was obvious that Devotha understood that life was difficult and painful and that all people may desert her in time of difficulty except Jesus Christ who could never leave her alone. Jesus was someone they could put their trust on. In Hebrews 13:5-6, the Scripture state, "I will never fail you. I will never abandon you." The biblical text continues to state, "The Lord is my helper, so I will have no fear. What can mere people do to me?" These verses were very encouraging and empowering to Devotha as we talked and conversed together. Devotha memorized them and took these verses into her heart as a motto for her life.

In order to help her, we tried to make several visits at her house. We talked different issues relating to life especially concerning her future dreams. Devotha wanted to be a prosperous woman in her future life after acquiring good education. She wanted to become a business woman. We talked about issues which she wrote in her memory book, especially concerning her feelings and emotions which she went through, the feelings of sadness and worry about her future. As we talked, she seemed to be very receptive and willing to cope with her difficult situations.

One of the ways she managed her emotions was through stories which were so empowering for her. The stories she learnt from her grandmother and from her friends helped her to feel more secure and belong to society. She learned from a Swahili saying which says that, "*Kutokuwa na rafiki ni kuwa maskini kweli,*" which means, "to be without a friend is to be poor indeed." We also tried to share biblical stories which became a way of defeating some of the bad feelings and emotions she went through. Devotha became a social person; she liked to be and talk to people. She liked to share her stories and sing different songs with her friends, which were very encouraging to her and her friends.

However, Devotha required support and help from the vulnerable life she lived. Peer-pressures from her friends had to be looked with caution. She also required support in understanding her sexuality very well so that she did not fall into traps of peer-pressures and end up in sexual relationships at that early age. Being open to issues relating to sexuality was very important at that time they lived. Talking about issues openly and in non-threatening ways helped children to understand their responsibility and staying away from every kind of bad behavior. Through narratives, the stories that related to sexual issues were helpful for such children as Devotha. Stories and metaphors helped children to talk about sexual issues in non-judgmental ways, ways which were friendly and understandable.

Case Number 12: Scola and Secilia

Background

The twelfth case concerned Scola and Secilia. Scola was 15 years old in 2007 and was born at Uyole in Mbeya. She was then in standard seven at Nsalaga primary school. She liked to study and play different games when had a chance of doing so. In her family, they were three children. Scola was the first born and Secilia (12 years old in 2007) was the second born and had the last born whose name was not known to us until we completed writing this book. In the *Amani* Orphanage Center Scola and Secilia were parts of people whom the authors saw. Scola liked to read and sing in the church as she told her story. They belonged to the Tanzania Assemblies of God church at Uyole. Scola and Secilia lost their father in 2004. Their mother was the one whom they lived with and the one who took care of them. She did small businesses at Uyole market. Sometimes Scola helped her mother to do those small businesses such as selling bananas and tomatoes. Other Scola's interests were drawing and playing games such as netball. In her drawings, she inserted some religious words which gave some comfort and hope for her life. In one of her drawings of a flower she wrote, "*Yesu ni jibu la maisha yangu*," which means, "Jesus is the answer for my life."

Scola's Story

One of her stories which she wrote on her memory book went like this: "Long time ago, there was a man who had two wives. The first wife bore a human son and the second wife bore a snake son. One day when the time came for the registration for the pre-primary school education, the first wife took her son to school, but the second wife did not. The snake son asked his mother that he also wanted to go to school like his brother, the son of the first wife. His mother told him, 'you are a snake son; I don't think the teachers will accept you!' But the snake son insisted in going to school for the registration hoping that he would be accepted. Finally, the mother agreed to send this snake son to school. When they reached at school, the mother introduced her son and expressed the need for her son to be registered at the school. The teachers did not accept him saying that the son was not a human being but a snake! The teachers expressed their fears to accept him because of the way he was, that he might even bite them. The mother and her son went back home very disappointed! When they reached home the mother told her son, 'Did I not tell you that you are a snake and that they will not accept you!' When the father of that son heard about that, he chased them out of the house.

The snake son and his mother went out looking for a place to stay, and when were going they reached in the interior of the forest. Then the snake son climbed up on the tree without being seen by his mother; his mother started looking for him and started to cry. The snake son heard her cry and saw his mother crying and called her saying, 'mother, come, I have already built a house to stay.' In that village a great famine happened and the father of that snake son began looking for a job and he came to the house which his second wife and his snake son built. He began asking for a job to a snake son, and the snake son asked him, 'Are you not the father who chased us out of your house?' The father began asking and begging for forgiveness in regard to all what he did to them." Scola finished her story from what she learned from it saying, "We should not disregard or look down upon our children no matter how they look like; they have great potential in them for building up the family, the church, and the nation as a whole."

Therapeutic Intervention

Scola and her sister Secilia who lived with their mother did not have much difficulty in life as compared to other childen at *Amani* Orphanage Center. The support they required was mostly the material needs not so much with psychosocial needs. As we talked and listened to stories we found that the major thing these two children required was finding a good network with friends, being connected to other children at home, school and at the Center. This would help them feel more comfortable and more acceptable in society. Games and telling stories would be good ways they could be connected and feel more secure in society. The best way we used for intervention with Scola and Secialia was establishing and building a healthy relationship which ultimately brought healing and wholeness (*shalom*) in their lives. These were implemented and seen to be the best ways in coping with various life situations.

A healthy relationship is very central to the ministry of healing. The Holy Spirit is the one who ministers the healing through the healing community. This healing community must experience the health relationships that ultimately bring healing to the wounded and broken child.[18] We are in line with Coetsee who says, "healing is the ministry of he Holy Spirit to bring restoration ('peace') to wounded and broken children in caring relationships with a compassionate community of believers."[19] Orphans and vulnerable children should be regarded for the Church and society as an opportunity for them to grow into maturity and not be regarded as troublesome or misfortunes to society. Orphans and vulnerable children do not cause problems of illnesses, poverty and other problems or difficulties. In that case, they should not be despised and put down because of the situation they go through. They are people like other normal people who are physically and materially well.

The feelings of sadness to these orphans because of who they are in society should be dealt with in order to make them feel more comfortable, acceptable, and respected. From the story of Scola and her little sister Secilia, it was obvious that they sometimes felt that they were the worst in society, that they were rejected and despised in society. However, as we continued visiting and conversing with them, this problem-saturated story was transformed to a story that transformed and empowered them to live a life of hope, faith, and success. Secilia discovered that it was in Jesus alone where there was a true answer for her life problems and struggles. She trusted in

---

18. Coetsee, "Walking with Wounded Children."
19. Ibid.

God to fulfill her dreams and for that reason she aimed at studying hard and being strong. She tried to break the bondage of shame and guilt of thinking that they were the worst and sinners in the world. She also learned that a wise person would not despise his or her friend as written in the book of Proverbs 11:12.

We once also shared the gospel narrative which was so empowering for Scola and her little sister Secilia. The story was about the rich person and Lazarus (Luke 16:19–31). The emphasis of this story as we conversed together was on how we should know to respect others no matter how they are, as is in the lesson of the story of Scola above. We should know how to talk and listen to all people despite their differences. Our life should be a good model for disciplined life so that we cannot find a word of excuse to stay irresponsible. There is a Swahili proverb which says, "*Majuto ni mjukuu,*" which means, "the mourning can become too late, if you don't take precaution of what you already know and act responsibly. Act responsibly and there will be no regret." The memory verse we learned from the story of rich person and Lazarus says, "Let me hear in the morning of thy steadfast love, for in thee I put my trust. Teach me the way I should go, for to thee I lift up my soul" (Psalms 143:8). This is what was reflected in the story above where Scola wrote on two children on which one of them was rejected and despised in society and the other accepted. There is a Swahili saying which says, "*Mpanda ngazi, hushuka*" which means, "the one who climbs the ladder will obviously come down again." So, whenever one feels to be above others or high, one day he or she will also come down. There is no use to despise others who are not like us. There was another proverb in Swahili which was so empowering in our relationship with Scola; it goes like this, "*Mdharau mwiba, utamchoma*" which means that the one who despises the thorn, it will pierce him or her. Therefore, Scola and Secilia also learned from biblical stories about humility which required one not holding to pride, which could ultimately bring that person down (James 4:6).

Case Number 13: Paschal

Background

Case number thirteen concerned about Paschal. By 2007, Paschal was 15 years old, born in Sumbawanga, Rukwa region. He began his primary education at Katandala in Sumbawanga. He belonged to the Roman Catholic Church. Paschal explained that he began suffering from life after the death of his mother, though his father was still alive. Paschal moved from

Sumbawanga, Rukwa region to Mbeya region after the death of his father. In Mbeya, Paschal lived with his grandfather and went to Itezi primary school at Uyole where he began standard five.

According to Paschal's story, he progressed well healthwise. He was not troubled by any bad sicknesses. Paschal said that he liked to study hard and at the same time liked to play football and other games. He also liked to live a descent life and a good moral life being obedient to all people and live a godly life without being involved in any kind of drugs and smoking, or any kind of life that could be considered as sin before God and before people. In Paschal's family, they were born three children, one of them by the name of Esther who died in 2002 and only two children were left, Paschal and his young brother Daudi. Paschal's mother died in 2002 followed by his father who also died in 2005.

Our Observation and Interpretation

Despite his grandfather's support, Paschal had some good networks with his relatives such as his aunt, uncle, and young father. Still the life of Paschal required some extra support from the *Amani* Orphanage Center for his psychosocial needs and progress in general because the life he lived was still very hard economically, socially, and psychologically. However, Paschal was a hard working boy who did not wait to be told what to do. He volunteered himself to do different activities to his grandparents such as going to the fields (*shamba*), cleaning the house, and doing the house chores and its environments.

In his memory book, Paschal wrote a will which his father left for him and his brother. This will was about them, that they should love and respect each other; and that they should work hard and not lust for other people's things. They should stay together in unity with the bond of love. Some of the family customs and traditions which Paschal remembered from his parents were that they were forbidden to marry more than one wife. Moreover, they were forbidden to believe in witchcraft.

Therapeutic Intervention

In building a good and healthy relationship, visiting and conversing with Paschal was a very important step in his developmental stage. Despite the difficulties he had, he was able to talk about his issues freely. For example, the issues of his parents' death and about witchcraft were not very easy to talk about. However, for Paschal, it was easy to share his stories with his counselors. Being able to talk about the issues which were so troubling was itself the healing process for Paschal.

Paschal was good in writing the memory book or letters which described his emotions and feelings of what he was going through. It was through his stories in the memory book and letters where we could find the issues to talk about. Through his stories and memories we talked, it became a healing process itself. Paschal's feelings of fear and grief for his parents' death was the big issue; however, through visiting and talking about them through his own writings, it was easy to find alternative stories that were empowering and positive for his resilience.

Paschal's religious background was also fairly strong; he did not want to concentrate in believing about witchcraft. He liked to think of God who was love and stronger than all the witches. The Bible stories he learned at *Amani* Orphanage Center helped him to hold on something godly and had the memory verse which he held on in his writings (i.e. memory book) and in his mind. The Bible verse which he liked said, "What then shall we say to this? If God is for us, who is against us?" (Romans 8:31)

Case Number 14: Tumaini M.

Background

The fourteenth case was that of Tumaini. Tumaini was 15 years old by 2007. His childhood was not very good due to his parent's economic difficulties. His health condition was not good as well as his educational progress. Tumaini explained his childhood story in very sad ways. He said that when he was about one year old, he walked using his stomach! His parents took him to traditional doctors who advised them to look for the skin of a snake and tie the child on his waist. Tumaini continued to tell his story that after following the advice of the traditional doctor he began to walk with his knees and after six months he began to stand up and walking slowly, yet by stumbling. As he explained himself, in this stage he was very fat.

Tumaini was baptized in his church in Chunya district, Mbeya region. Unfortunately, Tumaini did not continue with his primary education because of his parents' failure to support him. Another childhood story which Tumaini had was about a certain time when he was nearly eaten by the hyena at night when he troubled his parents. In his memory book, Tumaini said, "*Maisha ni safari ndefu,*" which means, "life is a long journey." Through those difficulties in life, Tumaini still seemed to show up some courage and hope in God. He also had this to write in his memory book, "*Mungu ni kiboko cha Shetani*," which means, "God is a stripe for Satan." Tumaini said that whenever his mother prepared a traditional alcohol she had to put it at the corner of the house. This was a kind of customs and traditions which Tumaini's parents believed in for the welfare of what they were doing. The family of Tumaini was very much influenced by the African culture, customs, and traditions. They were also influenced by some beliefs and taboos which made Tumaini to be filled by worry and fear; these included witchcraft and sorcery. Below we consider one of his stories he told and wrote in his memory book.

Tumaini's Story

Tumaini's story goes like this: "Once upon a time, there was an old woman in a certain village whose name was Simya. She was a very good person who liked to visit people in their houses around the village. The village had several people who practiced witchcraft. The people in that village lived in fear and uncertainty of their lives and the progress in various affairs was not that good. The old woman who came in that village was sometimes visiting the houses looking for the witches. Fortunately, she found twenty two witches in that village. In those houses she found the flesh of people who had died and also found cats that were stealing people's food and also found little children who had died (or lost) in their homes. She also obtained big cats in their houses.

The old woman took all these things and burned them, destroying all the evil works of the witches. From that day people felt in their deep sleep and nothing bad was in that village again. People thanked the old woman and gave her gifts to take with her at home. If the person got sick or had been bewitched they took him or her to that old woman to be healed. When people came to that old woman, she asked who had done such a thing and what has he or she done? The one who had done that could have gone to the ten cell leader of the village instead of doing such evil thing.

When the old woman died, many people were very sorry for her death. People cried a lot in her funeral. Many people said different things about her. Some people said that she saved them from afflictions and sufferings from witches, but the witches themselves were very happy and rejoiced at her death because they said that the old woman took off their witches. So these witches resumed their bad practices of witchcraft.

One month passed from that day when the old woman died. That village began to be worse again, bad things happened. One day, when children went for swimming in the stream of a river they found that one of them was drowning and finally was lost in the river; therefore, others decided to run back to their houses. The mother of the boy who was lost began asking where their friend was. They answered, 'he is drowned in the river.' The mother began calling the villagers and they came out of the river where the child had been drowned. The villagers began looking for the boy who had been lost in the river. Finally, they found the child lying beside the river already dead. And this was the end of the story."

Therapeutic Intervention

Tumaini's story and his life in general were full of fear and anxiety as we saw in his story above. His life and surroundings were confronted by witches and by some customs, myths, and taboos. Using narratives was ways of helping Tumaini cope with his feelings of fear and anxiety. The stories of fear were discarded through stories of hope and faith. Tumaini looked at the ways which would help him be a better person. One of the ways he found to be helpful for his spiritual life was being obedient to his people, a thing which he thought to be a way of succeeding in life here on earth and in heaven.

The struggle between good and evil, between the good people and bad people was one of Tumaini's concerns. He dreamt for his future life that he would continue fighting against what was evil and bad, whether poverty or illnesses. Tumaini believed in the miracles of life where he hoped and prayed that life should be treated with dignity. The alternative story of Tumaini was no longer filled with sadness, fear and worry but with hope and faith in God who would ultimately prevail against all evil things such as witchcraft. Good things always prevail against evil things.

One of the biblical narratives which was in line with this concept of good versus evil was about king Saul and David in the Old Testament (1 Samuel 18–22). King Saul was so envious to the success of the young boy David, or the story of Peter and John with the magician Simon in the book of Acts 8: 9–24. These biblical stories were used for the purpose of discarding unreasonable fears and building up good relationship filled with hope, faith, and love. Finally, Tumaini understood the mighty power of God over Satan and his evil deeds. He had a quote which he liked which said, "Don't play with God!" He remembered his own life as was very difficult during his childhood. Tumaini went through many difficulties in his life; however, he survived and continued to struggle. His struggle was made by the ambition that one day he would be able to help other children who faced similar situations, especially orphaned children. That was the reason he remembered and honored what the Swahili people said concerning life that, "*Maisha ni safari ndefu*," which means, "Life is a long journey that needs perseverance." Tumaini came to understand that the way we treat each other now, is the way the life will treat someone in the future. Despite his difficulties, Tumaini liked to study and continue with his education. His aim and dreams for his future life was to be a pastor and the one who would be concerned with orphans and other children from difficult environments. He hoped to be helpful to them as God gave him the opportunity of doing so.

Case Number 15: Israel

Background

Case number fifteen concerned about Israel. Israel was 12 years old by 2007. He was standard five at Itezi primary school. His mother died in October 2001. His father left him and ran away after his mother's death. Israel met his father after six years since he left him. When Israel met him, his father was sick. At this time he lived at Iwambi, outside Mbeya town center. According to Israel's story concerning his father, his father could not be cured from his sickness though was hospitalized several times. Israel's father was sick for a long time and his relatives could not know exactly what was he suffering from. In April 2007, Israel's father passed away.

Since Israel's mother died, Israel lived with his maternal grandparents at Uyole in Mbeya. They were like parents to him for how they lived with him since he was a little boy. They supported him in all his needs; however, he also had some support from other relatives such as his young mother who had a small business and also from his uncle who was not very far from where they lived. Israel was the first born of his family. His second brother Kevin died while was still a baby, and the third child was Tulinagwe who lived at Iwambi with her paternal grandmother.

Israel's Story

Israel narrated to us his story thus: "Once upon a time there was a rabbit and a man. The man had three children. One day the rabbit went to the man's groundnuts field and started stealing the groundnuts. The man had been troubled with the stealing behavior of the rabbit for a long time. Then the man decided to put a person-like sculpture in that field. On that sculpture he put some strong glue so that the rabbit can be trapped. One day, as usual, the rabbit went to steal the groundnuts in the man's field. The rabbit looked at that sculpture and said to it, 'forgive me. . .forgive me' but he could not obtain any reply. Then the rabbit said, 'Why don't you like to reply to me?' So the rabbit went closer to the sculpture and touched it firmly; and the rabbit was caught by the sculpture totally. He began screaming and shouting loudly. The noise was heard by the owner of those groundnuts who went to the groundnuts field and caught the rabbit. Finally, despite the rabbit's craftiness and cleverness, he was caught and could not do anything."

Israel wrote in his memory book: "this story teaches us that we should not be stealing other people's things. No matter how we think of ourselves as intelligent, clever and wise, we should not try to show off what we can do without considering other people." The Swahili people have the proverb which says, "*Za mwizi arobaini*," which means, "the thief has forty days only, because after that he or she will be caught."

Our Observation and Interpretation

Israel's grandparents were a good support and comfort to Israel. They were not very old. They had energy and passion for life. They engaged themselves in various activities such as cultivation and tailoring. In that way they could support themselves and Israel. They were good caregivers to Israel because they reared him in a disciplined Christian life. Israel himself was a good singer, actor and someone who attended church and Sunday school regularly. Israel liked to play football; he liked to sing and act in the drama, especially in church, the Moravian Church at Uyole where he belonged. Israel also liked school, but at the same time he liked to play too much. We could say that he was very naughty, mischievous and sometimes delinquent. In that way he could not concentrate well to his studies. He therefore did not pass well at school. He was an average student; however, if he minimized some of his playing, he could be very good and bright student.

When we talked to Israel about his parents' death, he did not feel good talking about them. He failed to explain himself about them and therefore, stayed quiet. When we asked him where he went for help or talk to when he had something in his heart, he told us he went to his aunt and his young father (uncle) and not to his grandfather to whom he stayed with. It was obvious that Israel was not very free and open to talk to his grandparents who took care of him. His grandparents did not have good relationship with Israel's parents as we noticed in the stories we had about the family. Israel's grandparents did not want to talk about Israel's parents to Israel. That was why Israel sometimes went to his aunt or his young father who could listen to him. There was a kind of hatred between the two families where Israel came from, from his father's family and his mother's family.

Therapeutic Intervention

Israel was a very charming boy, very active, and very busy playing different games with his friends. His parents' death was one of the things which distracted him with his school progress. The hatred of the two families from his mother's and father's sides affected him as well. These problems caused Israel to have poor performance at school and his delinquency. The visits and narrative activities such as stories, and proverbs and other activities which were done by children at the Center helped Israel in trying to cope with life's situation. *Amani* Orphanage Center became a healing community to most children who attended there. Building good relationships, and talking the issues over and helping Israel to write some of the good memories about his life's background in his memory book were very helpful for his healing.

We provided different things which Israel could use to tell his stories. Some of the things included papers and exercise books in which he was able to draw or paint some pictures and write some of his memories. Through these things Israel was able to talk more about his family; however, without them, it could be very difficult for him to tell his stories. As we observed Israel playing with his friends especially soccer, we saw clearly in his mood that it was more relaxed, happy, and friendly. After the game, we took some time to talk to him about the game. We asked him, "How do you feel playing the game with your friends"? The answer was very obvious that he was glad. This was another alternative for Israel to find a way which would help him not concentrate much on the problems he faced in his family.

Painting and drawing of pictures and images were also a way of coping up with life difficulties. The stories which were created out of these pictures were a healing process for the psychological and social development of Israel. The pictures which portrayed a negative message were then translated to make the pictures look more positive and hopeful. Sometimes, his anger and sadness towards his family were portrayed by his violent pictures or images; however, through talking about them, Israel was able to draw other images and pictures that portrayed positive messages of friendship and peace, faith and hope. He drew a family that was united and sometimes eating food together or the family seating together and talking. The hatred attitude which was observed in their grandparents towards other relatives especially from the sides of Israel's father were openly discussed and talked about so that they came out of their minds and especially from their grandson, Israel. Biblical stories became a good guide for them to understand about love and faith no matter how life treated them; they had to forget, forgive, and move forward with life that was acceptable to all people and God.

On his delinquent behavior we used the following story: "In a certain village there were two dogs. One of the dogs was very naughty but the other one was very cool. One day these two dogs went to look for food in the forest and decided to help each other. The one which first obtained the meat had to make a noise and call the other one so that they could share the meat together because they were friends. When they reached the forest they reminded themselves of the rules of the game on how to hunt and what not to do. They agreed and started hunting looking for some animals for their food. The first dog to obtain the meat was the cool dog. So it decided to call its friend so that they could share together. It shouted once, second, and third but the naughty dog did not want to respond. As naught as it was, it came making much noise, jumping happily, and running from there to here, forward and backward because of the meat. The cool dog said, 'Hey, do not make much noise; otherwise, other animals will come and take our share because of your acting out.' The naughty dog did not want to listen; it kept on making nonsense noises until when it saw many other animals coming towards the cool dog which held the meat. These other animals included hyenas, lions, and more other animals which were stronger than them. The cool dog decided to run away and leave the meat behind and the naughty dog tried to rescues the meat from those hyenas without success and ended up being hurt and wounded by the hyenas because of the fight. The naughty dog lost the food because of its bad behavior of being so mischievous, naughty, and noisy."

When we asked Israel what he learned from the story, he was able to relate the story with what the wise people of Tanzania said in the proverb, "*Debe tupu lina makelele mengi,*" which means "an empty tin has much noise." This means that people who talk too much thinking that they know many things, they actually have nothing; they are just empty like a tin. It is better to be cool and allow people to see your richness and success at the end. Being noisy and showing off your character ends up like a naughty dog in the story. It is better to be cool while being creative and clever just like the cool dog.

Another Swahili wisdom saying goes like this, "*Kunguru mwoga huishi miaka mingi,*" which means, "the scary clove lives many years." This is because whenever he sees the danger or even one tries to scare the clove with an empty hand, it just runs away. In that way the clove lives many years. But those who think are clever and bold will not live long. They can be snatched one day. Our only trust should be in the Lord Jesus Christ who knows our lives better than ourselves. The Bible text says, "Trust in the Lord with all your heart, and do not depend on your own insight. In all your ways acknowledge him, and he will make straight your paths." (Proverbs 3:5–6) We also shared some of the biblical stories which told us the same thing that the one who thinks he is stable must make sure that he doesn't stumble and fall (1 Corinthians 10:12). Moreover, we learned that the one who is bold and proud of himself or herself should not be proud because of who he or she is, but should be proud because of the one who is greater than him or her, i.e., God the almighty, whom he or she knows as his or her Lord (Jeremiah 9: 23–24).

Case Number 16: Juliana

Background

The sixteenth case was that of Juliana. Juliana was 15 years old by 2007. Both of her parents died. She was then being reared by her grandmother. Juliana was the last born of three children in their family. She had two older brothers of 18 and 21 years old respectively. Juliana went to school and was standard seven. She belonged to the Nyakyusa ethnic group, and was a Moravian Christian attending church at Uyole in Mbeya. Most of Juliana's support depended on her grandmother. Her grandmother was still strong and healthy, though was old and did not have any dependable means of generating income for the family needs on what she could take care of children she lived with. Juliana's grandmother depended on other family relatives to support her family such as Juliana's uncle and aunt who lived not far from Uyole area. Apart from Juliana and her two brothers, Juliana's grandmother also took care of other two children, the daughters from her uncle and the other one from her young mother. Therefore, they were six people all together in the family.

The deaths of Juliana's parents were not clearly understood from what caused their deaths. Juliana's mother died in 1993 just one year after her birth. She became sick for a short while and died. Her father died in June 2003; since then, Juliana lived with her grandmother. Apart from Juliana's grandmother, Juliana also received support from *Amani* Orphanage Center, which provided most of her school needs like uniforms, exercise books, soap, and even some clothing. Juliana's perspective was reflected in her story below.

Juliana's Story

"Once upon a time there was a king. The king had a daughter. The daughter lived in the twelve storey of a big flat. No one entered in her room. All the supplies were sent to her inside her room. One day the thieves broke the house and entered her room where she stayed. And they ordered her to take everything that was hers and not to scream. Then they took her to another flat in another storey of the flat. In that flat there was a servant by the name of John Best Kuku. In the room, where the King's daughter lived, no one was allowed to enter. If the food was required she just rang the bell and the food was brought in. One day, the King's daughter heard someone chopping firewood and decided to look at the window and saw a young boy named John Best Kuku. The King's daughter called and told him to open the door for her. John went up and opened the door. The king's daughter went out, and John fell down three times as he saw the beauty of that King's daughter. When John woke up, the king's daughter told him that the thieves kidnapped her from her room; so she told him, 'let us run and go out of here.' Therefore, they ran away and took the car left by the thieves and drove it away.

When they reached somewhere far, the car broke down and came out of the car. When they looked around for help, they saw seven people and were those thieves. The king's daughter said, 'let us borrow a spanner number 12 so that we can fix the car quickly and continue with our journey.' But those people did not provide them the spanner. The king's daughter then had to ask for a place to sleep and those seven people allowed them to sleep where they were. It happened that, those seven people fell in love with the King's daughter, because of her beauty. Therefore, they decided to separate them the rooms they were going to sleep. Therefore, John slept room number six and the king's daughter slept room number seven. Then John said to her, 'Why do they separate us while we have come together?' The intention of those seven people was to kill John at night and then take the King's daughter away. Then those seven people went away, and John told the king's daughter let us escape from here and in our beds we should put on the pigs to sleep over them. Then they run away taking the thieves car again. Those seven thieves who kidnapped the king's daughter began chasing them. When they reached to those thieves, they began to ask people if they saw a beautiful daughter and a young man. They told them that they had gone away just then.

Then those seven people and seven thieves joined together and became fourteen and together began looking for John and the King's daughter. John and the King's daughter decided to speed up the car until they reached the harbor where they found a ship and quickly boarded it; and the ship sailed away; and they could not be caught again. When the thieves reached at the harbor, they found that the ship had already gone with John and the King's daughter.

It happened that when the king could not find her daughter in the room she was, he announced and proclaimed to all people that whoever saw his daughter would be rewarded greatly. In that ship there were some people who saw the king's daughter and decided to throw John in the sea so that they could easily take the king's daughter. John in the sea was swallowed by the hippo and then the hippo vomited out John on the dry land. When John woke up, he found himself hungry and began looking for food. He found a restaurant and asked for a job. The owner of the restaurant asked him which kind of job he liked to do. He asked whether John could cook or sell in the restaurant. John chose to cook and began eating and then working.

The king's daughter was taken to her place, to the king, by those people who drowned John in the sea. One day the king told those people, but each one, to prepare tea and bread and write names on each of them and the tea which would be better than others, the person who made it would be provided the king's daughter for a hand of marriage and would also be rewarded for a portion of the kingdom's inheritance. Therefore, all went to prepare tea. When they were ready, the king's daughter began to taste the tea. When she tasted the tea which John Best prepared, she saw that it was the best tea she had; and when looked what was the name of the person who prepared it, she saw that it was John's tea. She asked her father to call the person who has prepared that tea—John Best.

Those people who threw John in the sea went and called the person who employed John and took him to the king. Then the king asked them who had prepared that good tea. John's boss replied that it was his servant and he commanded to be brought in the king's presence. When John was brought there, his daughter said, 'father let those people who brought John be killed because this man saved my life, and without him I would have been dead by now.' Therefore, John was provided the King's daughter to marry her and also was provided a portion of the kingdom to inherit and both lived happily."

Our Observation, Interpretation and Intervention

Juliana wrote in her memory book that the above story teaches us not to harm other people, but should try to do good to every person we meet in our lives. There is a Swahili proverb which says, "*Tenda wema nenda zako, usingoje shukrani*," which means, "do good deeds to people and go away, do not wait for an appreciation". Or another proverb, "*Usimtendee neno baya jirani yako*," which means, "do not do bad things to your neighbor." Life is striving to do good things to all people, and if possible, to live in peace with all people. Paul writes in Romans 12:16–21,

> Live in harmony with each other. Don't be too proud to enjoy the company of ordinary people. And don't think you know it

all! Never pay back evil with more evil. Do things in such a way that everyone can see you are honorable. Do all that you can to live in peace with everyone. Dear friends, never take revenge. Leave that to the righteous anger of God. For the Scriptures say, "I will take revenge; I will pay them back," says the Lord. Instead, "If your enemies are hungry, feed them. If they are thirsty, give them something to drink. In doing this, you will heap burning coals of shame on their heads." Don't let evil conquer you, but conquer evil by doing good.

The story shows the real intention of Juliana. Juliana was a good girl who wanted to do what was right and good in society. The story shows how people in society struggle between good and evil. As the story shows, always all the people who try to do their best and what is right win the fight, but bad people eventually fail even if they seem to be succeeding at the beginning in life.

Juliana's story was very helpful to her since she knew that her difficult life would eventually end. She knew that even in the midst of difficulties people are called to act justly. Her favorite biblical story relating to this issue was the story of Job in the Bible. Bad things may happen in life and most people may seem to be against someone; however, the most important thing is to stand up for what is right to do and what is just and true to God and to ones conscience. Always good things prevail against the bad ones! Therefore, it is obvious that the story of Juliana had something to do with her life. Juliana's model was in that story where she wished to be and do. Juliana sought good relationship which would benefit her and not ruin her life. Despite the troubles of life Juliana learned to do good things in life and not evil things to neighbors.

Juliana was a disciplined girl. She respected her grandmother and relatives; moreover, she respected her teachers, counselors, volunteers, and other people in society where she came from. In general, she did well in her studies at school. Soon she finished her primary school education. She was very eager to go to secondary school if she passed the exams.

Juliana liked to draw pictures especially different kinds of flowers. To her, they were like an inspiration for her life. Moreover, she liked to play netball, cooking, singing, and reading books. She had a good circle of friends around her. In her own words she said, "When I don't meet with even one of my friends in a day, I feel weak and sick." Therefore, for Juliana, meeting with friends was one of the healing processes for her in whatever circumstances she passed through.

In our observation, Juliana's loss of parents seemed to be very hard for her even to talk about them. It took time to talk about issues of her parents' deaths. Fortunately, through different narrative means, we were able to find ways that allowed her to cope with her feelings and emotions of sadness and worry. For example, Juliana was a social person, she was cool and quiet; but when she was with her friends, she talked a lot. This being with people she loved was one of the ways she could do to cope with the life of grief, sadness and loneliness.

As time went on, Juliana learned to accept her condition of being an orphan. She did not feel shy of her condition and situation she was in; she accepted who she was. She had drawn what she called the symbol of her life, which was the heart and the sun showing love and life. Juliana decided to love her life and live the best life she could, understanding that life was so precious but delicate that required to be respected and taken care of. We observed that she had several drawings of flowers in her house. In Juliana's life, she dreamt of becoming a minister of education. But she also dreamt of being a successful and wealthy woman in future. Through hard work and many risks in life, Juliana understood that one day those dreams were going to be fulfilled in God's time.

The house of Juliana's grandmother was full of good pictures and drawings in the walls of the house, which Juliana had drawn herself. These drawings became a healing for Juliana since they empowered and strengthened her as she looked and meditated on them. She also used her memory book to draw pictures and images. For example, some of the images which were most important to her were pictures of the heart and the sun, which for her had many meanings to talk about as mentioned above. They symbolized the life of love.

Case Number 17: Giveni

Background

Case number seventeen concerned about Giveni. Giveni's story was very sensitive and emotional. His life was very difficult. Giveni was 16 years old by the year 2007. He was standard five at Nsalaga primary school. He was the last born of six children in his family, and was the only son. Giveni's parents died. His mother died in 2001 from tuberculosis infection. His father also died from tuberculosis in 2006. The family had a grave yard where all relatives were being buried. Their grandparents were also buried at this graveyard. Giveni lived on himself to the family's house. He was supported by his second born sister who involved herself in small petty businesses.

All other Giveni's sisters were scattered in various places in the region of Mbeya; therefore, he had very minor support from his relatives.

Giveni explained himself that when in standard four, he was very troublesome, naughty, and delinquent. For that reason, most of his relatives did not like him. In this stage of life at one occasion, when he was playing the hide and seek game with his friends, he suddenly had a thought in his mind that he should commit suicide. Then, he decided to take the rope from his jacket which he wore and entered the house and tied himself on the roof of the house attempying to kill himself. Fortunately, there was an old man close to their house. This neighbor heard him crying, he rushed inside the house to rescue him. The old man rescued him. And that was his escape from the danger of attempting to kill himself.

Giveni told the authors of this book about his story on what made him to come into that thought of suicide. According to him, it was after seeing that the torturing and suffering in his life was too much for him to bear. He explained that his relatives hated and segregated him especially his aunts who left him without food or any kind of care. Most of the time, Giveni ate his meal once a day. Moreover, when he was provided something to eat, his aunts began gossiping about him, which made him feel very bad about himself, and could not eat the food in peace.

Our Observation and Interpretation

Giveni lived in the house which was very poor health-wise. The place where he slept was also the place he cooked, washed the dishes, stored the utensils, and put the water to drink. Giveni's school progress was improving daily. He required much attention from his teachers and counselors for his psychological development, from his emotions and feelings about his life. According to his age, Giveni was not supposed to be Standard Five, but in secondary school. All these problems in his academic progress were caused by his family problems and the difficulties he was went through. All these family circumstances caused some mental and psychological problems to Giveni's life, such as low self-esteem.

Giveni was also a member of a scout club in his school. This was very helpful to him because it involved with discipline, physical exercises, and various games which were good for him to develop his character and personality. Giveni's life was very difficult. Most of his relatives abandoned him. His school's progress was not good and did not like school so much. This was caused by various reasons, particularly from his family or relatives. He did not have enough support from his family. His age also was by then bigger than that of his classmates; therefore, he felt shy in the class where he looked older than his classmates. To have his daily needs such as food was also very difficult for him. All these factors caused him to lag behind in his school development.

Therapeutic Intervention

Giveni required much support from *Amani* Orphanage Center. He also required support from counselors, relatives, and the community as a whole. His suicide attempt came as the result of his life situation which became unbearable for him. Intervention was required in order to help him cope with his life difficulties, the abandonment from his relatives, school problems, and psychosocial problems. Visiting and talking to him was one of the ways which helped him to be aware of what was going on. Moreover, narratives such as stories, proverbs, and otherwise Swahili sayings, became the means to help him cope with his life difficulties. We did all these through talking as friends and relatives who entered his life, but also being careful with the problem of transferences because this would ruin the intervention process. This kind of relationship helped Giveni to acquire a sense of his self-esteem and self-control. His personality had to be strengthened and empowered so that he came out of feelings which made him to be down and nothing. Hence, building positive relationship with Giveni was the basic ground for his healing process.

Giveni liked to draw pictures and through his own pictures we could help him to talk about several issues relating to his problems and how we could change the destructive dominating thoughts and stories into stories that empower and provided him a sense of self-esteem and self-control. In the long run Giveni learned that "*Hasira ni hasara*" as Swahili people said, which literally means, "anger is a loss." He learned that he should never act or respond in anger, which would ultimately bring disaster or chaos. He also learned from the biblical proverb which said, "A soft answer turns away wrath: but a harsh answer word stir up anger." (Proverbs 15:1)

Giveni then learned to cope with his problems especially when he felt down and liked committing suicide. He had self-control for what came out of his mind. He kept himself busy by playing social games with his friends, or used the memory book to go through and reading it or writing and drawing something in it, that was joyful, hopeful, and strengthening to him. At that moment Giveni seemed to be very responsible to his own life; he was the person who could take care of his life and do his things without depending too much from his relatives or neighbors. His progress was promising.

However, he required more connection to build a strong relationship with his friends and relatives.

Case Number 18: Devotha and Christina

Background

The eighteenth case concerned Devotha and Christina. Devotha was 14 years old by 2007. She was standard six at Mwanyanje primary school. The family, which Devotha and Christina belonged was originally from Makete district in Njombe region and their home language was Kinga. Devotha lived with her mother and her young sister Christina who was 12 years old by then. Christina was in standard four at the same school with her sister Devotha. Their father died when Devotha was in standard two in 2003. According to their family history, their father became sick from stomachache for only two days until he died. Devotha's mother worked in small businesses of selling bread, firewoods and other small things. However, most of the time she did not do anything because of her frequent and various illnesses. Devotha's mother was very free to talk to authors of this book about her sickness and her family successes and problems unlike others people who were visited. She was also open to tell her stories about her husband's death and other stories relating to the family.

Religiously, this family was Christian belonging to the Moravian church at Uyole in Mbeya. They were good Christian believers. Due to difficult circumstances they lived, they devoted life much to Christ's hope and his promises. Ultimately, they believed that God would look over their problems and help them. We can say that their difficult circumstances and problems drew them closer to God than was ever before. The family had various ways of remembering their father such as pictures. Devotha's mother also lost her last born daughter called Yustina. Yustina died while was still four months old. Devotha and Christina remembered their young sister with the picture they kept in the album of the family, which they were willing to share to authors of this book.

Our Observation and Interpretation

The context of the family where these two children and their mother lived was very difficult. First of all, they did not have a house of their own. They lived in the house they had rented, where they had to pay about Tanzanian shillings 5000 per month (which by then was equivalent to 5 US Dollars). According to the situation they had and lived, it was very difficult for them to meet that cost and other costs. The condition of the house itself was not that good. The house was dirty, muddy, and built by mud; during the rainy season, the water went inside the house. The place where they cooked, put utensils, and slept was not that clean. However, by God's grace, they survived and continued living. Clothing, food, and other needs were also difficult to find because of their economic situation. The family depended on support from various places such as friends, relatives, and the church.

Devotha and her young sister Christina accepted their situation of being poor and orphans with only a single parent. Their mother who also was often sick required much support from her children. In this case, according to their mother's story to the authors, the children worked hard in order to survive and live a descent life. They went for distance to look for firewood and worked hard in the farm in order to have some money to buy food and other necessary needs. They also obtained some crops from their small farms for their food at home without much depending on outside support. Devotha and Christina liked to go to school despite the difficulties they faced. They were students who tried to study hard as as they could, and became average students when it came to their academic performances. However, they required more support in order to become better students at school, such as obtaining more financial support from outside the school to enable them attend evening school tuitions. Their dreams of life after school were obvious to them. Devotha wanted to be a teacher after her studies in the college. Christina wanted to be a police, particularly a traffic police after acquiring her higher education.

In her story, Devotha explained that during childhood she was very naughty. One day she burned her nose purposely. She said that she grew up in a difficult situation where she did not have clothing, food and sometimes relatives had to provide them food and could eat just a single meal per day. Devotha's mother liked to talk to her children. She did not become tired of telling them about their lives then and for the future. She hoped and prayed for them to be good Christians who loved God and lived a good Christian life. She also wished for them to have good respect and relationship with all people if possible, especially neighbors. She has the dream for them that they would finally have good jobs after their studies in universities or colleges.

Therapeutic Intervention

Through her stories, and as we talked together, it was obvious that Devotha's mother regretted the life she and her husband went through in their youth, the life of carelessness and unfaithfulness. In that case, she did not want that kind of life to be imparted to her children. Devotha was very clear and open to talk about things she did not like such as gossiping, adultery, fornication, hatred, evil desires, deceitfulness, and other things relating to these bad things which even God did not like. Devotha was very sensitive to disabled people. It was clear in her drawings that she cared for people who were not able to do things like other people. In one of her pictures, she drew the person who broke a leg and underneath she wrote that people should help those who broke their legs. Moreover, she liked to draw flowers. Flowers were beautiful and attractive with their scent and colors. For Devotha flowers symbolized goodness and life. Devotha was also interested in stories and proverbs.

It should be taken into account that memory working through stories, pictures, and other things are very important for the healing process to the child. Remembering our lost friends and relatives through pictures and other things which belonged to them is a very important step and crucial process in the healing and coping from grief. Therefore, we walked together with the family of Mahenge to encourage them about some things they were doing for their family. We also encouraged them to talk about their relatives who died. Actually, in the African concept and philosophy, it is believed that all our people who died still have some kind of relationship or connection with people who are alive. This is to say that we have to honor the things they did for us; people die but the things they did and their influences are still with us who are live.

Through narratives, metaphors, stories, pictures, and plays Devotha and her sister Christina were able to cope with their life situations. Their mother, who was most of the time sick, was very good in stories, and especially biblical narratives. Devotha's mother accepted her situation and was free to talk about her health and that she was HIV positive. In that understanding, she was also able to talk to her children about life, the life that was disciplined and full of the fear of God. She cautioned them that they should not end up with the life she lived; rather, they should start living their lives and prepare their future life which would be a successful life, the life of faith and hope, the life of health and prosperity. She taught her children to be responsible for their own lives.

The biblical narratives were very helpful to them in particular. The stories of the Bible became a model for them. They took biblical promises very seriously. For example, there was a story of a poor widow who kept asking for the justice to be done, but the judge could not listen to her; however, since the widow kept on asking persistently, the judge decided to grant her what was her right at the end (Luke 18:1–8). This story helped these two children to stand up for their rights and keep asking (praying) to God what was the right for them as children of God. They believed that at the end their lives would eventually become successful and prosperous no matter what happened. They believed and hoped that they would have what they dreamt and asked for their lives. In cementing their hope, they memorized the verse which said, "Rejoice always, pray constantly, give thanks in all circumstances; for this is the will of God in Jesus Christ for you." (1 Thessalonians 5:17–18)

The family of Mahenge lived optimistically despite problems and difficulties they were in. Poverty and illnesses, especially the HIV positive status of Devotha's mother was challenging; however, they still kept on hoping and believing in the good things out of their belief in God who made them Christians. They ultimately hoped for life, not only of then and of now, the eternal one in the coming kingdom of God where God's children live happier for ever and ever.

Summary of Case Studies

The presentation of the eighteen case studies is complete. These case studies described and explored in detail the lives and theology of OVC in Mbeya. The life experiences of these children differed from one child to another, and their understanding of God in relation to their lives; however, they were all grouped together as OVC. It was a group of people who required special consideration from the Church and society as a whole. They faced many risks of life that was why they were vulnerable. The HIV and AIDS was the major problem in the area of research, although was difficult to point out from the case studies of children or parent/s who exactly were infected. That was because of some myths, ignorance and stigma which surrounded the pandemic. The children faced many psychosocial problems such as poverty and sicknesses; they also went through difficult times because of guilt, shame, fear, grief, and uncertainty in life. They required finding ways to live the life that was peaceful, happy, free, worthy, and whole.

The case studies above journeyed through the life stories of children (narratives). Children in the case studies explored their own experiences through stories, metaphors, proverbs, riddles, songs, and games (arts and plays). Exploring and communicating in narratives was the best way for them to find healing, peace and wholeness. In the pastoral counseling process, that communication through narratives conveyed healing and wholeness as they identified themselves with heroes of similar lives in counter stories from the Bible.

Children as human beings have stories to tell; they also have needs and problems just like any person on earth which they would like to talk about. They travel in the world experiencing and longing for better life of wholeness. It was obvious in the case studies that the children's life cycle was almost the same no matter how each child experienced life. The model of this life cycle is clearly explored in the next Chapter. It is the model which explains the life cycle of the child from what lies inside him or her and the struggles he or she passes through until when one finds a way to healing and wholeness.

Results from Focus Group Activities

After the above explored case studies of individual children, we had an opportunity to work together in groups with children. This subtopic forms the discussions of the focus group activities we had. Normally, this kind of interviews is conducted with a group of children who share some common base of experience. Hence, the discussions with a focus group helped to understand people in a naturalistic way and how they experience their daily lives.[20]

The focus group we worked with consisted of children who were orphans and vulnerable between the ages of 12 to 18. These included children we had in case studies. Children liked to work in groups. What children required was guidance and procedures of what they had to do. Children liked to communicate through narratives. It was the art of telling and listening to stories, proverbs, and sayings, but went further than that. Narratives also involved some arts such as plays, songs, and games. Children interacted in ways that were sometimes metaphoric, symbolic and imaginatively. In this case, we argue that the language which children use is through playing; and their words are seen through the toys they play with.

In the focus group activities, we were mainly facilitators of what children discussed. The facilitator requires being attentive to observe how children understand and experience life in a group so that the purpose of research is reached and met at the end. Different and various subjects are discussed to fulfill the objectives set. In our case, the group was interviewed through open-ended questions which allowed the group to talk freely and even go further than what was being asked. Children payed attention to whether they were provided enough space and freedom to express in ways that were easy to them. Sometimes, children expressed themselves through non-verbal expressions; however these had to be recorded and taken notes (process notes) to know what was going on.

20. Terre-Blanche, Durrheim, and Painter (eds.), *Research in Practice*, 304.

The focus group activities allowed for the free discussion in the planned group of people where specific themes or concepts were discussed and analyzed. In order to obtain the specific information, we required to follow the procedures and guidelines for focus group activities. The focus group was done at *Amani* Orphanage Center in a chosen classroom that fitted 15 to 20 children. Participants liked the sessions because they arouse shared feelings as the process went on. We conducted five (5) focus group activities of 45 minutes to 1 hour each week. The sessions were open for discussions, comments, questions, and observations.

Specific themes and topics were introduced to the group by the facilitators. Beginning from very general and easy topics to specific and difficult topics (deductive approach), the sessions were introduced and conducted. The detailed notes were taken from the discussions that went on. Moreover, the observations were noticed for the better analysis and interpretation. Both the discussions and the observations provided were reflected at the end of the session to make sure that the conclusion reached was right for the group and nothing was left out.

The purpose of focus group discussions was to verify the themes and topics which emerged during the survey which was conducted in the participants' families in the case studies as elaborated above. The analysis and interpretation of focus group discussions based on activities which were narratively focused. These narrative activities were such as the following: Bible stories, parables, dramas, African stories, proverbs, sayings, games, arts, plays, symbols and images. Below we explore the themes which were discussed using these different activities to make sure that the message was conveyed.

Different Themes Discussed

Psychosocial Needs, Problems and Support

The first theme discussed concerned the psychosocial needs, problems and supports. The Swahili saying so goes, *"Mtaka cha uvunguni sharti ainame"* (if one wants something which is underneath, he or she should bend down in order to take it). This Swahili proverb implies that to live life is to work hard; it is a struggle in the midst of challenges and problems, such as the existing poverty in society. Therefore, the focus group discussions discovered that poverty was one of the main factors which made OVC live a devastating life with their caregivers. Poverty was one of the big factors which accelerated the spread of HIV in Tanzania. Some of the issues discussed which children liked to talk about were such as the need to study, health, food, and clothing. These needs and problems came as the result of economic difficulties in society. The focus group activities concentrated on discussing issues that troubled them as children. Children recognized and accepted their needs and problems and were willing to move ahead with life, to struggle and work hard and find ways of coping with their problems.

One of the biblical proverbs used by these children who struggled with poverty says, "He who oppresses a poor man insults his Maker, he who is kind to the needy honors him." (Proverbs 14:31 cf. 17:5) The proverb calls for the Church and society to be kind to all people who are in need, such as orphans. We should not despise the poor people. Unfortunately, society always despises poor people and are looked as untrustworthy in society as one of the Swahili proverbs says, "*Maskini haokoti, akiokota huambiwa kaiba,*" which means, "a poor person does not pick something up, if he or she picks up, he or she is told she or she stole it." The poor person is always despised by people especially the rich people; they would not even dare even to ask him or her anything as the Swahili proverb says, "*Maskini haulizwi*" (a poor person is not asked). Hence, the Christian teaching is clear that Christians should honor and take care of poor people around them.

One of the ways to struggle and fight in order to cope with life and find peace in children's life, especially during the interview sessions, was to use dramas and sing songs that empowered, revived, encouraged, and steered their emotions to act for what was right and good for their lives physically and spiritually. To them, these narratives were like a request or prayer and thanksgiving to people and God. Here are some of the verses of the poem which they used to sing during the sessions:

1. *Kituo hiki Amani, kimetutoa ukiwa*
   (This Amani Orphanage Center, has taken our sorrows)
   Kimetupa na amani, tumebaki tunatawa
   (It has provided us peace; we have remained calm)
   Moyoni tuna amani, kituo hiki ni dawa
   (We have in our hearts, this Center is a medicine)
   Bwana Mungu awalinde, na tena awabariki.
   (May God protect you, and bless you)

2. *Mazingira ni magumu, yatima twaongezeka*
   (The context is tough, orphans increase)
   Maisha kweli magumu, kwa mawazo tumezeeka
   (Life is real hard, in thinking we become old)
   Twaombea wahudumu, awabariki Rabuka
   (We pray for the servants, May God bless you)

>   *Dumuni kwenye maombi, hakika hali ni mbaya.*
>   (Stay in prayers, the situation is real worse)
>
> 3. *Maisha haya magumu, tunaishi kwa lazima*
>   (This life is hard, we live by force)
>   *Tunaikosa elimu, na mioyo inauma*
>   (We miss education, and our hearts are hurt)
>   *Kweli hii ni hukumu, tuoneeni huruma*
>   (This is real a condemnation, have mercy on us)
>   *Tuko mbele zako Baba, twaomba tuhurumie.*
>   (We are before you Father, have mercy on us)
>
> 4. *Ni huruma zake Bwana, kwamba hatuangamii*
>   (It is God's mercy, that we do not perish)
>   *Ndiye Bwana wa mabwana, na sisi tunamwamini*
>   (The Lord is Lord of lords, and we believe in the Lord)
>   *Sisi kwake ni watwana, katutoa utumwani*
>   (To the Lord we are slaves, the d Lor delivered us from slavery)
>   *Wageni lete habari, sisi tuko mbele zenu.*
>   (Guests bring good news, we stand before you).

Another poem which followed talked about the life of orphans. The life of these children became like bats without no place to stay. They always lived as refugees, however by the help of churches they found a place to stay and not only stay but also had found peace, hope, encouragement, and joy in God. This poem went like this:

> 1. *Tuliishi kama popo, Makazi tuliyakosa,*
>   (We lived like bates, missing places to stay)
>   *Huzuni ilikuwepo, Malezi tuliyakosa,*
>   (The sorrow was there, we missed to be reared)
>   *Kituo hiki kuwepo, Jamani kimetakasa,*
>   (This Center to be here, has been a cleansing)
>   *Twamshukuru Rabuka, Kituo kukiendesha.*
>   (We thank God, to take care of the Center)
>
> 2. *Hakika twafarijika, Tufikapo kituoni,*
>   (We are truly consoled, when are at the Center)
>   *Wazazi walitutoka, Tumepata kanisani,*
>   (Our parents left us, we have found others from church)
>   *Kutuona wanafika, Wanatupa tumaini,*
>   (They come to visit us, and give us hope)

Twamshukuru Rabuka, Kituo kukiendesha.
(We thank God, for taking care of the center)

The narratives also helped children to gain different skills on how to communicate and talk to each other on various issues of life. Narratives helped children to live in the community and stay together as they usually say in Swahili, "*Umoja ni nguvu, bali utengano in udhaifu*," which means, "unity is strength, but disunity is weakness." This Swahili proverb was very much used by the late President Mwalimu Julius K. Nyerere when he tried to establish the politics of *Ujamaa* (socialism) in Tanzania. Staying together was not enough, but working together and helping each other were most important things. The focus of *Amani* Orphanage Center was to help children find skills that help them to respect each other; and the self-esteem of every individual was respected despite the differences they had from one child to another. Through games and plays and other activities, they were able to work together and understand each other much better. They learned from the group that every one was vulnerable and weak, and that every individual was strong and important. When these were shared together and were willing to help and support each other; then, they became stronger. This Swahili proverb called them to unity and solidarity, it said, "*Kuwa watoto wa baba mmoja ni kusaidiana*," which means, "to be of the same father is to help one another." The biblical proverb which was parallel or portrayed the same message went like this, "*Ajitengaye na wenzake, hutafuta matakwa yake mwenyewe; Hushindana na kila shauri jema*" (Proverbs 18:1), which means, "He who is estranged seeks pretexts to break out against all sound judgment." Therefore, children in the focus group activities were able to use their daily words and sayings for communication to understand and apply them to deal with issues in their daily lives. Solidarity and respect for each other, support, and unity among themselves helped them to cope with difficulties of life such as sorrow, fear, low self-esteem, loneliness, shame, and guilt in great deal.

The Child's Experience of Adversity

Orphans and vulnerable children experience many problems apart from those just mentioned and discussed above. Because of poor non-governmental and governmental systems, or lack of resources and knowledge, ignorance, stigma, inequality, biasness, segregation, rejection and many other reasons, made children to undergo many ill-experiences. These experiences which emerged in the focus group activities should not be ignored; they should be heard by the Church and society. These experiences were part of who they were. Hence, they indicated the need for a way of helping OVC on how to cope with those situations.

At the focus group activities, children were able to talk why they liked to run in streets to beg for money or work in silly jobs or very hard jobs for their age (i.e., child labor). This was because of the reality of life which they lived under their caregivers; or it was because there was no one at all to take care of them in regard to their daily needs. Society labeled those children as "street children." Other experiences which children talked about in the focus groups were the abuse, whether physical, sexual or verbal abuse. They were abused in different ways. In the conversations during focus group activities, it was very difficult for them to talk; however, through figures of speech or sayings, and proverbs they were able to talk more openly and freely. They learned how to use some words which we could call in Swahili *Nahau,* which were sayings built by pictures or symbols used with regular words but delivered alternative meanings that were not normal. For example, someone could have sharp and harsh words that would hurt the person despite the truth presented. Those people who did not know how to speak wisely and only spoke to hurt, we would say to them that they had a sword-like tongue in Swahili "*wana ulimi wa upanga,*" or "*wana maneno ya kukata maini,*" which means, "they have the words that make the stomach ache." The conversations about all those abuses were a good stage for them to heal their wounds. Furthermore, children were helped by pastoral counselors to deal with some deep issues relating to their lives, especially those who were abused. They were helped to gain respect and self-esteem and move on with life instead of despairing and acting out.

Some other experiences which OVC were able to talk about included the behavior of stealing, acting out, delinquency, violence, and truancy from school.[21] These behaviors and experiences were results of society's and church's ignorance and denial of these children. These behaviors were an alert to people that "we are here, don't ignore us, we are people like anybody else. We have the needs and have to be heard and supported. For example, on truancy," children could speak openly that the reason for that behavior was because they did not have exercise books, or did not obtain any food or breakfast to eat in the morning so could not stay at school.

---

21. Cf. Dyregrov, *Grief in Children*.

Spiritual Problems and Needs

Like grown up people, children can experience God in their lives too. Children have to experience their lives in an open and free space. They must also be allowed to experience their own spirituality. The center of spirituality is love, as we also said about the centrality of our human sexuality. Love is the basic doctrine in the Christian life. The Bible text points out clearly that in love there is no fear (I John 4:18); and also that love is the fulfillment of the law (Romans 13:8). Love always covers up the multitudes of sins and mistakes people commit every time. The Bible text warns people not to mistreat and disregard children because theirs is the kingdom of God (Matthew 18:1-6). We should love children and treat them as people and will also be able to imitate what the grown people do to them.

Unfortunately, orphans and vulnerable children experience rejection, fear, shame and guilt most of the time. The Church and society should be aware of this and if possible change for the better. Therefore, children require spiritual help and support to cope with feelings they go through. One way of helping and supporting children is through narratives which are theologically interpreted and applied to bring purpose and meaning in their lives. Bible study, Bible dramas, hymns, songs, and Christian choruses were used in focus group activities for empowering, encouraging, and reviving their souls to a sense which God wanted them to be. The *Amani* Orphanage Center composed songs, and hymns that touched their spiritual life, and hopefully changed them from inside out. The Bible study was also chosen; different texts were discussed for the goal of giving children their intimate and spiritual needs. When children sang, they usually liked it because they felt happier and found a real peace in singing and studying the Bible and acting it in the form of drama to make it more practical.

Here was one of the songs they usually liked to sing in the focus group activity and sometimes individually. This song was about orphans. They portrayed the kind of life they lived. Therefore, through this song, they prayed and cried for help and support from society:

Watoto Yatima Jamani

1. *Wote: Watoto yatima jamani kweli wanapata shida maisha wanayoishi sasa kweli yanasikitisha x2*
   (ALL: Orphans really have problems, they live a very terrible life x 2)
   Solo: Ona kule mitaani majararani nako nenda utawaona jamani kweli wanasikitisha x2

(SOLO: See there at the dumps, go there you will see them; it is truly sorrowful x 2)

Chorus:

WOTE: *Ni nani awasaidie hao watoto yatima bila ya wewe baba, mama kweli muwasaidie x2.*

(CHORUS: Who should help those orphans if not you father and mother, please help them x 2)

2. WOTE: *Bwana Mungu nae anapenda watu wanojitolea mali zao hata kwa chakula chao watoto yatima x2*

(ALL: *The Lord God likes those who voluntarily offer their wealth, even the food for orphans x 2*)

SOLO: *Hata hapa duniani baraka mtazipata jaribu kusaidia hao watoto yatima x2*

(Solo: You will receive blessings just here on earth, try to help those orphans x 2)

Chorus:

WOTE: *Ni nani awasaidie hao watoto yatima bila ya wewe baba, mama kweli muwasaidie x2.*

(CHORUS: Who should help those orphans if not you father and mother, please help them x 2)

Furthermore, the following poem (*ngonjera*) talked about the cry of children to the Church. It talked about how they were rejected and lost the hope, wandered in the streets, and did not have a place to stay. They asked believers to hear their cry and be merciful on them and trusted in God to make their work and support to be more effective. Part of the poem went like this:

1. *Yatima wengi jamani, wakosa matumaini*
   (Orphans are many, and have no hope)

   Waacha makanisani, mwakimbilia porini
   (They run away from churches, they run to bushes)

   Wazazi huko porini, wataishi kwa amani.
   (Parents, to these bushes, will they live peacefully)

   Kilio chetu sikia, kifike kwenu wapendwa.
   (Listen to our cry, to reach to you beloved)

2. *Yatima waangaika, sababu yake dunia*
   (Orphans are wandering, because of the world)

   Gonjwa lililoanguka, hapa kwetu Tanzania
   (The dangerous disease that has fallen, here in Tanzania)

Wazazi wameanguka, watuacha tunalia.
(Parents have fallen, they have left us crying)
Kilio chetu sikia, kifike kwenu wapendwa.
(Listen to our cry, it should reach you beloved)

3. *Nyumbani nako kwa moto, kanisani nako joto*
   (The home is also hot, the church is also hot)
   Mitaani nako moto, na shuleni ni viboko
   (In the streets there is heat, at school there are stripes)
   Ndugu yangu ona moto, utakipata cha moto.
   (My friend look at the fire, you will taste fire)
   Kilio chetu sikia, kifike kwenu wapendwa.
   (Hear our cry, it should reach you beloved)

4. *Ndugu zetu waumini, twaomba msikie*
   (Our beloved faithful, we ask you to listen)
   Moyoni mkiamini, haya basi mtulie
   (Believe in your hearts, and calm down)
   Mungu mumtumaini, na kwake tukimbilie.
   (Trust in God, and to whom we should run)
   Kilio chetu sikia, kifike kwenu wapendwa.
   (Hear our cry, it should reach you beloved)

5. *Nadhani mumetupata, wazazi wetu hakika*
   (I hope you have got us, our true parents)
   Popote mtawapata, watoto hao hakika
   (You will have them everywhere, the children indeed)
   Wahurumie okota, waishi kwake Rabuka.
   (Have mercy find for them, to live under God)
   Kilio chetu sikia, kifike kwenu wapendwa.
   (Hear our cry, should reach you beloved)

Human Sexuality

Children also struggled with the issue of sexuality. They always curious to understand who they were and why they were in the way they were, or the way they did. Sexuality was one of the subjects which created misunderstandings and divisions among people. The Church and society were quite or ignorant about it as we discussed in Chapter three above. In order to help OVC in our area we had to open a sacred space to talk about it and remove all the wrong information, the myths, taboos, and misunderstandings, they had about sexuality. This was done in order to help the OVC to cope with their situation and find ways to resilience for their wellbeing and wholeness. Through metaphoric narratives such as proverbs and other sayings, children were able to talk about issues of sexuality in ways that were familiar and comfortable. Through metaphors and stories told in group activities, children were able to learn different skills on how to be safe about their sexuality. They learned how to respond to issues that could entice them to unsafe sex. Using these African sayings and stories they learned to respect themselves and others, and to take control of their sexual life. For example, we discussed the temptation of doing sex carelessly. One of the Swahili proverbs from which children took a hint said, "*Uzuri wa mkakasi, ndani kipande cha mti,*" which means, "the sweetness of a pineapple, there is a peace of log inside it." That was to say that something could be seen as good or sweet, but at the end of it was a big loss. It also meant that "we should judge things deeply and not just outwardly." From the lessons of these narratives children could learn to say no to sex before the proper time. They were also able to talk and discuss issues of sex without shame. They also learned that "*Usipoziba ufa, utajenga ukuta,*" which means, "if you do not fill up the cracks, you will end up building the entire wall." That is to say, prevention is better than cure. Throuhg the group conversations, children were also able to control their emotions and feelings through keeping themselves busy with studying, playing, and helping their caregivers with house works.

The HIV and AIDS

The focus group also concentrated on discussing and debating about the HIV and AIDS. Several questions were posed for opening up the discussion. The leading proverb in this activity went in Swahili thus, "*Mfichaficha maradhi kilio kitamuumbua*" (The one who hides his or her sicknesses death will embarrass him or her). Through proverbs children talked about the meanings behind proverbs which usually had hidden and deeper meanings. Proverbs and sayings teach and warn people about being careful with life. The proverb above says that the one who hides his or her sickness, the death reveals him or her. The proverb calls for openness to our problems and weaknesses to others who can possibly help us. At the group activity, children discussed and talked how people could hide their weaknesses and problems which hurt them more. Living examples were shared in the group of some children who experienced similar problems.

As we have discussed, the HIV and AIDS have been subjects which people are not free to talk about in our society. The HIV and AIDS relate to sin, promiscuity, and condemnation. Therefore, many people who have the problem of the HIV and AIDS are blamed and condemned as sinners. Obviously, these people will hardly be able to open up for their sickness and problems. Guilt and shame will always be upon their faces. And people who discover that they are infected by the HIV will not be willing to go for testing because of stigma which surrounds people infected by HIV virus.

At the end of the focus group activity children were more open to talk about issues which troubled them because they learned to be open and not secretive. They learned that one is hurted greatly when he or she hides his or her true feelings. As the Swahili people would say, "*Msema kweli ni mpenzi wa Mungu*," which means, "the one who speaks the truth is the friend of God." Children learned that God healed people who were truthful and open to their issues.

Children learned that life was something to be kept and respected. Death was their enemy and very secretive to them; it had to be avoided as much as possible. They contemplated upon the riddle of Swahili peple. The Swahili people had a riddle in regard to the secret of death which said, "*Baba yangu amesoma mpaka chuo kikuu lakini hajui 'A' inakogeukia*," which means, "my father has learned to a level of university, but he does not know where 'A' is supposed to turn when writing it." Also there was another riddle which children liked to use when talking about issues of death; it went like this, "*Hamwogopi mtu yeyote—kifo*," which means that he or she does not fear anyone, and that is—death." Death has no respect of anyone, whether young or old, rich or poor, white or black, female or male, all are destined to dying; and no one knows the time of his or her death. As long as we have life, let us keep it with all dignity and strength, because life is too precious to loose it. Some of the symbols and images which children liked to use in their memory books or in the discussion about life during focus group activity sessions were water, plants, and the sun.

Witchcraft and Curses

In Swahili we have a proverb which says, "*Aliyekuloga wewe ni jamaa wa familia yako*," which means, "the one who has bewitched you is a member of your family." The issues of witchcraft and curses were seen in most of children's cases. In African customs and tradition these two things were very common. In every corner of Tanzania, especially in different tribes of Bantu people, one heard stories related to issues of witchcraft and curses as part and parcel of the African people. Therefore, it was difficult or almost impossible to escape talking about these things. People's minds were filled by the notion of the other world which was full of evil and bad things. The evil things became part and parcel of people's lives.

Before going further discussing the concept of witchcraft, let us survey the different translations or meanings of such a term as used in relation to witchcraft practices. These translations are such as superstition, fortune-telling, sorcery, and wizardry; other words which may be used in relation to witchcraft are demons, evil powers, satanic powers, spells, curses, and magic. The witches (*wachawi*) are different people from witch doctors (*waganga*). The witchdoctors are considered as good doctors whom their intentions are good towards people; but witches or sorcerers are bad people who intend to do evil in society or toward an individual purposely or without any purpose. In that case, many people in Tanzania live under fear because of witches and sorcerers, that they may curse or do any evil toward them. According to African culture many people believe that in every case of evil thing in society or towards an individual there must be a reason for that. Whether it is sickness, deformity, death, drought, calamities, misfortunes or anything bad or evil, there must be a reason for that. Usually people say "*amelogwa*" that means, "the person has been bewitched by a witch." And people find out who or what caused the problem and why. This is where witch doctors try to use their knowledge to solve the problem.

The fear of witches and their activities is not limited to non-Christians; even some Christians live under this fear of witches. Healey and Sybertz point out that, "Belief in witchcraft is greater than belief in Christianity. To be bewitched is worse than anything else. It seems that, if pastoral workers could lead people to fear sin as much as they fear witches, evangelization would be much easier and more successful. Among local Christians in East Africa the influence of witchcraft is often greater than the influence of Christian values. . . ."[22]

As we saw from children's cases above, some Christian's children live under the fear of curses and witchcraft. In the African culture we do not underestimate the power of witchcraft and the fear involved with it. The fear of witchcraft causes many illnesses towards children and their families; this may be mental or physical illnesses. As Christians and pastoral counselors, we should recognize the power of witchcraft because the Bible also clearly speaks about it (cf. Deuteronomy 18:10–11; Micah 5:12; Isaiah 47:9, 12; Mark 5:1–8; Acts 8:9–24). However, the Bible clearly condemns practices of witchcraft as evil (see Leviticus 19:26 and 2 Kings 21:6).

---

22. Healey and Sybertz, *Towards an African Narrative Theology*, 293.

Pastoral counselors who work with children have to apply biblical narratives to convey the message that will be a healing and a way to wholeness. The fear of evil and bad things, especially from witches, should to be dealt with by applying biblical narratives that show the greatness and powerfulness of Christ the King, the one who is all powerful, the omnipotent one (1 John 4:4). The powers of demons and witches cannot overpower Jesus Christ and his followers. Christ has provided his people the authority over the power of Satan and his demons. Therefore, Christ's followers should not live under the fear of witches and their demons. No matter how strange or terrible the things they can do, they are not to be trusted; only God is the one to be trusted. God is in the charge of our lives, not witches. The pastoral counselor is there to help the child to move away from the dominating story of worry and fear and turn the story to an alternative story that is uplifting, empowering, and hopeful. The Bible has many such stories that can be used to remove the fear of witches, sorcerers, and demons, and gain the hope and trust in God (for instance the story in Acts 8:9–24).

Reflections and General Assessments

Through this study one learns and experiences several things. The case studies and the themes and concepts from children were great lesson. One can find great pleasure working with children despite the difficulties and challenges he or she can face. Children are great gifts from God. They are people just like other grown up people. They must be respected, honored, listened to, and provided space to do things they like. Through children, we learned many things such as trust, openness, transparency, and friendship. We also observed and learned that in order to understand children well we have to go down to their own language and understanding. In most of the time, children's language is through plays. It is through plays children are able to share their stories more safely, freely and openly. Play is children's language. Their feelings can be expressed through plays; in that way, they gain some control over the situation that frightens or threatens and traumatizes. The whole purpose of this intervention is to build a trusting relationship between the child and the counselor. This positive relationship is the basis for health growth, which brings about healing and wholeness in the child.

Through this study it has been obvious that this kind of research, especially with vulnerable children, is not only sensitive and difficult, but also very challenging. One has to consider very well the ethical issues because of delicate matters. The context of this study with children had some limitations. The context of this research with children in the research was very different from the context of other developed countries. When it came to using some of play methods, we used things that were available in the Tanzanian context and which were cheaper and easy to obtain. The materials we used were such as the plain sand ground instead of sand box; we also used clays, sticks, stones, seeds instead of special made toys. Another challenge faced in this study with children we chose as a sample of 12 to 17 years was that they had different interests. The child of 17 years did not like to play much with toys like the child of 12 years old. They all liked to play but with different games. For example the child of 17 liked to play games such as football, table tennis, and drawing. But, the child of 12 was more interested in games such as painting, drawing, and telling and listening to stories.

From the case studies and the themes which were explored, the major common theme or issue which came up as a dominating factor was grief. Grief came as a result of the loss of their loved ones, i.e., the parent/s. Grief made children to be sad, anxious, and worry about their future life. The loss of their parent/s made them to be sad and worry because of the uncertainty of their lives.[23] They did not know exactly how much they were affected by the HIV and AIDS or by any other problems. The poverty in their homes and families was another fear of not knowing what will be their destiny. These problems and difficulties which came as a result of grief affected children's self-esteem. Children ended up feeling ashamed, guilty, and fearful. Another good intervention with children under grief was through singing. Songs or music was such a powerful tool for grievous children who were sad and lonely. For example one of the songs they liked to sing was as the following:

1. *Maisha Ee, maisha mazuri*
   (Life Oh, life is good)
   Tunatamani sisi maisha Ee
   (We desire good life Oh)
   Lakini tutaishije Eh bila msaada wenu x2
   (But how can we survive, without your keen help)

2. *Kudeka Eh Kudeka kuzuri*
   (To be loved, it is good to be loved)
   Tunatamani sis kudeka Eeh
   (We desire to be loved oh)
   Lakini tutadekaje Eeh bila msaada wenu x2
   (But how can we be loved without your help?)

---

23. Cf. Boss, "The Trauma and Complicated Grief"; Price, "Walking through the Dackness"; Jones, "A Theology of Hope."

3. *Elimu Eeh Elimu ni nzuri*
   (Education, Oh education is so good)
   Tunatamani sisi elimu eeh
   (We desire oh, we desire to have education)
   Lakini tutasomaje Eeh bila msaada wenu x2
   (But oh how can we be educated without your help?)
   Kibwagizo
   (Chorus):
   Kina baba, tusaidieee, tusaidieee
   (You fathers, help us, help us)
   Kina mama tusaidieee, tusaidieee
   (You mothers, help us, help us)
   Kuishi maisha haya hatukupenda
   (We did not choose, to live this kind of life)
   Tusaidies, tusaidiee
   (Help us, help us)
   Kusoma bila msaada wenu hatuwezi
   (We are not able to study without your help.

As pointed out above, the basis of a good therapeutic intervention with children is building up a trusting and positive relationship. Grief can be a problem to the child if we think that children are the problem. Grief in the child must be handled carefully with good procedures so that the process of healing does not hurt or traumatize him or her. Trusting relationship is a way out to help the child find peace, self-esteem, and love. Trusting relationship can be found through good communication with the child. This good communication can be done through a play, which is the child's language. As pastoral counselors we must be with the child to listen, understand and care for what he or she tries to convey. It is not the matter of manipulating the child, but building a healing relationship that helps the child to communicate more freely and safely. The technique of play comes up in a variety of things which we must be attentive to observe, feel and listen to. A good relationship which we as counselors have to facilitate to the child is the relationship with self, with others, with the environment, and with God. Therefore, we must always remember that the key to healing and wholeness is not in the techniques we use in the counseling process; rather, it is in the relationship. The important thing is to be with the child, to show that we hear, understand, and care for the child.[24]

24. Sweeney, *Counseling Children*.

The focus group schedule was very helpful for children because it provided them power to talk about issues together; it was a session that enabled the sharing together by everyone in the group. This kind of intervention helped them to recognize that the problems shared were more easily solved. From the group they were able to learn different skills of coping up from one another. They also increased the sense of self-esteem, and coping mechanism. The conversation was easier because of the intervention or approach used which was by narratives such as metaphors, stories, songs, plays, proverbs, riddles and others. Narratives were very important in working with children whether they were in groups or in individual base. Narratives gave them an opportunity of not only sharing the pain together, but also gaving them freedom of expression and open space that was not threatening or scaring to children.

Conclusion

Generally, this chapter dealt with research results, analysis, and interpretation and discussion of the collected data. Through narratives, we were able to collect detailed stories of children, their background and the challenges they faced in their lives. Children were open and collaborative to tell their stories from which we were able to converse different issues relating to their problems and other challenges of life. Different opportunities were encouraged for children to feel at ease to talk about their issues more freely. The discussion or conversation was sometimes done one by one, and sometimes with family members, and also with all children in the same group of age and gender. Through narratives (stories) and metaphors children were able to know who they were accepting who they were and where they came from. They were also able to discover (map) their problems and be able to talk about their problems in ways that were not threatening or very difficult for them. In such a way, children were able to discuss and communicate with themselves and with people who took care of them (i.e., caregivers, teachers, counselors, pastors, etc.). This openness and freedom of sharing their stories became itself a healing process for them to cope with their difficult and challenging situation. Children found ways of understanding alternative stories, the stories of hope and future, the stories which empowered and encouraged them to remain at peace, self-esteem, and self-control for their whole life. Therefore, narrative, through stories and metaphors, became one of the ways for OVC to demonstrate their resilience in the process of healing and wholeness.

What challenge do we face from the theologies of orphans and vulnerable children in the cases and focus group discussions with children discussed in this chapter? We can summarize the challenge to us, as a Church, of theological reflections done by children in their narratives by the words of Grobbelaar thus: "CT [Child Theology] calls us to revisit our understanding of Scripture, our dogmatic truths, our Church history, and our faith and Church practices by placing the child in the midst of all of our theological reflections. A key question in this regard is: How do children influence what we are seeing and hearing?"[25] Therefore, "A church that starts to live as a story God is telling or people who allow God to 'tell their stories' are on a journey full of possibilities. Narrative [in] children's ministry means allowing children to live inside the stories that God is telling, to hear and see and copy and borrow from others' stories and to become storytellers in their own right."[26]

25. Grobbelaar, *Child Theology*, 11.
26. Coetsee & Grobbelaar, "The Church Where Children are Welcome," 813.

CHAPTER 6

Towards an Integrative Model for Pastoral Counseling to Ovc

Introduction

NARRATIVE APPROACH IN PASTORAL counseling is an applicable model for working with OVC in Tanzania as it has been pointed out in the previous chapters. However, when we talk about narrative, it comprises of several aspects which relate to each other. Narrative is a term which is broad and has been used by different scholars in various fields of study. Therefore, in this chapter, we want to suggest a new model which can make the narrative more integrative in its approach especially in the context of practical theology, and pastoral counseling in particular. This model came out of results of field research with children in Mbeya region Tanzania as discussed in the previous chapters.

Narratives

In the previous discussions, it was found that when talking about narratives with children there was a need to consider some other approaches or techniques that would be helpful in working with children in pastoral counseling. These approaches or techniques were such as metaphor, play, art, family systems, and analytical theories. The most important thing was to look for an approach that would be more integrative, i.e., to use other approaches or methods that would facilitate holistic growth of the person. These methods were such as family systems, psychoanalytic, and play and art therapy. It is our view that an integrative approach can be used for more holistic growth of the person instead of having a single or a unique type of approach which misses the richness of other ideas or approaches. Therefore, in the following subtitles, we discuss narrative approach with other approaches which can be integrated or applied with it to make the approach more effective and broad in its application.

Narratives and Play Therapy

Narratives can very well suite with play theories as we saw in chapter three where we discussed about play therapy and its theories in relation to narrative theories. For example, we discovered that narratives as stories could not be more effective if we did not employ play theories in the approach, where the play theories assumed that the human being was a social being and play was a natural phenomenon for all human beings. In regard to this, Axline says that "play is the child's natural medium of self-expression."[1] Moreover, Klein emphasizes the power of playing for children indicating that, "play is the child's most important medium of expression."[2] She continues to point out that, "by means of play analysis we gain access to the child's most deeply repressed experiences and fixations and are thus able to exert a radical influence on its development."[3] Therefore, listening to their language and communication opens ways of understanding and healing. One significant way of reaching that end for children is through the narrative process, where even words themselves cannot express the depths of our inner being and its complexity.

From the above understanding of play theory, we can generalize that play comes in a variety of forms. Narrative is a very general term which also refers to stories told through metaphors, games, arts, rituals, images and symbols, drawings and paintings; it even goes beyond what is physical or seen with naked eyes. Play is a kind of media which helps the person to communicate with the universe and its environment. Play is part of what we are. Our body mechanisms are always in activity and play. Playing is a natural reaction we have been created with. Therefore, narratives and plays can be integrated when we work with children, especially as we try to help them to cope with life's problems and situations.

In order for the person to find peace, healing and wholeness one has to be conscious of what happens around him or her. The most important thing is to pay attention to the happenings of life; this is called lives events. Events happen in life no matter whether we like or not. Events are

1. Axline, *Play Therapy*, 8.
2. Ibid., 30.
3. Ibid., 38.

part of who we are as human beings. Human beings must also recognize that we are vulnerable. We live in the world with ups and downs, with some strengths and weaknesses. When we pay attention to these events we provide the chance to our unconscious mind to be conscious with what is going on around us and in us. However, we should not stop there in observing the events of our lives; what is required is how we do with what happens to our lives. Playing and thinking with the happenings in our lives is what is called 'fantasizing'.[4] Fantasizing is a process of playing with these events in our minds. The *Dictionary of Pastoral Care and Counseling* defines fantasizing as "the creative process of mental imagery. Flowing as a visual stream of images, metaphors, symbols, and dramatic sequences, fantasy forms a major part of the internal world of experiencing."[5] Fantasy produces creativity in someone's mind. The mind is filled with symbols, dreams, and images in which, we have to fantasize with them. This process helps the mind to bring into consciousness what is unconscious or subconscious. Therefore, play becomes a means of obtaining the events to the surface through fantasizing. People play with symbols, images, pictures, dreams, and other things that help the person to become aware of what is going on in life. Fantasy helps the person to move forward into a meaningful life that is more of explorative and purposeful. However, what does the fantasy come into a play or in consciousness? It is through narratives by guiding, provoking and engaged conversation. Conversations through stories and playing help the person to move forward with understanding and experiencing the life in ways that are meaningful.

In working with OVC at Nsalaga, in Mbeya, it was found that some of the children were very good at playing with things such as playing games and drawings; however, it was very difficult for them in talking their issues verbally. Therefore, in order to understand such children one had to follow what they liked doing and in that way playing with them and through their games or play one found a way of communicating with them. The story in conversation can be much easy if one finds a way of integrating narratives through stories in the play they engaged in. This was true because most children were able to draw pictures, play different games, and other activities, which in themselves became part of their healing process.

In order for someone to find peace, healing, and wholeness, he or she required to understand how life went. First of all, it was to be aware of the events that were going on in someone's life. Second, one required to fantasize about the images, or symbols that he or she experienced in his or

---

4. Jung, *Memories, Dreams and Reflections*.
5. Hunter (ed.), *Dictionary of Pastoral Care*, 429.

her life events. The third stage was through play which was like a media for the fantasy to take place. It mediated the events and what was going on inside the person's mind. When the process goes well with good guidance, then play provides a way to the next level of being able to talk. Play cannot or becomes very difficult to understand without talking about them or without an engaged conversation. When people talk about their issues openly, it heals their feelings, emotions and actions. The things which were repressed down are allowed to come out in the surface and become easy to deal with them. This was the situation found to OVC involved in this study, that most of the time had all these feelings and emotions (i.e., anger, resentment, delinquent, sadness, truancy, fear, etc.), which were very difficult to be talked about. It was therefore hoped that through this proper process children would be able to come to their self-realization.

Healing or wholeness is a process that requires time. We have seen that events in life happen for a reason; therefore, one has to rethink of why and what goes on in life, the process that we have called fantasizing the events. Narratives become meaningful if one understands the potential of person's life and what is within the person. When the person or the child plays, it is a natural phenomenon of a human being; however, one has to find out what does that play portray in the real life of the person. Using play methods one can understand the person's feelings and uncover the problems lying inside that person. Narrative approach is the way of understanding and helping the person to map the problem, externalize, empower the person to deconstruct the problem, and finally thicken the alternative story, the story which changes one's life and brings the life with full of hope; this is what is called the healing process (MEET process).

Narratives and Family Systems

A family system as an approach to counseling is also an integrative model which tries to combine other theories. Such other theories include: Client-centered, Gestalt, Play, and Systems theory. Narrative approach also tries to use some ideas from the family systems theory. For example, when worked with some of the families at *Amani* Orphanage Center in Nsalaga, Uyole, we employed the family systems theory. Family systems theory looks at an individual through the eyes of other members in the family. Therefore, understanding an individual story one has to understand how communication goes on in the particular family. Also we tried to follow what the family systems liked to use in understanding the historical background of the family and that was 'genogram'[6], the family history. In the following paragraphs we examine how the narrative approach can be enriched by the family systems theories.

According to Hunter, "family system theory is a way to conceptualize the life of the family unit. Family systems involve understanding the individual within the context of a dynamic family system with its own unique developmental stages, history, and cultural relatedness."[7] Looking at our African context, it is our contention that the above definition is very much applicable in this context where this study was undertaken. The African way of living is different in many ways from the Western way of living. The kind of life the Western world live, even in small units of the family, is very individualistic. In the opposite, the families are still in contact to one another and even have what is known as extended families in the African context. The African families are not as individualistic as one can see the Western families are. Therefore, we find that working within the African context and using family systems theory is more applicable and effective than in the Western families which are more disintegrated.

Some of the pioneers of the family systems theory are such as Virginia Satir, Murray Bowen and Salvadore Minuchin. Family systems theory is all about the communication between the family members. The structure of the family is dynamic and each individual as a unit of the family tries to look for a balance within the family which is known as the process of *homeostasis*. It is further pointed out that, "family system theory hypothesizes that changes in the context will produce changes in the individual."[8] The question to ask ourselves according to the above explanation is the following: how effective it is when we work with an individual who comes from the disintegrated family? Otherwise, we should start working with making sure that the context which an individual comes from is first fixed.

The family systems theory emphasizes on seeing an individual in a context of the whole family. Furthermore, an individual is also traced back from where he or she came from. This is what is known as "generational histories" (genogram) of the person. Generational history helps the therapist or counselor to know the person in an intimate way and in detail. The problem of the person can be traced back through his or her

---

6. Using genogram for children was difficult for them; however, in their memory books we explored something similar to genogram which was a family tree in which they drew the family lineage. Whenever, we used genogram, as family therapists use, this meant the 'family tree' as explored by children at *Amani Orphanage Center*.

7. Hunter (ed.), *Dictionary of Pastor Care*, 423.

8. Hunter (ed.), *Dictionary of Pastoral Care*, 423.

grandparents.[9] However, most counselors use the generational history of the person to gather data. They use family stories (narratives) to gather information that help in the process of establishing good relationships in the family or to an individual.

Family systems theory employs some kind of communications, histories, stories, and family traditions. We believe that the family systems theory is very much applicable in the African culture because most African families still live their lives in extended families, where the communication system is very broad, very close and intact as we have just pointed out above. In the western countries, the family systems are very small, limited, and isolated; helping such families may be very difficult.

The communications, histories, stories, and traditions are also employed with narrative theorists as we have seen above. Therefore, integration of narrative and family theory enriches the process of working with OVC in the context of Tanzania. As we work with OVC, we do not only talk to children individually, but also follow up with what is going on in their families. We see and talk issues that involve the whole family. The dynamics and structures of families are also taken into consideration for the betterment of an individual and the whole family.

Understanding the person through his or her historical background is very crucial in the process of children's resilience. This is what is known as a family historical background (genogram). Genogram is a family sculpture or, the structure that seeks to understand the person through understanding his or her family system or context. It is a generational history which traces the family dynamics of strengths and weaknesses. It looks on an individual for the balance of the whole family. The systems theory looks for an individual within the family context for the good of the whole person.[10] Through genogram, it is anticipated that the therapist or pastoral counselor will then try to gather stories or contents of the genogram. That is what is called the narrative approach where the person gathers information through observing and listening to stories of the family and the events surrounding the family. Through narratives, counselors are able to fill the gaps and other shortcomings in the genogram. African families have stories to tell according to different circumstances they are in. For example in times of birth, wedding, worship, death, and other celebrations of life, Africans have ways of performing these activities through narratives such as metaphors, stories, myths, proverbs, symbols and images.

---

9. Ibid.

10. Bowen, *Family Therapy*; cf. Hunter (ed.), *Dictionary of Pastoral Care*, 423–424.

Narrative approaches or methods through histories and stories of people's lives which we know them through the family systems process help the person to grow into maturity for the purpose of reaching out into the process of wholeness. Understanding our lives of where we have come from and all sorts of our historical background is one of the ways to resilience. Resilience is a way of coping with difficult circumstances in life. It is the ability to deal with issues that happen in our lives. Resilience process helps the person to move forward with life that is more meaningful and purposeful. Genograms and narratives become meaningful and applicable when they are being translated or integrated for the goal of bringing meaning and purpose in life. The human being has been created in God's image and, therefore, he or she looks at life that would be fulfilling God's kingdom and its systems.

Theology is what is hoped to bring about the meaning, healing, and wholeness in someone's life. Theology translates life's events for the purpose of bringing life's meaning. Theology is the way of understanding our lives in God's ways. Our experiences and our ways of living must be applied in the context of God's system. This system is all about the right relationship with oneself, people, God, and the whole creation in the universe. The joining factor of this relationship is based on love, and love happens in the midst of communication. This kind of communication comes in different ways not only in verbal and written communication, but also through images and symbols, through action and none action activities. The goal is to make the balance in life, the life of peace and harmony, but more specifically the life of wholeness. God in his creation, as we read the book of Genesis, saw that everything created was very good (Genesis 1: 31). Later in the process of creation God's system did not go well. Sin entered the system. Therefore, we are always not perfect and long for something in our system to make things alright. God had to intervene to make things or the system work properly again. It is only through Jesus Christ that we can maintain the system which was broken. God loves the creation and wants to restore it; and through Jesus Christ everything became possible. Therefore, in Jesus alone we find healing, peace, harmony, and wholeness.

Genogram is the foundation or the basis of how we understand and help our counselees, if we want to make our ministry effective. The counselors have to build such a relationship with an individual through the context of the person concerned. Genograms enable the counselor to understand the communication and relationships within the family. Through genogram one finds many things to explore and work out with the counselee concerned. Genogram is not something to rush about and make it easy; it is sometimes very complicated and difficult to understand. Relationships must be established; and that is where the next process or stage comes in—the narratives.

Narratives are about life stories. Stories help someone to be interested in knowing each other more closely. Narrative process is a non-threatening approach to make relationships with people. Narrative approach invites people to talk more freely about their lives. Through their stories people can make their own genogram very easily and in an open arm. Many things, knowingly and unknowingly, can be talked about and that is where the pastoral counselor has to pay attention to listen and note all details from his or her counselee. This process leads the pastoral counselor to try to understand and interpret the life of his or her counselee theologically.

Theological understanding is the foundation for the pastoral counselors. Pastoral counseling bases its ground in practical theology. All what people go through in their lives, whether fear, shame, guilt, sickness, sadness, grief, death and any other kind of crisis must be interpreted theologically to bring about positive changes (i.e., hope, faith, love, purpose and meaning) in their lives. When these undesirable things happen in life and people know how to respond to them, the world becomes a better place to live.

Narratives and Analytical Theories

Analytical theory (Jungian) founded by Carl Gustav Jung (1875—1961) is a theory that emphasizes the creativity of the person through the soul (*psyche*). The psyche experiences many events and happenings; however, not all of these remain conscious, some of these remain in the subconscious mind. The things in the unconsciousness usually are repressed down. Something has to be done to make the things which are repressed down to come up to the consciousness for the person to be whole or to become integrated in his or her *psyche*.[11]

Analytical theories have been used by different therapists and counselors in their methods to help their clients. The psychologists, psychotherapists and other professionals have employed the theories and methods learned from what Jung found and wrote down. The goal of analytical theory is to make the person grow into maturity and fulfillment through the process which Jung called '*individuation*.' It is the process where through creativity someone becomes aware of his or her life. It is sometimes known as a self-realization process. Hence, individuation (self-realization) process

---

11. Jung, *Memories, Dreams and Reflections.*

is the situation where one finds the fullness of life according to the clinical or medical paradigm of pastoral care and counseling.[12]

Theologically, this individuation or self-realization is what is called wholeness or salvation. Analytical theory through creativity and awareness in the *psyche* helps the person to find oneself who and what he or she is. Several things are analyzed and these are such as myths, arts, rituals, symbols, images, dreams, shadows, and letters. Therefore, the process of individuation through the analysis of these archetypal images brings the person to self-fulfillment and this is what is called wholeness.[13]

In this process of individuation, narrative approach integrates some of the analytical theories. Narrative approach uses memories, stories, metaphors, dreams, symbols, myths, and letters, especially when we work with children. These can also be analyzed through the process which Jung uses when dealing with symbols and images. For example, the narrative approach uses the memory book or memory box as a healing tool for children who are searching ways to resilience in coping with difficulties or crises of life. Analysts also use the memory book/box for recording and keeping some important things and events in the life of the person such as dreams and other life images and symbols (e.g., pictures and arts). These are ways which help people become aware of who they are and how they are supposed to cope with the happenings of life (i.e., events).

Narrative approach and analytical theories can be used and finally be integrated into a better process of healing and coping mechanisms in pastoral counseling. The soul (psyche) is the place where things and happenings of life dwell. Many things enter in the soul of the person. These can be things that are good as well as that are not good. Things that people do not like are suppressed or repressed down; and these things will remain in the subconscious or unconscious minds. When these things or events stay in the unconscious state without dealing with them, the person will not be able to grow into a maturity and his or her life will be disconnected. The person ends up with different problems and even sicknesses such as depression, grief, anxiety, fear, and many other psychosocial problems.

In order to deal with things or events in the subconscious mind the person has to be creative and find a way of becoming aware of the happenings. Through the process of fantasizing the events one become aware of understanding what goes on in his or her life. Paying attention to images, symbols, and other life events helps the person to move to a healthy stage of distinguishing or discerning what is good and what is bad as life

12. Hunter (ed.), *Dictionary of Pastoral Care*, 30.
13. Ibid., 33–35.

is a package of both good and bad. Becoming aware of what is going on in one's life is a necessary stage for healing and development. This is the stage whereby you bring the unconscious to consciousness (i.e., becoming aware of life' events). This transition is not easy; it requires discipline and training. First of all, it depends on how one works using his or her creativity as one experiences life, the life that is full of narratives, symbols, and images. One has to take time, stop and wander with what is going on in his or her life.

We agree with Jung who says, "If you can not take *a hint* from life, then the life will hit you" (emphasis ours). A good example which we like to share here is the parable or a story of a prodigal son found in the Gospel of Luke 15: 11–32. The parable talks about a man who had two sons. The younger son of that man told his father to provide him a share of his inheritance so that he may be independent and live the life he liked. The father did as the son was pleased. The son went away and decided to live a luxurious life of squandering the money and at the end he found himself empty handed that he had spent all the money he had, and lost everything he owned. Then the economic crisis happened in that country and he did not have anything to spend for his life. He then started looking for a job so that he could find something to put into his empty stomach. He succeeded to obtain one work of feeding swine; however, it did not pay him very well, and he even shared the food with those swine. The emphasis of this story comes when the Scripture says, "But when he came to himself. . . . ." another translation similarly reads "And when *he came to himself. . . .*" (Emphasis in verse 17 is ours) (KJV) The text says that the lost son "*came to himself*", that means, before that crisis, he did not know who he was. He was lost and was out of himself. But he took sometime to look around and think of what happened with him. He thought of life which he lived with his parents at home, and compared with the life which he lived at that moment (i.e., life experiences), then he came to his mind or to his senses, to his new discoveries and understanding of who he was. That was the time we call the time of "self-realization," the time of salvation for him. The end of this story is very positive. The son realizes who he was and accepts his weaknesses and confesses of all what he has been and moves forward to go and face his father. Fortunately enough the father accepts him unconditionally though the son himself puts the condition himself of being one of his father's servants, not the father's son. Worse enough the son did not think that he would be accepted at all. But the father accepts him unconditionally as his own son; he does not punish him or complain at all. Instead he provides him favorable things which even make the older brother to be angry with his father.

For the healing and wholeness to happen one has to use his or her imagination for translating events and things that happen in life. The human being is a disintegrated person who requires gathering and putting together the disintegrating things in life. One has to be aware of his or her life, that is to 'take a hint' from life. This comes out in the process of individuation. During this process of creativity one comes to a climax, a crisis point, the turning point where the revolution of life begins. This is the process of individuation, where the person finds himself or herself. Theologically, it is the process where someone becomes a new creature or a born again Christian (2 Corinthians 5:17). Salvation is not the end of the journey, but the beginning of a new life which is integrative and continuous. It is not the end of bad things or sufferings in life, but the new perspective in life. Events of life happen daily in our lives; however, when we are aware (conscious) of these things in life, we deal with them differently and positively and not suppressing them down making the person sick or disintegrated in his or her life. This is a life-cycle which revolves around; however, it does not pass to the same point, it passes to different place and at a different orbit. This cycle is continuous and grows gradually as someone experiences life. Orphans and vulnerable children also have to see the reality of life and its complexity. They must come to a point where they are able to use their creativity through narratives, metaphors, symbols, images, dreams and other methods to help them integrate their lives for their resilience in times of sufferings and other hardships of life.

In the following paragraphs we propose a model which comprises the ideas or explanations we have discussed above. It is a narrative approach which integrates other approaches or methods in pastoral counseling of OVC. It is a cyclical model of a life of the child or person and how he or she experiences life; it is a journey to wholeness.

An Integrative Narrative Model for Healing and Resilience for OVC

In developing an ingegrated model, practical theology is involved. Practical theology creates ways that are integrated in its methods. It is based on the real life of people's experiences and activities of the Church in practical ways. It is also a theory of action. Practical theology is about the two concepts of praxis and theory.[14] Pastoral counselors work within practical theology. They must make sure that counseling is beneficial to the whole person as a human being created in the image of God. Therefore, love should

14. See Heitink, *Practical Theology*, 151.

be the dominant factor in pastoral counseling especially when working with orphans and vulnerable children.

Pastoral counseling should employ methods that are more effective in helping the person grow into a Christian maturity in every way that is spiritual, physical, mental, and emotional. As we have seen in the above discussion, narrative approach can also employ or pick up some ideas, methods, or approaches from other disciplines such as play, analytical, and family systems. When these are integrated together and used in a systematic ways, and if that can be understood and applied well, people will obviously grow into the fullness of life, the life of wholeness.

We can generalize that a model which follows is a life journey of every individual human being. The processes or stages in the cycle are sometimes not easy to be aware of and sometimes even recognize them or explain as people experience life in this world; however, these stages are there in the person's life. The following model explains how healing and wholeness can be reached by OVC in particular as seen and experienced in working with children in our context of study. The life experience in the circle is not a fixed one; it is flexible and the process is sometimes not that systematic and can go either way. However, the goal of each soul is to reach the process or stage which Jung called individuation (i.e., wholeness), no matter what way you take to reach there. What follows is our own creativity of the process. The model came to Mwenisongole when he usually played with children in the river. When one throws stones in the river, something happen there; it is the rings of small waves moving from inside to the outside. We compare this action of the water with the life of the person. The model is called an integrative narrative cycle for pastoral counseling of OVC. This model is shown in the concentric circles below.

Diagram (hand-drawn concentric circles, from outer to inner):

- WHOLENESS / HEALING
- EXPERIENCES / STORIES
- HOPES — FANTASIES — EVENTS — IMAGINATIONS — COPING
- SOUL (Psyche)
- MEMORIES
- PLAYS
- MEANINGS
- SALVATION

A Model: An Integrative Narrative Cycle for Pastoral Counseling of OVC

This model is a cyclical model. In Swahili there is a saying which says, "*Maisha ni mzunguko/duara*," which means, "life is a circle." Life is a rotation which goes around and around. Life is a continuous ring which goes around on and on until when someone dies; however, according to African belief in the African Tradition Religion (ATR), this cycle of life continues even after death where the person meets with ancestors and another arena of life continues in another world.[15] Therefore, life is a process. One passes one stage to another stage continuously. The ultimate stage is when we find a true meaning of our lives, the lives of fulfillment, self-realization, and

---

15. Mbiti, *African Religions*; cf. Mligo, *Elements of African Traditional Religion*.

individuation. This is the life of salvation and wholeness. In the paragraphs below, we provide explanations of the model sketched above.

The human being is created with a soul (*psyche*). The soul is the source of our personality and being. This is what makes us human. We experience life through the soul within us. The psyche experiences many *events* in life, not only negative and positive ones, but also the unconscious and conscious ones. The goal of soul is the wholeness of our personality. Therefore, one has to go beyond things that go inside the soul. This is what is called the "psychic process" where the soul seeks for integrative and the totality of the person (personality).[16]

The next stage in this circle in the model after the events is *memory*. Events are all the happening things that person experiences since birth. Then the memory is the stage where the events are being stored. What the memory does here is to store the things that are experienced. This might be good or bad. The tendency of a human being is to repress down those things that were so difficult to handle or accept. The work of memory is to restore the events whether are bad or good; the memory will restore them. The negative things which are repressed down usually go to the place called unconscious or subconscious mind, while the other regular or usual events remain in the conscious mind. When the memory keeps on holding the repressed things or events, the person ends up in a situation that is disintegrated or becomes what is known as disorder in someone's personality. In other words, the person becomes sick if the things that are repressed down are not dealt with whether through the person's interventions, or with psychiatrists help, or counseling services. Through professional help one can be helped to move forward with life that is more integrated rather than remaining with life that is disintegrated.[17] How could someone move forward to a more mature life, the life that is more integrated? This is the next stage in our circle of life, and that is fantasy.

Through *fantasy* one uses the potentials that are within him or her. The happenings in life happen for a reason. Therefore, the person must become aware of asking himself or herself to know what is going on in his or her life. Someone must start fantasizing with all the events and the happening in his or her life. Through guidance the person can know and understand himself or herself by the whole process of integration, which includes fantasy as "the creative process of mental imagery."[18] This process is followed by being imaginative of all the things that go inside, such as

---

16. Cf. Hunter (ed.), *Dictionary of Pastoral Care*, 970.
17. Jung, *Memories, Dreams and Reflections*, 165.
18. Hunter (ed.), *Dictionary of Pastoral Care*, 429.

symbols, images, dreams, stories, metaphors, and other life experiences. Jung calls this process "active imagination."[19]

As the process of *imagination* continues in the mind of the person, the actions come into the *play*. Acting out what is inside is the next stage in the person's life.[20] For children in particular, their imaginations are being translated or manifested in arts and playing. Children like to play and use their imagination in arts. The problems and other feelings that children have experienced in life are not talked easily; but through arts and play, they find easier to talk and provide stories about their problems and life in general. Children sometimes play through *fantasies* and *imaginations*. That is why when working with children, it is important to use stories and metaphors because it is the place where they find at ease and free to express their feelings and emotions. They *experience* the world in different ways and express themselves in various ways too. *Narrative* approach through *stories*, metaphors, songs, proverbs, and games are the ways of expression through which children like to communicate for their coping and healing. It is through narrative approach children find *meanings* and *hopes* in lives that lead them to *wholeness*.

It is through integrative narrative approach that we find the integration of other methods helpful in the healing and coping mechanisms for OVC in the Tanzanian context. Integrative narrative approach helps the counselor map the child's problem through stories or other narrative methods to be able to deconstruct the dominating story in order to empower the child to an alternative story that is healing and hopeful. Narrative approches are ways or paths to a healing stage as you can see in the figure above. Stories that are alternative to dominating stories are ways to moving forward to bring what is unconscious to conscious. The repressed things must be dealt with through fantasy, and imaginations and being aware of the happenings in order to reconstruct that is denied and disintegrated. According to Jung, the life of the soul is both good and evil, or light and darkness. The persona or shadow side of the person is part of who we are. A human being likes to wear a mask to imitate the image of what he or she wants to be. The disguising of our personality is what is called a "mask in our face." This part of a shadow side must be recognized as holding the healing power. It is only God who is perfect, but not a human being. As human beings we should always remember that we are vulnerable and weak. The person's life is disintegrated and must be integrated to be whole. The two sides of the person must be integrated for the holistic development of the person. It is

19. Jung, *Man and His Symbols*.
20. Cf. Dyregrov, *Grief in Children*.

pointed out that "the goal of wholeness depends on conscious as well as unconscious seeking."[21]

The integration process is what brings meaning and purpose in someone's life. The person has to face the life squarely, to be aware of life in the other side of the being, no matter how dark it is or how hurtful the experience might be. As human beings we have to recognize the dark side of our being and come to consciousness of the things that have been repressed down in our souls. By this process then, a human being finds healing and wholeness; otherwise, he or she is doomed to sickness and disintegrated life. The text in the Bible teaches that, "If we say we have no sin, we deceive ourselves, and the truth is not in us. If we confess our sins, he is faithful and just, and will forgive our sins and cleanse us from all unrighteousness." (1 John 1:8–9) After the fall, sin became part of us as human beings who have predicaments, corrupt, full of misery, and evil. Acknowledgement of our sinful nature, of our weaknesses, and of our vulnerability is an important step to a true healing which comes as a result of salvation. The response of the person to what he or she is responsible is a way to salvation. This response is a matter of one recognizing the responsibility of accepting of who he or she is in relation to the creator and God's creation. When the link between accepting the vulnerabilities and the Higher Being (God) is found, healing and wholeness happen.

According to the figure above, the model which we have called as an integrative narrative cycle for pastoral counseling of OVC is a life long process of the person. The source of life is in the soul itself. A human being is not a static being; a human being is the person who grows experiencing many different things. The things that happen in life are not typically new every time, they just repeat every time in life but in different ways and in different stages. That is why we concur with the Swahili saying which says, "*Maisha ni mzunguko*," which means, "life is a continuous circle." In order to grow healthier one has to go with what is suggested above and these things are not disconnected, they are connected and related to each other. Growth happens in dealing with and being aware of events, memories, fantasies, imaginations, stories, and experiences, which lead to the life that is meaningful, hopeful, healing, and whole. Hence, it is in exploring and being creative to the self (*psyche*) in us that we can find the Self (God) in us who can lead us to wholeness.

OVC experience their lives in different ways, although the process explaind above stays the same to every individual human being whether child or adult. The children at Mbeya, our study area, for example, faced different

21. Hunter (ed.), *Dictionary of Pastoral Care*, 38.

kinds of problems and challenges, which were economic, spiritual, and emotional. They experienced poverty, guilt, shame, rejection, anger, sicknesses, loss, grief, and abuse. All these experiences became as the dark side of their lives.[22] These challenges had to be talked about openly and freely and not in threatening ways. Children had to express their needs and problems in ways that could be simple and easy for them. Through narrative approach, stories, plays, metaphors and other methods children are allowed to respond to issues that are hurtful to them. Children must be guided to map their problems in ways that are easy for them, in ways mentioned above. Through plays and other imagination techniques children must be guided to tell their stories in an artistic ways, the ways that are non-threatening to them. In this way, children can be able to find new stories that are thickened and are empowering to dominating stories. These are stories that are hopeful, empowering, and healing.

Narrative Approach to Pastoral Counseling

The intervention which was done by OVC at Nsalaga in Mbeya Tanzania proved that the Narrative approach to pastoral counseling was an applicable approach in the Tanzanian context. Evaluation was conducted to see whether the changes happened in children for a period of one year 2007. The evaluation determined whether the caregivers and children themselves saw any changes compared to the time when they began using this narrative approach. Several indicators were used to measure their understandings and feeling to see where and how children felt since the program began. These indicators were analyzed to see how and where they were according to their own understanding. Children were provided a safe and open space to express themselves whether they saw any changes in their lives according to things which the authors used. These were the feelings of joy, sadness, worry, anxiety, anger, love and peace. The evaluation showed that most children who participated in the study (75%), and filled the evaluation form were more in the feelings of joy, love, and peace rather than sadness, worry, and anger they had before.

Through narrative approach children were able to cope with different problems they faced which included anger, sadness, acting out, anxiety, shame, guilt, fear, and loneliness.[23] Children were open to talk about other things which they thought might be helpful or added for them at *Amani*

---

22. Cf. Boss, "The Trauma and Complicated Grief"; Price, "Walking through the Dackness"; Jones, "A Theology of Hope."

23. Cf. Dyregrov, *Grief in Children*.

Orphanage Center or at their homes to make them more responsible, confident, and self-esteem. These other things which helped children to become more active and cope with psychosocial problems are such as material support for their family (house), for their school needs, games, gardening, and Bible study materials.

Caregivers and volunteers (teachers) also had their evaluation form to fill in. They had the opportunity to say which ways they thought to be useful in teaching children and helping them to cope with their problems. They also had to mention the success and/or the failure they encountered during the whole year of 2007 while using the narratives approach. The form they had to fill had the scale of 1 to 5, one to be very bad, and five to be a very good. The indicators based on the feelings of children they have been working with, which are sadness, anger, worry, happiness, love, and peace. The evaluation with teachers and volunteers who were interviewed were five of them. The average scale they had were between 3 to 5, which means that they saw that children tremendously changed for good, number three being the average, the four being good, and five being very good. These also showed that children were no longer feeling sad, angry, or lonely for that much.

Integrating Practical Theology and Narrative Approaches

Narrative approaches have been used by different scholars and different faculties in the academic arena. Narrative approach has become very popular especially at this postmodern time. The world experiences the fast advancement of science and technology and more generally in the educational system. It is also when the world becomes like a village because of such advancements. This is known as the globalization time. In this time, narrative approaches have become very familiar and applicable with social scientists in particular and in the humanities departments. Narrative approach has been accepted as one of the ways or theories which academicians use as a scientific method in their research works. Theologians have for a long time also employed narratives in biblical analysis. Narrative theology is all about using biblical stories and images to understand and interpret the Bible through people's events and relationships.[24]

Practical theology seeks to make theology more practical in its experience. Müller as quoted in Streets writes: "Practical Theology happens whenever and wherever there is a reflection on practice, from the perspective of

---

24. Hunter (ed.), *Dictionary of Pastoral Care*, 592; Ganzevoort, "Narrative Approaches."

the experience of the presence of God. There are obviously various levels of Practical Theology. It can be very spontaneous, informal and local. It can also be very formal, systematic and organized. It can be part of ministerial activities on the congregational level, or it can be highly academic on university level. In any case, it is always guided by the moment of praxis (always local, embodied, and situated)."[25] Following the above quotation, practical theology with narrative approach seeks to integrate the methods to make people's events, life, and relationships more meaningful and that brings about wholeness. Stories, parables, metaphors, symbols, images, and myths in people's lives are used to interpret and understand the relationships of people and their life events. These are all used in the biblical context as well as in the social context. Working within practical theology, the pastoral counselor looks at a theology that is closer to people's lives. Narratives (stories) are something that happens to our lives everyday. It is part of who we are and what we are. The theology which uses or applies narrative analysis is very much close to people's lives. Every corner of our lives is full of and surrounded by narratives. Narratives (stories) have to be interpreted and understood in ways that are helpful and healing to people's lives. Narrative approach has to be integrated with theology to bring about healing and wholeness. The integration of narrative approach with practical theology looks for the healing that is whole. The integration looks for the harmony and peace between the human web and its creation. It looks for the relationship that is more balanced. The whole systems in the human arena must be integrated for the wholeness in the life of the person.

The ministry of the pastoral counselor is to support an individual, the family or any group to come to their self-realization which is a process of individuation or salvation of the person. Through narrative approach, the pastoral counselor guides and uses the approach to allow people understand their problems (dominating story) and further allows them to move forward to the coping and healing process (alternative story). This process leads for the life that is more integrated, the life that is worthwhile, with purpose and meaning, the life of wholeness.

Conclusion

This chapter presented and discussed a model that is useful in working with OVC through the narrative approach in the context of Tanzania. The model

---

25. Streets, "Love: A Philosophy of Pastoral Care," 6; cf. Van Wyk, "From 'Applied Theology' to 'Practical Theology' 90–93; Woodward, "Theological Reflection," 130–133.

is the result of the conducted field study, analysis, and interpretation of the data collected. This model is ultimately integrated with theories from different approaches so that it can be appropriate and be used to OVC in pastoral counseling. The model is very integrative in its approach because of relying on other theories as it has been discussed above. The main aim of this model as discussed above is to enable the child read his or her self-realization, individuatioan or salvation, which will eventually lead to creating alternative stories of hope and joy in order to suppress the dominating stories of grief, anger, and hatred. Therefore, an integrative narrative cycle model for pastoral counseling to OVC fulfills the thesis statement and objectives of this study.

In our suggestion of the model, however, we are aware of the many possible limitations of any narrative apporoach to counseling. One possible limitation of the approach (narrative approach) is that it is not the only one in the provision of pastoral counseling; and the second is that the approach is effective to literate people and those knowledgeable with biblical narratives as were the children at *Amani* Orphanage Center. The approach hardly speaks about how illiterates and ignorants of biblical narratives can use the bible for their self-realization. Despite these, and other possible, limitations, we confess that the approach is effective and appropriate in enhancing the release from suffering to those who use it in counseling people facing traumas due to the loss of beloved ones, such as the children who were involved in our study.

CHAPTER 7

Conclusion

Summary of the Book

THIS BOOK WAS ABOUT how narrative approach with the use of stories and metaphors in pastoral counseling could be used to orphans and vulnerable children in Tanzania. A study was done in Mbeya region to represent the other regions in the country. Mbeya was one of the regions severely impacted by the HIV and AIDS in Tanzania. This pandemic affected the region leaving many people affected by it whether directly or indirectly. The pandemic caused many deaths and left more problems and challenges in society such as poverty, the increase of orphans, street children, and more other vulnerable children.

The study surveyed different related literature to see various theories, methods, and responses from different fields in the academic arena. The literatures surveyed based on the objectives of the book. Furthermore, the book based on the study conducted in the field where specific case studies, focus group and activities and discussions were conducted and applied using narrative approach. Concepts and themes were also discovered and discussed for analysis. These meant to find a theory and model that could suit for and fit in the context of Tanzania. The model discovered was the integrative narrative approach which was used because it appeared to be very effective in working with OVC in Tanzania.

This book has discussed and explored in detail that the narrative approach is an applicable approach in pastoral counseling and in practical theology as a whole. In this case it is probably true that narrative theories contribute much in practical theology in particular. The narrative approach through stories and metaphors is found to be at home in Tanzania which means that it is an approach that is applicable, reliable, and viable in the context where the research was undertaken—in Mbeya the selected study area. Narrative approach is found to be an integral approach involving or incorporating other theories and methods to make it more effective and interesting to work with in the context of the African people in Tanzania. Narrative theories can therefore be applied very well and in effective ways with our theological contexts and doctrines. In other words, narrative theories can be integrated very well with theology as we have seen in the case studies with OVC. The model proposed concurs well with the Swahili saying which says, "*maisha ni mzunguko*," meaning that "life is a circle." The life of the person is a story which goes around in its circle where inside it the person experiences and goes through many life challenges. The end of the circle is not the end of life (death), but the maturity of life and wholeness. The circles or rings in an integrative narrative cycle model for pastoral counseling to OVC have no definite boundaries; they are a continuous process of life. The African Traditional Religion and its philosophy believe that people continue to live even after their physical death. That means, life continues in the other side of the world.[1]

Challenges Encountered during Study Process

As in other academic fields, narrative approach with the use of stories and metaphors in pastoral counseling faces challenges, and even this book will most likely face criticisms from other scholars. Narrative, as a phenomenon of post-modernism, has been a challenging theory not only to others but also to our own journey as researchers and pastoral counselors. In this study we have found that narrative approach in pastoral counseling requires special attention especially if one works with children. Working with children requires much time and patience to work with them in order to understand them properly. Despite the skills one might have, pastoral counseling to OVC requires perseverance, commitment, and interest. Otherwise, one will fail to do what is right and just for children and end up hurting and traumatizing them psychologically and spiritually.

Another challenge faced in the study with OVC was collecting the data and trying to integrate them for analysis. As pointed out above, the approach used was an integral one. We integrated narrative approach with different theories from other counseling approaches from systems, plays, to analytical theories. Therefore, one had to pay more attention to not only what children were saying, thinking and doing, but also having something from their context at home, school or at the Center as they engaged with

1. Mbiti, *African Religions*; cf. Mligo, *Elements of African Traditional Religion*.

others. Narrative approach is one of the proper effective communications for conversing with children in non-threatening ways. Using stories and metaphors in narrative approach, detailed description has to be well collected, organized, and analyzed in order to understand children in ways they understand the world and their circumstances.

The challenge of narrative approach in pastoral counseling in a religious context has also been a challenge to us and others. The challenge has also been how narratives can be interpreted spiritually and theologically to be able to help children understand their regular or dominant stories of desperation and hopelessness to stories that are empowering, lifting, and helping them to grow into maturity and wholeness! However, through this book we attempted to prove that narrative approach by the use of metaphors, stories, proverbs, plays, and arts can be theologically effective in pastoral counseling to OVC in other different contexts apart from Tanzania.

Pastoral counseling to orphans and vulnerable children, in particular, requires more attention and seriousness from pastoral counselors. Pastoral counselors have to walk with wounded children by being with them in order to listen, understand, and care for them. Children's ministry must be established in the doctrine of love and relationship. We must establish the community that would be able to understand God's plan of healing and wholeness.[2] We should build the community that facilitates healing relationships to wounded children. This is what we tried to establish in this research which has to be explored more by other researchers.

The most challenging things in our lives are lives themselves. If we want to understand our lives we first have to know and understand our stories and tell ourselves and listen to them. We also have to hear stories from others and from the community of which stories have to tell. All stories of our lives contain points that show strengths and weaknesses of a human being. Biblical narratives especially in the book of Proverbs and Ecclesiastes tell us about our vulnerabilities. The condition of our vulnerability makes us more cautious of our lives, that we are weak, limited, and cannot control everything that happens in this world. It is only God who is perfect and is in control of everything; however, we as human beings are vulnerable and desperate. Our only hope is Christ alone. Therefore, we have to understand who we are by understanding our personal and communal stories that make us who we are and change for the better. Every time and always, we have to

---

2. Petra College in White River has established a good ministry for children, which facilitates the idea we try to establish here. They have produced a training manual which is the course one can take at Petra College, the manuscript is known as "Walking with wounded children."

keep learning and experiencing life in God's way so that we grow into the life that is mature and whole.

The book of Proverbs 12:1 states, "Whoever loves discipline loves knowledge, but he who hates reproof is stupid." Therefore, we and our children should be wise and learn from what God shows us in our daily stories and experiences in life and live a life of individuation (not individualistic life), the life of discernment, maturity, and wholeness. Stories of our lives are lessons themselves for all of us to tell and hear for the better change of people and the community.

Recommendations

Basing on the discussion in the whole of this study, we provide the following recommendations for action: first, the Church, theologians, counselors, and other scholars should apply narrative approach with the use of stories and metaphors in their context for the welfare of children, especially in the ministry to OVC. We particularly urge pastoral counselors to integrate their methods in practical theology with narrative theories. In doing that they will reach children taking into account their safe space where they are able to express their feelings and emotions.

Second, narrative approach in African Christian theology should be paid more attention because it is part and parcel of the life of the African people. Narratives are such great resources we have as Africans. Narrative approach affects the way we interpret and understand theology and Scriptures. In other words, narrative theories and approaches affect us on how we do our African Christian theology.

Third, the Church in Africa should try to reframe its theological understanding to fit into the context that is serving its people. The Church should be more creative and open to challenging issues related to the African context and their theology, such as human sexuality, the HIV and AIDS, poverty, and other critical and sensitive issues. In taking into account the African context, dealing with narrative approaches will make pastoral counseling at home to OVC and other groups in miserable situations.

Fourth, the ministry to children should be paid more attention as other ministries in the Church. Children's ministry should not be treated as an extra ministry; it should be in an upfront in our churches because of their vulnerability and other risks they face in our societies today. Children are human beings as any other human beings who have experiences both good and bad. In emphasizing on the ministry to children builds the Church of Jesus Christ because children of today are adults of tomorrow.

There are several aspects which are not explored in this study as were supposed to be explored. We leave them as challenges to other scholars and researchers to explore them in their studies. Some of these aspects are as follows: narrative approach in other children rather than the OVC, other approaches or methods that can be more applicable and effective in working with OVC other than the narrative approach used in this study, and practical theology and particularly pastoral counseling methods that can be more applicable in the context of Tanzania with the ministry of children other than the one developed in this study.

Finally, but not least, we urge other scholars to conduct further researches in this particular subject. It is our hope that we have triggered some new thoughts and challenges that can be researched further for the betterment of the Church and society as a whole. We also welcome challenges and criticisms to the model developed and used in this study in order to enrich the academic field especially in practical theology as said in the Swahili proverb that, "*Asiyekubali kushindwa si mshindani*" (the one who does not accept his or her failures or weaknesses is not a competent person). In following this proverb, we can hardly claim this study to be exhaustive; it is still subject to criticisms and nourishments for the better one possible.

References

Abashula, Gudina, Jibat, Nega and Ayele, Tariku. "The Situation of Orphans and Vulnerable Children in Selected Woredas and Towns in Jimma Town." *International Journal of Sociology and Anthropology* 6:9 (2014) 246–256.

Addo, Peter. "Proverbs in African Narrative Theology: Looking at Ourselves in Africa: Ghana at 50," 2006. Online at http://www.timbooktu.com/addo/proverbs.htm (Accessed on 11 October 2017).

Ammicht-Quinn, Regina and Hacker, Hille (eds.). *AIDS*. London: SCM, 2007.

Andrews, Molly, Squire, Corinne, and Tamboukou, Maria. (eds.). *Doing Narrative Research*. London: SAGE, 2008.

Atkinson, David J. and David. F. Field; Holmes, Arthur F., and O'Donovan, Oliver (eds.). *New Dictionary of Christian Ethics and Pastoral Theology*. Leicester and Downers Grove: Inter-Varsity, 1995.

Axline, Virginia M. *Play Therapy: The Inner Dynamics of Childhood*. New York,NY.: Ballantine Books, 1989.

Babbie, Earl R. *The Practice of Social Research*. Thirteenth Edition. Belmont, CA. Wadsworth, 2013.

Basson, Nerine Celeste. "Narrative Pastoral Practice at a Primary School." MTh thesis, University of South Africa, 2001.

Bate, Stuart C. "The Mission to Heal in a Global Context." *International Review of Mission* 90 (2004) 70–80.

———. *Inculturation and Healing: Coping-Healing in South African Christianity*. Pietermaritzburg: Cluster, 1995.

———. (ed.). *Serving Humanity: A Sabbath Reflection*. Pietermaritzburg: Cluster, 1996.

———. "A Theological Model of Healing to Inform an Authentic Healing Ministry." *Journal of Theology for Southern Africa* 144 (2012) 69–91.

Benner, David G. *Strategic Pastoral Counseling: A Short-Term Structured Model*. Grand Rapids, MI.: Baker, 2003.

Berinyuu, Abraham A. "An African Therapy in Dialogue with Freudian Psychoanalysis." *The Journal of Pastoral Care and Counseling* 56:1 (2002)11–20.

———. "Change, Ritual, and Grief: Continuity and Discontinuity of Pastoral Theology in Ghana." *Journal of Pastoral Care* 46:2 (1992)141–152.

Bertram, Carol. *Understanding Research: An Introduction to Reading Research*. Second Edition. Pietermaritzburg: University of KwaZulu-Natal, 2004.

Besley, Tina. "Foulcouldian Influences in Narrative Therapy: An Approach for Schools." *Journal of Educational Inquiry* 2:2 (2001) 72–93.

Bevans, Stephen B. *Models of Contextual Theology*. Revised and Expanded Edition. Maryknoll, NY.: Orbis Books, 1992.

———. "Models of Contextual Theology." *Missiology: An International Review* 13:2 (1985) 185–202.

Bless, Claire And Higson-Smith, Craig. *Fundamentals of Social Research Methods: An African Perspective*. Third Edition. Cape Town: Juta & Co, 2000.

Bloor, Michael, Frankland, Jane, Thomas, Michelle and Robson, Kate. *Focus Groups in Social Research*. London: Sage, 2001.

Boje, David. M. "Narrative Therapy," 2005. Online at https://business.nmsu.edu/~dboje/narrativetherapy.html [Accessed 11 October 2017]).

Bongmba, Elias K. *Facing a Pandemic: The African Church and the Crisis of AIDS*. Waco, Texas: Baylor University, 2007.

Boss, Pauline. "The Trauma and Complicated Grief of Ambiguous Loss." *Pastoral Psychology* 59 (2010) 137–145.

Bowen, Murray. *Family Therapy in Clinical Practice*. New York, NY.: Jason Aronson, 1978.

Boyd, Glenn E. "Pastoral Conversation: Relational Listening and Open-ended Questions." *Pastoral Psychology* 51:5 (2003) 345–360.

Brink, Anna Margaretha. "Lighting His Way Home: Pastoral Conversations with a missing Child's Mother." MTh Thesis. University of South Africa, 2003.

Brunn, Stanley D. "The World Council of Churches as a Global Actor: Ecumenical Space as a Geographical Space." *Geographica Slovenica* 34: 1 (2001) 65–78.

Burns, George W. (ed.). *Healing with Stories: Your Casebook Collection for using Therapeutic Metaphors*. New Jersey: John Wiley & Sons, 2007.

Byamugisha, Gideon and others. *Journeys of Faith: Church-based Responses to HIV and AIDS in Three Southern African Countries*. Pietermaritzburg: Cluster, 2002.

Capps, Donald. "Ricoeur's Theory of Hermeneutics." UNISA E-Reserves (Accessed on 25 February 2008).

———. *Pastoral Care and Hermeneutics*. Philadelphia, PA.: Fortress, 1984.

———. *The Poet's Gift: Toward the Renewal of Pastoral Care*. Louisville, Kentucky: Westminster/John Knox, 1993.

———. *Reframing: A New Method in Pastoral Care*. Minneapolis: Fortress, 1990.

———. *Living Stories: Pastoral Counseling in Congregational Context*. Minneapolis, Minnesota: Fortress, 1998.

———. "Situating System and Giving Self Its due: A Story-based Counseling Model." *Pastoral Psychology* 48:4 (2000) 293–313.

Case, Caroline and Dalley, Tessa. *Working with Children in Art Therapy*. London: Tavistock/Routledge, 1990.

Cattanach, Ann (ed.). *The Story so far: Play Therapy Narratives*. Philadelphia, PA.: Jessica Kingsley, 2002.

Carr-Hill, Roy, Katabaro, Kamugisha Jovita, Anne Ruhweza Katahoire, Anne Ruhweza and Oula, Dramane. *The impact of HIV/AIDS on Education and Institutionalizing Preventive Education*. Paris: International Institute of Educational Planning/UNESCO, 2002.

Carroll, Janell L. and. Wolpe, Paul R. *Sexuality and Gender in Society*. London: HarperCollins, 1996.

Charon, Joel M. *Symbolic Interactionism: An Introduction, An Interpretation, An Integration*. Seventh Edition. Upper Saddle River, NJ.: Prentice-Hall, 2001.

Chogo, Pamela. "Improved Income for Centers of Orphan and Vulnerable Children through Poultry Production at Kibowa Orphanage Center in Arusha District." MSc in Community Economic Development, Dar es Salaam: The Open University of Tanzania, 2015.

Christensen, Pia M. and James, Allison (eds.). *Research with Children: Perspectives and Practices*. New York,NY.: Falmer, 2000.

Clandinin, D. Jean. (ed.). *Handbook of Narrative Inquiry: Mapping a Methodology*. Thousand Oaks, CA.: Sage, 2007.

Clebsch, William A. and. Jaekle, Charles R. *Pastoral Care in Historical Perspective*. New York, NY.: Jason Aronson, 1983.

Clinebell, Howard J. "Toward Envisioning the Future of Pastoral Counseling and AAPC." *Journal of Pastoral Care* 37:3 (2004) 180–194.

———. *Basic Types of Pastoral Care and Counseling: Resources for the Ministry of Healing and Growth*. Revised and enlarged edition. Nashville, TN.: Abingdon, 1984.

———. *Counseling for Spiritually Empowered Wholeness: A Hope-Centered Approach*. New York and London: The Haworth Pastoral Press, 1995.

Coetsee, Dirk. "Walking with Wounded Children." A training manual compiled by Dirk Coetsee. Unpublished Material, Petra College: White River, 2005.

Coetsee, Dirk and Grobbelaar, Jan. "A Church Where Children are Welcome. A New Paradigm for Children's Ministry in Africa." In *Handbook of Theological Education in Africa*, edited by Phiri, Isabel Apawo and Werner, Dietrich, 803–817. Oxford: Regnum Books, 2013.

Concise Oxford Dictionary, 2001 (CD Rom).

Corbetta, Piergiorgio. *Social Research: Theory, Methods and Techniques*. London: Sage, 2003.

Cortez, Marc. "Creation and Context: A Theological Framework for Contextual Theology." *Westminster Theological Journal* 67:2 (2005) 347–362.

Couture, Pamela D. and Hunter, Rodney J. (eds.). *Pastoral Care and Social Conflict: Essays in Honor of Charles V. Gerkin*. Nashville, TN.: Abingdon, 1995.

Couture, Pamela D. "The Effect of the Postmodern on Pastoral/Practical Theology and Care and Counseling." *Journal of Pastoral Theology* 13: 1 (2003) 85–104.

Crollius, Ary Roest. "Inculturation: Newness and Ongoing Process." *In Inculturation: Its Meaning and Urgency*. Edited by John Mary Walligo, Ary Roest Crollius, Theoneste Nkeramihigo and John Mutiso-Mbinda, 31–45. Nairobi: St. Paul, 1986.

Culbertson, Phillip L. *Caring for God's People: Counseling and Christian Wholeness*. Minneapolis, Minnesota: Fortress, 2000.

Daigneault, Susan D. "Narrative means to Adlerian ends: An illustrated Comparison of Narrative Therapy and Adlerian Play Therapy." *The Journal of Individual Psychology* 55:3 (1999) 298–315.

Denis, Phillipe. "Sharing Family Stories in Times of AIDS." *Missionalia* 29: 2 (2001) 258–281.

———. (ed.). *Never Too Small to Remember: Memory Work and Resilience in times of AIDS*. Pietermaritzburg: Cluster, 2005.

Dinkins, Burell David. *Narrative Pastoral Counseling* Longwood, FL.: Xulon, 2005.

Doehring, Carrie. *The Practice of Pastoral Care*. Louisville, Kentucky, Westminster/ John Knox, 2006.

Donkor, Rose. "Criteria for Developing a Relevant Contextual Theology." *Journal of Applied Thought* 4:1 (2015) 12 – 20.
Dreyer, J.S. "Doing Empirical Research in Theology: A Supervisor's Guide for Master's and Doctoral Students." Unpublished Handout Notes. Pretoria: University of South Africa, 2007.
Dube, Musa.W. (ed.). *HIV and AIDS and the Curriculum: Methods of integrating HIV and AIDS in Theological Programs*. Geneva: WCC, 2003.
———. (ed.). *Africa Praying: A Handbook on HIV/AIDS sensitive sermon guidelines and Liturgy*. Geneva: WCC, 2003.
———. *Fifty years of Bleeding: A Storytelling Feminist Reading of Mark 5:24–43*. Geneva/Atlanta: WCC, 2001.
Dube, Musa.W. and Njoroge, N.J. (eds.). *Talitha Cum! Theologies of African Women*: Pietermaritzburg: Cluster, 2001.
Dube, Musa.W. and Kanyoro, MusimbiR.A. (eds.). *HIV and AIDS and Gender Readings of the Bible*. Pietermaritzburg: Cluster, 2004.
Dunn, Mikaela R. "Narrative Therapy: Similarities Among Clinicians and Practice Implications." Master of Social Work Thesis. St. Paul, Minnesota. St. Catherine University and The University of St. Thomas, 2014. Online at htp://sophia.stkate.edu/msw_papers/311 [Accessed 15 October 2017].
Dyregrov, Atle. *Grief in Children: A Handbook for Adults*. London: Jessica Kingsley, 1991.
Eide, Oyvind.M. et al. (eds.). *Restoring Life in Christ: Dialogues of Care in Christian Communities an African Perspective*. Arusha: Makumira Publication Nineteen, 2008.
Elliot, Jane. *Using Narrative in Social Research: Qualitative and Quantitative Approaches*. Thousand Oaks, CA.: Sage, 2005.
Elwell, Walter A. and Comfort, Phillip W. (eds.). "Jacob." *Tyndale Bible Dictionary*. CD Rom Database, 2006 WORD search Corp. Tyndale, 2001.
Engedal, Leif Gunnar. "The Theological Foundation of Pastoral Care and Counseling." In *Restoring Life in Christ: Dialogues of Care in Christian Communities: An African Perspective*. Edited by Eide, Oyvind M., Engedal, Leif Gunnar, Kimilike, Lechion Peter and Ndossi, Emeline, 52–70. Makumira Publication Nineteen. Neuendetelssau Erlanger Verlag fur Mission und Oukumene, 2008.
———. 2008. "The Counselor's Competence." In *Restoring Life in Christ: Dialogues of Care in Christian Communities: An African Perspective*. Edited by Eide, Oyvind M., Engedal, Leif Gunnar, Kimilike, Lechion Peter and Ndossi, Emeline, 108–122. Makumira Publication Nineteen. Neuendetelssau Erlanger Verlag fur Mission und Oukumene, 2008.
Erikson, Erik H. *Identity: Youth and Crisis*. New York: W.W. Norton, 1968.
———. *Childhood and Society*. New York: Norton, 1964.
Evans, Bernard F. *Lazarus at the Table: Catholics and Social Justice*. Collegeville, Minnesota: Liturgical Press, 2006.
Eybers, Howard H. *Pastoral Care to Black South Africans*. Atlanta: Scholars, 1991.
Finucane, Colin. "In Search of Pastoral Care in the Seventh-day Adventist Church: A Narrative Approach." DTh Thesis. Pretoria: University of South Africa, 2009.
Foster, Geoff,, Levine, C. and Williamson, John (eds.). *A Generation at Risk: The Global Impact of HIV/AIDS on Orphans and Vulnerable Children*. New York, NY.: Cambridge University Press, 2005.

REFERENCES

Freedman, Jill. and Combs, Gene. *Narrative Therapy: The Social Construction of Preferred Realities*. New York, NY.: Norton, 1996.

Freeman. A. "Sexuality". Unpublished materials, Bethlehem, PA. January 1999.

Ganzevoort, R. Ruard. "Narrative Approaches." In *The Willey-Blackwell Companion to Practical Theology*. Edited by B. Miller-McLemore, 214–223. Chichester: Wiley-Blackwell, 2011.

Garner, Stephen. "Contextual and Public Theology: Passing Fads or Theological Imperatives?" Stimulus 22:1 (2015) 21–28.

Geldard, Kathryn and Geldard, David. *Counselling Children: A Practical Introduction*. Second Edition. Thousand Oaks, CA: Sage, 2002.

Gerkin, Charles V. *The Living Human Document: Re-visioning Pastoral Counseling in Hermeneutical Mode*. Nashville, TN.: Abingdon, 1984.

———. *Widening the Horizons*. Philadelphia, PA.: Westminster, 1986.

Graham, Elaine. " Pastoral Theology in an Age of Uncertainty." HTS 62:3 (2006) 845–865.

Grobblelaar, Maryna Susanna. "Inviting Faith Communities to Re(-)member Their Identity as Community-of-friends." DTh Thesis: UNISA, South Africa, 2006.

Grobbelaar, Jan. *Child Theology and the African Context*. London: Child Theology Movement, 2012.

GTZ (Deutsche Gesellschaft fur Technische Zusammenarbeit). 2003. "AIDS Control Project in Mbeya Region," 2003. www.gtz.de (Accessed 13 June 2007).

Haddad, Beverley. "We Pray but We cannot Heal: Theological Challenges posed by the HIV/AIDS Crisis." *Journal of Theology for Southern Africa* 125 (2006) 80–90.

Haley, Jay. *Uncommon Therapy: The Psychiatric Techniques of Milton H. Erickson, M.D.* New York, NY.: W.W. Norton & Company, 1986.

Hawley, Keeley. "Shepherding Lambs: The Church's Response to Children at Risk." *Evangel: The British Evangelical Review* 22:1(2004) 10–16.

Healey, Joseph G and Sybertz, Donald. *Towards an African Narrative Theology*. Nairobi: Paulines, 2005.

Heitink, Gerben. *Practical Theology: History, Theory, Action Domains: Manual for Practical Theology*. Translated by R. Bruinsma. Grand Rapids, MI.: W.B. Eerdmans, 1999.

Henry, Matthew. *Matthew Henry Concise Bible Commentary*. CD Rom, Database: Wordsearch, 2008.

Herman, David, Jahn, Manfred., and Ryan, Marie-Laure (eds.). *Routledge Encyclopedia of Narrative Theory*. London: Routledge, 2005.

Hiltner, Seward. *Preface to Pastoral Theology: The Ministry of Theory and Shepherding*. Nashville, TN.: Abingdon Press, 1958.

Hogue, David A. *Remembering the future: Imagining the Past*. Cleveland: The Pilgrim, 2003.

Hoopes, Marva L. "The Power of Story in the Spiritual Development of Children." D.Ed. Dissertation. Ann Arbor, MI: Beola University, 2013.

Holland, Scott. *How do Stories Save us? An Essay on the Question with the Theological Hermeneutics of David Tracy in View*. Louvan, Dudley: Peeters, 2006.

Hunter, Rodney J. (ed.). *Dictionary of Pastoral Care and Counseling*. Nashville, TN.: Abingdon, 1990.

———. *Dictionary of Pastoral Care and Counseling. The New Edition*. CD Rom, 2007.

Igo, Robert. *Listening with Love: Pastoral Counselling: A Christian Response to People Living with HIV/AIDS*. Geneva: WCC, 2005.
Irinoye, Omolola. "Counseling People affected by HIV and AIDS." *The Continuing HIV/AIDS Epidemic* (1999) 181–192.
Israel, Mark and Hay, Lain. *Research Ethics for Social Scientists: Between Ethical Conduct and Regulatory Compliance*. London: Sage, 2006.
Jackson, Edgar N. *Understanding Grief: Its Roots, Dynamics, and Treatment*. London: SCM, 1985.
Jenkins, Suzanne. "Counseling and Storytelling: How did We Get there?" *Psychotherapy and Politics International*, 11:2 (2013) 140–151.
Jones, Daniel C. "A Theology of Hope for Pastoral Care: Reframing Life's Losses in the Context of God's Future." PhD Thesis. Garland Texas: Austin Presbyterian Theological Seminary, 2012.
Jun, Chul Min. "The Paradigm Shift of Practical Theology and Theological Practice to Overcome Modernism and Postmodernism." *Pacific Science Review* 16 (2014) 156–166.
Jung, Carl G. *Man and His Symbols*. New York: Dell, 1964.
———. *Memories, Dreams, and Reflections*. Translated by Richard and Clara Winston. London: Collins and Routledge & Kegan Paul, 1963.
———. *Modern Man in Search of a Soul*. Translated by. W.S. Dell and C. F. Baynes, New York, NY.: Harcourt Brace Jovanovich, 1933.
Kacholi, Godfrey. "Assessment of Factors Influencing Identification of the Most Vulnerable Children in Tanzania: Experiences from Morogoro Rural District." MA Thesis in Health Policy and Management. Dar es Salaam, Muhimbili University of Health and Allied Sciences, 2012.
Kimilike, Lechion P. "An African Perspective on Poverty Proverbs in the Book of Proverbs: An Analysis for Transformational Possibilities." DTh Thesis, Pretoria: University of South Africa, 2006.
Kiriswa, B. "Pastoral Care and Counseling of Persons Living with HIV and AIDS." *AFER* 46:1 (2004) 80–99.
Kirkpatrick, Bill. *AIDS sharing the Pain: Pastoral Guidelines*. London: Darton, Longman and Todd, 1988.
Kistemaker, Simon J. "Jesus as Story Teller: Literary Perspectives on the Parables." *The Master's Seminary Journal* 16:1 (2005) 49–55.
Kistner, U. "Reconciliation Unjustifiable, Justice Irreconcilable? Story and Narrative in Testimony before the South African Truth and Reconciliation Commission." Public Lecture at UNISA 2005, Pretoria South Africa, 2005.
Klein, Melanie. *The Psycho-analysis of Children*. London: The Hogarth, 1963.
Koening, Harold G. and Grossoehme, Daniel H. *The Pastoral Care of Children*. New York, NY.: The Haworth Pastoral Press, 1999.
Kothari, C. R. *Research Methodology: Methods and Techniques*. Second Edition. New Delhi: New Age, 2004.
Kotzé, E. and D. Kotzé (eds.). *Telling Narratives*. Spellbound Edition. Pretoria: Ethics Alive, 2001.
Kunene, Mazisi. "Research in African Literature." *The Language-Question* 23:1 (1992) 27–44.
Landman, Christina. "Doing Narrative Counseling in the Context of Township Spiritualities." DTh Thesis. Pretoria: University of South Africa, 2007.

Landreth, Garry and Bratton, Sue. "Play Therapy." In *ERIC Digest* 1999. Online at https://static1.squarespace.com/static/587c153d17bffc8c1edof6bc/t/588bc56 35016e17565bbcb69/1485555043348/Landreth+Bratton+play+therapy+.pdf [Accessed 31 March 2018]

Lebacqz, Karen and Driskill, J.D. *Ethics and Spiritual Care: A Guide for Pastors, Chaplains, and Spiritual Directors*. Nashville, TN.: Abingdon, 2000.

Lekule, Chrispina. "Investigating School Experiences of Vulnerable Children in Singida, Tanzania: Challenges, Strategies and Possible Interventions." PhD Dissertation, University of Windsor, Ontario Canada. 2014.

Lester, Andrew D. *Hope in Pastoral Counseling*. Louisville, Kentucky: Westminster John Knox, 1995.

———. *Pastoral Care with Children in Crisis*. Philadelphia, PA.: The Westiminster, 1985.

———. (ed.). *When Children Suffer: A Sourcebook for Ministry with Children in Crisis*. Philadelphia, PA.: The Westminster, 1987.

Loue, Sana. *Textbook of Research Ethics: Theory and Practice*. New York, NY.: Kluwer Academic Publishers, 2002.

Louw, Daniel J. *A Pastoral Hermeneutics of Care and Encounter: A Theological Design for a Basic Theory, Anthropology, Method and Therapy*. Wellington: Lux Verbi, 2003.

———. "A Theological Model for Pastoral Anthropology within the Dynamics of Interculturality: *Cura Animarum* and the Quest for *Wholeness* in a Colo-spirituality." In *Die Skriflig/In Luce Verbi* 46:2 (2012) 1–9. Online at: http://dx.doi.org/10.4102/ids.v46i2.57 (Accessed 23 October 2017).

———. *Wholeness in Hope Care. On Nurturing the Beauty of the Human Soul in Spiritual Healing*. Zurich: LIT Verlag, 2014.

———. *A Pastoral Hermeneutics of Care and Encounter: A Theological Design for a Basic Theory, Anthropology, Method and Therapy*. Wellington: Lux Verbi B.M., 1998.

———. *Meaning in suffering: A Theological Reflection on the Cross and the Resurrection for Pastoral Care and Counseling*. Frankfurt am Main: Peter Lang, 2000.

———. *Illness as Crisis and Challenge: Guidelines for Pastoral Care*. Orion, 1994.

———. *Cura Vitae: Illness and the Healing of Life in Pastoral Care and Counseling: A Guide for Caregivers*. Wellington: Lux Verbi. B.M., 2008.

———. "Ministering and Counseling the Person with AIDS." *Journal of Theology for Southern Africa* 71 (1990) 37–50.

Lull, Patricia J. "Telling the Truth: Introducing Death and Resurrection to the Young." *Word and World: Theology for Christian Ministry. Death and Resurrection* XI:1 (1991) 36–43.

Magesa, Laurent. *Anatomy of Inculturation: Transforming the Church in Africa*. Nairobi: Paulines, 2004.

———. A Theological Journey." *Exchange* 32:1 (2003) 43–53.

Mageto, Peter Maiko. "A Silent Church = Death: A Critical Look at the Church's Response to HIV/AIDS." *Currents in Theology and Mission*. 32:4 (2005) 291–298.

Majiyasoda, P. L. *Fasihi Simulizi: Methali, Nahau, na Vitendawili*. Unpublished Material PLM, Mbeya, 2007.

Ma Mpolo, Jean Masamba and. Nwachuku, Daisy (eds). *Pastoral Care and Counseling in Africa Today*. Vol. 1. New York, NY.: Peter Lang, 1991.

May, H.G. and Metzger, Bruce M. (eds.). *The New Oxford Annotated Bible: Revised Standard Version*. New York: Oxford University Press, 1973.

Matheny, Duane Paul. *Contextual Theology: The Drama of Our Times*. Eugene, OR.: Wipf and Stock/Pickwick, 2011.

Mbiti, John S. *African Religions and Philosophy*. Second Edition. Heinemann, 1989.

McClurre, Barbara J. *Moving Beyond Individualism in Pastoral Care and Couseling: Reflections on Theory, Theology and Practice*. Cambridge: The Lutherworth Press, 2011.

McFague, Sallie. *Metaphorical Theology: Models of God in Religious Language*. London: SCM, 1982.

McLeod, John. *An Introduction to Counseling*. Second Edition. Philadelphia, PA.: Open University Press, 1998.

———. *Doing Counseling Research*. Second Edition. Thousand Oaks, CA.: Sage, 2003.

———. *Qualitative Research in Counseling and Psychotherapy*. Thousand Oaks, CA.: Sage, 2002.

McMahon, Linnet. *The Handbook of Play Therapy*. New York: Routledge, 1992.

Metzger, Bruce M and Murphy, R.E. *The New Oxford Annotated Bible*. NRSV. New York: Oxford University Press, 1991.

Microsoft Encarta Encyclopedia. "Tanzania", CD Rom on line, 2004.

Minuchin, Salvador. *Families and Family Theory*. London: Tavistock, 1974.

Mligo, Elia Shabani and Mikael Kaombeka Mwashilindi. *English as Language of Teaching and Learning for Community Secondary Schools in Tanzania: A Critical Analysis*. Eugene, Oregon: Wipf and Stock/Resource, 2017.

Mligo, Elia Shabani. *Teolojia ya Kimazingira*. Mbeya: AJ Technologies, 2017.

———. *Writing effective Course Assignments: A Guide to Non-Degree and Undergraduate Students*. Eugene, Oregon: Wipf and Stock/Resource, 2017.

———. *Introduction to Research and Report Writing: A Practical Guide to Students and Researchers in Social Sciences and the Humanities*. Eugene, OR.: Wipf and Stock/Resource, 2016.

———. "Jesus Christ, the Compassionate Companion: Christological Reflections in the Time of the HIV/AIDS Pandemic," *Acta Theologica* 34:2 (2014) 56–71.

———. *Symbolic Interactionism in the Gospel according to John: A Contextual Study on the Symbolism of Water*. Eugene, OR.: Wipf and Stock, 2014.

———. *Elements of African Traditional Religion: A Textbook for Students of Comparative Religion*. Eugene, OR.: Wipf and Stock/Resource, 2013.

———. *Jesus and the Divorce Commandment: Reading the Gospel of Mark in a Context of Divorce and Remarriage in Tanzania*. Saarbrucken, Germany: LAP Lambert Academic Publishing, 2012.

———. *The Kingdom of God: A Challenge to the Poor and the Rich*. Saarbrucken, Germany: LAP Lambert Academic Publishing.

———. *Jesus and the Stigmatized: Reading the Gospel of John in a Context of HIV/AIDS-Related Stigmatization in Tanzania*. Eugene, OR.: Wipf and Stock/Pickwick, 2011.

Mlilo, Luke G. and Soédé, Nathanael.Y. (eds.). *Doing Theology and Philosophy in the African Context*. Frankfurt: Verlag für Interkulturelle Kommunikation, 2003.

Monk, Gerald, Winslade, John, Crocket, Kathie and Epson, David (eds.). *Narrative Therapy in Practice: The Archaeology of Hope*. First Edition. San Francisco, CA.: Jossey-Bass, 1997.

Moore, Kelsey, Gomez-Garibello, Carlos, Bosacki, Sandra and Talwar, Victoria. "Children's Spiritual Lives: The Development of a Children's Spirituality Measure." *Religions* 7:95 (2016). Online: doi:10.3390/rel7080095; www.mdpi.com/journal/religionsMorgan, Alice. *What is Narrative Therapy?* Adelaide: Dulwich Centre, 2000.

———. "Beginning to Use a Narrative Approach in Therapy." *The International Journal of Narrative Therapy* 2 (2002) 85–90.

Morkel, Elizabeth. "When Narratives Create Community: Standing with Children against Stealing." MTh Thesis. Pretoria: University of South Africa, 2002.

Mouton, Johann. *How to Succeed in Your Master's and Doctoral Studies: A South African Guide and Resource Book.* Pretoria: Van Schaik, 2001.

———. "Autumn School on Research Methods: African Doctoral Academy." Unpublished material. Stellenbosch University 15–18 March 2010.

Mucherera, Tapiwa N. *Pastoral Care from a Third World Perspective: A Pastoral Theology of Care for the Urban Contemporary Shona in Zimbabwe.* New York, NY.: Peter Lang, 2001.

Mugambi, Jesse. N. K. *Christian Theology and Social Reconstruction.* Nairobi: Acton, 2003.

———. *From Liberation to Reconstruction: African Christian Theology after the* Cold War. Nairobi: East African Educational, 1995.

Mukoyogo, Christian M. and Glen. Williams. *AIDS Orphans: A Community Perspective from Tanzania.* Nairobi, Dar es Salaam, London: Action/Amref/World, 1991.

Müller, Julian. "HIV/AIDS, "Narrative Practical Theology, and Postfoundationalism: The Emergence of a New Story." *HTS Theological Studies* 60:1&2 (2004) 293–306.

Murphy. Francesca Aran. *God is Not a Story: Realism Revisited.* Oxford: Oxford University Press, 2007.

Musopole, Augustine C. *Spirituality, Sexuality and HIV/AIDS in Malawi: Theological Strategies for Behavior Change.* Zomba: Kachere Series, 2006.

Mwaura, Philomena Njeri. "Response." *International Review of Mission* 90 (2004) 65–69.

Mwendapole, J. "Kikwete: Tusiwanyanyapae wenye UKIMWI." *Nipashe*, 11 September 2006.

Mwenisongole, Tuntufye.Anangisye. "Religious Education of Children in the Old Testament in the Context of Deuterenomy 6:4–9." BD Thesis. Arusha: Makumira University College, 1997.

———. "The use of Symbols and Images from a Jungian Perspective in Pastoral Counseling with Young People." MAPC Thesis. Bethlehem, PA.: Moravian Theological Seminary, 2001.

———. 2002. "A Biblical and Theological Response to the Issues of HIV/AIDS in Tanzania." MATS Thesis. Bethlehem, PA. Moravian Theological Seminary.

Ndossi, Emeline. "The Significance of the Female Perspective." In *Restoring Life in Christ: Dialogies of Care in Christian Communities: An African Perspective.* Eide, Oyvind M., Engedal, Leif Gunnar, Kimilike, Lechion Peter and Ndossi, Emeline, 38–45. Makumira Publication Nineteen. Neuendetelssau Erlanger Verlag fur Mission und Oukumene, 2008.

Nelson, James B. *Embodiment: An Approach to Sexuality and Christian theology.* London: SPCK, 1978.

———. "A Continuing Sexual Revolution." *Christian Century*. June 1, 1988. Taken from *Religion-Online* at www.religion-online.org (Accessed 27 March 2006).

———. "Reuniting Sexuality and Spirituality." *Christian Century*. 25 February 1987, 187–190. Taken from Religion-online, www.religion-online.org (Accessed 27 March 2006).

Ng'ondi, Naftali Bernard. "Characteristics of Most Vulnerable Children and Their Guardians that determine Service Use in a Tanzanian Social Agency." *Sage Open* (2014) 1–8.

Neuger, Christie Cozad. *Counseling Women: A Narrative, Pastoral Approach*. Minneapolis, MIN.: Fortress, 2001.

Nicholls, Bruce J. *Contextualization: A Theology of Gospel and Culture*. Hong Kong: Regent College Publishing, 2003.

Nsangalufu, Musokwa Emmy. "'The Contributions of Local NGOs/CBO in Care and Support of Orphans' Mpiji Village." MSc.in Community Economic Development. Open University of Tanzania and the Southern New Hampshire University, 2005.

O'Connor, Thomas James, Davis, Andrea, Meakes, Elizabeth, Pickering, Ruth, and Schuman, Martha. "Narrative Therapy using a Reflecting Team: An Ethnographic Study of Therapists' Experiences." *Contemporary Family Therapy* 26:1 (2004) 29–33.

Okafor, Peter O. "The Challenge of Contextual Theology," *Ministerium-Journal of Contextual Theology* 1 (2014) 1–14.

Oliver, Paul. *The Student's Guide to Research Ethics*. Philadelphia, PA.: Open University Press, 2003.

Olsen, David C. *Integrative Family Therapy*. Minneapolis, MIN.: Fortress, 1993.

Osmer, Richard R. 2008. *Practical Theology: An Introduction*. Grand Rapids, MI.: WB Eerdmans Publishing Company, 2008.

Ozodi, ChristopherChinedu. "Clinical Pastoral Education for Igbo Society: A Cross Cultural Model for a Family/Community-Based Educational Process in Pastoral Care." PhD Dissertation. Pietermaritzburg: University of KwaZulu-Natal, 2005.

Patton, John H. *Pastoral Counseling: A Ministry of the Church*. Nashville, TN.: Abingdon, 1983.

———. *Pastoral Care in Context: An Introduction to Pastoral Care*. Kentucky: Westminster/John Knox, 1993.

Pearce, Stephen S. *Flash of Insight: Metaphor and Narrative in Therapy*. Boston, CA.: Allyn and Bacon, 1996.

Petta, Johnson. "In Search of a Contextual Pastoral Theology for Dalits in India." PhD Dissertation. University of Denver and Iliff School of Theology, USA, 2012.

Phiri, Isabel. A, B. Haddad and M. Masenya (ngwana Mphahlele) (eds.). *African Women, HIV and AIDS and Faith Communities*. Pietermaritzburg: Cluster, 2003.

Phiri, Isabel A. "A Theological Analysis of the Voices of Teenage Girls on 'Men's Role in the Fight against HIV/AIDS' in KwaZulu-Natal, South Africa." *Journal of Theology for Southern Africa* 120 (2004) 34–45.

Price, Mary M. "Walking through the Darkness: Pastoral Care to Survivors of Traumatic Loss." MA in Liberal Studies Thesis, Skidmore College.

Ramsay, Nancy J. (ed.). *Pastoral Care and Counseling: Redefining the Paradigms*. Nashville, TN.: Abingdon, 2004.

Riley, Shirley. *Contemporary Art Therapy with Adolescents*. London: Jessica Kingsley, 1999.

Robertson, Blair. "Storytelling in Pastoral Counseling: A Narrative Pastoral Theology." *Pastoral Psychology* 39:1 (1990) 33-45.
Roscoe, Karen. D. & Madoc, Iolo Jones. "Critical Social Work Practice a Narrative Approach." *International Journal of Narrative Practice* 1:1 (2009) 9-18.
Ross, Alistair. *Counselling Skills for Church and Faith Community Workers*. Maidenhead and Philadelphia, PA.: Open University Press, 2003.
Ryan, M. "Narrative." In *Routledge Encyclopedia of Narrative*, 2005. http://lamar.colostate.edu/~pwryan/narrentry.htm (Accessed 12 June 2006).
Sanders, Cody J. "An Exploration of Knowledge and Power in Narrative, Collaborative-Based, Postmodern Therapies: A Commentary." *The Professional Counselor* 1:3 (2011) 201-207.
Sahin, Z. Seda and McVicker, Melissa. "The Use of Optimism in Narrative Therapy with Sexual Abuse Survivors." *Journal of European Psychology Students* 1 (2009) 1-6.
Salt, Susan. "Healing in the Context of Pastoral Care." *The Reader* 107:1 (2010) 10-11.
Sasso, S. "The Role of Narrative in the Spiritual Formation of Children." *Journal of Family Ministry* 19:2 (2005) 13-26.
Schaefer, Charles E. and Kevin J. O'Connor (eds.). *Handbook of Play Therapy*. New York: John Wiley & Sons, 1983.
Segler, Franklin M. "The Concept of Ministry." *Review and Expositor* 66:2 (1969) 141-153.
Schlauch, Chris R. *Faithful Companioning: How Pastoral Counseling Heals*. Minneapolis, MIN.: Fortress, 1995.
Schoeman, J.P. and Merwe, M. *Entering the Child's World: A Play Therapy Approach*. Pretoria: Kagiso, 1996.
Setiloane, Gabriel M. *African Theology: An Introduction*. Cape Town: Lux Verbi, 1986.
Shelp, Earl.E and Ronald.H. Sunderland. "Faith Community Responses to HIV and AIDS: Care and Counseling. *AIDS and the Church*: The Second Decade, 1992. Online at: http://www.cedpa.org/publications/faithcommunity/faithcommunity4.pdf (Accessed 17 September 2005).
Shelp, Earl. E., E. R. DuBose, and Ronald H. Sunderland. 1990. "AIDS and the Church: A Status Report." *The Christian Century*. December 5 (1990) 1135-1137.
Shim, Y. H. K. "Pastoral Care and Counseling to and with Children." MTh Thesis. Cape Town: University of Stellenbosch, 1995.
Shorter, Aliward. "Book Review." *Towards an African Narrative Theology*. By Joseph Healey and Donald. Sybertz. Nairobi: Paulines, 1998.
Shreiter, Robert J. *The New Catholicity: Theology between the Global and the Local*. Maryknoll, NY.: Orbis Books, 1997.
Smart, Rose. *Policies for Orphans and Vulnerable Children: A Framework for Moving Ahead*. USAID and Policy, 2003.
Singhal, Arvind and Howard, Steve (eds.). *The Children of Africa Confront AIDS: From Vulnerability to Possibility*. Athens: Ohio University Press, 2003.
Sisemore, Timothy A. "Christian Counseling for Children: The Five Domains Model." *Journal of Psychology and Christianity* 22:2 (2003) 115-122.
Snodgrass, Jill L. "Pastoral Counseling: A Discipline of Unity amid Diversity." In *Understanding Pastoral Counseling*, edited by Maynard, Elizabeth and Snodgrass, Jill L., 1-16. New York, NY.: Springer, 2015.

SOS Children's Villages International. *Assessment Report of the Alternative Care System for Children in Tanzania.* Innsbruck, Austria: SOS Children's Villages International, 2014.
Speedy, Jane. *Narrative Inquiry and Psychotherapy.* New York, NY.: Palgrave Macmillan, 2008.
Stemler, Steve. "An Overviews of Content Analysis." *Practical Assessment, Research and Evaluation* 7:17 (2001). Available at: http://pareonline.net/getvn.asp?v=7&n=17 (Accessed 10 October 2017).
Stiemer, Harriet Russouw. "A narrative Pastoral Care Approach to a School Outreach Programme at a Private School in Gauteng." MTh Thesis: UNISA, 2007.
Stine, Gerald J. *AIDS Update 2010.* New York, NY.: McGraw-Hill, 2010.
Stone, Howard W. and Clements, William C. (eds.). *Handbook for Basic Types of Pastoral Care and Counseling.* Nashville, TN.: Abingdon, 1991.
Streets, Frederick J. "Love: A Philosophy of Pastoral Care and Counselling." *Verbum et Ecclesia* 35:2 (2014) 1–11. Online at http://dx.doi.org/10.4102/ve.v35i2.1323 [Accessed 06 November 2017]
———. "The Pastoral Care of Preaching and the Trauma of HIV and AIDS." *Verbum et Ecclesia* 29:3 (2008) 832–853.
Sunderland, Ronald H. and Earl E. Shelp. *Handle with Care: A Handbook for Care Teams Serving People with AIDS.* Nashville, TN.: Abingdon, 1990.
Sweeney, Daniel S. *Counseling Children through the World of Play.* Carol Stream, IL.: Tyndale House, 1997.
Swinton, John. and Mowat, Harriet. *Practical Theology and Qualitative Research.* London: SCM, 2006.
Switzer, David K. *The Minister as Crisis Counselor.* Nashville, TN.: Abingdon, 1974.
TACAIDS, The United Republic of Tanzania: The Prime Minister's Office, 2008. Online at: www.tacaids.go.tz [Accessed 20 May 2011].
Tanzania Daima. "Hakuna Takwimu za Wajane, Yatima wa UKIMWI." Jumatano, 12 Julai 2006.
Tanzania Prime Minister's Office. *National Policy on HIV/AIDS*, 2001. Online at: www.tacaids.co.tz.
Tanzania National Website. 2008. HIV/AIDS in Tanzania. www.tanzania.go.tz
The United States President's Emergency Plan for AIDS Relief. FY2008 Country Profile: Tanzania. www.usa.gov.
Terre Blanche, Martin, Durrheim, Kevin. and Painter, Desmond (eds.). *Research in Practice: Applied Methods for the Social Sciences.* Second Revised edition. Rondebosch: U.C.T., 2006.
Togarasei, Lovemore. "HIV/AIDS and the Role of the Churches in Zimbabwe." *Africa Theological Journal* 28:1 (2005) 3–20.
Trahar, Sheila (ed.). *Narrative Research on Learning: Comparative and International Perspectives.* Oxford: Symposium Books, 2006.
Truter, C.J. and Kotze, D.J. "Spirituality and Health: A Narrative-Pastoral Approach." *HTS* 61:3 (2005) 973–984.
UNAIDS/WHO/UNICEF. "Epidemiological Fact Sheets, 2008 Update." United Republic of Tanzania. Online at www.unaids.org (Accessed 27 December 2009).
UNICEF. "Unite for Children and Unite against AIDS," (n.d.). www.unicef.org/uniteforchildren/index.html (Accessed 05 September 2006).

REFERENCES

UNICEF, UNAIDS AND PEPFAR. "Africa's Orphaned and Vulnerable Generations: Children affected by AIDS," 2006. Online at www.unicef.org/uniteforchildren (Accessed 11 March 2008).

UNICEF, "Caring for Children affected by the HIV and AIDS." *Innocenti Research Centre*, 2006. Online at https://www.unicef-irc.org/publications/pdf/insight-hiv-eng.pdf [Accessed 22 October, 2017]

USAID. "From the American People." USAID Project profiles: Children affected by HIV and AIDS. January 2005. Fourth Edition. www.usaid.gov/our_work/global_health/aids/publications/docs (Accessed 18 September 2005).

USAID. "From the American People." USAID Project profiles: Children affected by HIV and AIDS. January 2007/2008. Fourth Edition. www.usaid.gov/our_work/global_health/aids/publications/docs (Accessed 11 November 2009).

Vahakangas, Auli. "The Church as a Healing Community? The Case of HIV/AIDS Stigma." *Africa Theological Journal* 28:1 (2005) 48–56.

Van Wyk, A.G. "From 'Applied Theology' to 'Practical Theology.'" *Andrews University Seminary Studies* 33:1 (1995) 85–101.

Van Duuren, Linda Anne. "Children's Voices on Bereavement and Loss." MTh Thesis. Pretoria: University of South Africa, 2002.

Van Dyk, Alta. *HIV/Aids Care and Counseling: A Multidisciplinary Approach.* Third Edition. Cape Town: Pearson Education South Africa, 2005.

Vosman, Frans and Baart, Andries. "Relationship based Care and Recognition." In *Care, Compassion and Recognition: An Ethical Discussion.* Edited by Leget, Carlo, Gastmaans, Chris and Verkerk, Marian, 201–227. Leuven: Peeters, 2011.

Walker-Jones, Kelli. "A Narrative Approach to Pastor-Congregational Relationships. Sustaining Pastoral Excellence." *Sustaining Pastoral Excellence,* 2005. Online at https://www.faithandleadership.com/programs/spe/articles/200508/narrative.html [Accessed on 11 October 2017].

Wallace, Catherine. M. "Storytelling, Doctrine, and Spiritual Formation." *Anglican Theological Review* 81:1 (1999) 39–59.

Walligo, John Mary. "Making a Church that is Truly African." In *Inculturation: Its Meaning and Urgency.* Edited by John Mary Walligo, Ary Roest Crollius, Theoneste Nkeramihigo and John Mutiso-Mbinda, 11–30. Nairobi: St. Paul, 1986.

Wanjohi, Gerald Joseph. *The Wisdom and Philosophy of African Proverbs: The Gikuyu World-View.* Nairobi: Paulines, 1997.

Ward, Edwina. D. "The Contribution of Clinical Pastoral Education to Pastoral Ministry in South Africa: Overview and Critique of its Method and Dynamic, in View of Adaptation and Implementation in a Cross Cultural Context." PhD Dissertation. Pietermaritzburg: University of Natal, 2001.

WCC. *Resource Material for Churches and Communities: Ecumenical HIV/AIDS Initiative in Africa (EHAIA).* Geneva: WCC, 2004. Online at http://archived.oikoumene.org/en/programmes/justice-diakonia-and-responsibility-for-creation/hivaids-initiative-in-africa-ehaia.html [Accessed 11 October 2017] WCC. 2005. www.oikoumene.org

WCC. *Facing AIDS: The Challenge, the Churches' Response.* A WCC Study Document. Geneva: WCC, 2004.

Webb-Mitchell, Brett. "The Importance of Stories in the Act of Caring." *Pastoral Psychology* 43:3 (1995) 215–225.

Webster, Leonard. and Mertova, Patricie.*Using Narrative Inquiry as a Research Method: AnIntroduction to using Critical Event Narrative Analysis in Research on Learning and Teaching*. London: Routledge, 2007.

Wendler, M. Cecilia. "Understanding Healing: A Conceptual Analysis." *Journal of Advanced Nursing* 24 (1996) 836–842.

Wheeler, Ray. "The Legacy of Shoki Coe." *International Bulletin of Missionary Research* 26:2 (2002) 77–80.

White, Michael and David Epston. *Narrative Means to Therapeutic Ends*. New York, NY.: Norton, 1990.

Wicks, Richard. J and Parsons, Robert. D. (eds.). *Clinical Handbook of Pastoral Counseling*. Volume 2. Mahwah: Paulist, 1993.

Wikipedia. Tanzania. www.wikipedia.org, 2008

Williams, Donna Relly and JoAnn. Starzl. *Grief Ministry: Helping Others Mourn*. Revised and Expanded Edition. San Jose: Resource, 1990.

Wimberly, Edward P. *Pastoral Care in the Black Church*. Nashville, TN.: Abingdon, 1979.

———. *Using Scripture in Pastoral Counseling*. Nashville, TN.: Abingdon, 1994.

———. *Moving from Shame to Self-Worth: Preaching and Pastoral Care*. Nashville, TN.: Abingdon, 1999.

———. *African American Pastoral Care*. Revised Edition. Nashville, TN.: Abingdon, 2008.

———. *No Shame in Wesley's Gospel: A Twenty-First Century Pastoral Theology*. Eugene, OR.: Wipf and Stock, 2011.

Winslade, John M. and Monk, Gerald D. *Narrative Counseling in Schools: Powerful and Brief*. Thousand Oaks, CA: Corwin, 1998.

Woodward, Peter. "Theological Reflection as Key to Practical Theology." AEJT 22:2 (2015) 128–141.

World Bank. *Education and HIV/AIDS: A Window of Hope*. Washington, DC: The International Bank for Reconstruction and Development, 2002.

Zeig, Jeffrey K. *Ericksonian Methods: The Essence of the Story*. New York, NY.: Brunner/Mazel, 1994.

www.ingramcontent.com/pod-product-compliance
Lightning Source LLC
Chambersburg PA
CBHW050434240426
43661CB00055B/2379